Lyndon B. Johnson School of Public Affairs
Policy Research Project Report
Number 69

An Assessment of Drunk Driving Policies in Texas and Other States

A report by the
Highway Safety Policy Research Project
The University of Texas at Austin
1985

Library of Congress Card Number: 85-81359
ISBN: 0-89940-671-8

© 1985 by the Board of Regents
The University of Texas

Printed in the U.S.A.
All rights reserved

POLICY RESEARCH PROJECT PARTICIPANTS

PROJECT DIRECTORS

Leigh B. Boske, Ph.D.
Associate Professor
Lyndon B. Johnson School of Public Affairs

Robert J. Macdonald, Ph.D.
Manager of Planning and Evaluation
Traffic Safety Section
Texas Department of Highways and Public Transportation

STUDENTS

Beth Beck, B.A. (Government), The University of Texas at Austin

Yvonne M. Brunson, B.A. (Political Science), University of Florida

Andrew D. Campbell, B.A. (Political Science and Psychology), Austin College

William E. Coll, B.A. (Health Education), Montclair State College

Peter T. Ginsberg, B.A. (Political Science), Northwestern University

Jo Anne Hawkins, B.S. (Art), M.L.S., The University of Texas at Austin

Susan K. Kelly, B.A. (English and Psychology), Austin College

Sue E. Masica, B.A. (Political Science), Austin College

Cary L. McDougal, B.A. (Political Science), Baylor University

Diane Mettenburg, B.A. (Public Administration), St. Cloud State University

Lisa C. Norman, B.A. (Political Science), University of Florida

Joanie Carson Raff, B.A. (Humanities), The University of Texas at Austin

Ann M. Setterlund, B.A. (Middle Eastern Studies), The University of Texas at Austin

Chris A. Vein, B.S. (Political Science), Miami University

Julie K. Ware, B.A. (Political Science and German), Trinity University

Terri R. Williams, B.A. (Business Administration), Austin College

TABLE OF CONTENTS

	Page
FOREWORD	ix
ACKNOWLEDGMENTS	xi
EXECUTIVE SUMMARY	xiii

CHAPTER 1: Legislative History of Federal and State DWI
Policy Initiatives.................................... 1

    Introduction... 1
    Federal DWI Program Activities........................... 1
    State Legislative Activity: 1983-84...................... 14
    Legislative History of Texas DWI Laws.................... 19
    Conclusions.. 27

CHAPTER 2: Description of the Texas DWI System................. 33

    Introduction... 33
    DWI System Components.................................... 34
    Agency Descriptions...................................... 38
    Agency-to-Agency Interactions............................ 47
    Conclusions.. 60

CHAPTER 3: DWI Information Collection Systems.................. 63

    Introduction... 63
    Federal Data Collection Systems.......................... 63
    Recording DWI Information at the State Level............. 72
    Recording DWI Information at the County Level............ 74
    Travis County Anti-DWI Project........................... 80
    Conclusions.. 83

CHAPTER 4: Local Perspectives on Texas County DWI Systems
and Senate Bill 1................................... 87

    Introduction... 87
    Texas County Interviews.................................. 92
    Mail-Out Servey of Texas County and District Attorneys... 100
    Conclusions.. 109

CHAPTER 5: Programs in Other States............................ 111

    Introduction... 111
    Florida.. 113
    Minnesota.. 128
    New York... 142
    Pennsylvania... 153
    Summary.. 165
    Conclusions.. 169

	Page
APPENDIX 1: Reports on Texas Counties	179
Introduction	179
Comal County	179
Dallas County	187
El Paso County	195
Gray County	203
Harris County	209
Harrison County	216
Webb County	223
Williamson County	229
APPENDIX 2: Questionnaire for Visited Texas Counties	239
APPENDIX 3: Mail-Out Questionnaire for Texas County and District Attorneys	247
APPENDIX 4: Questionnaire for Florida	251
APPENDIX 5: Questionnaire for Minnesota	259
APPENDIX 6: Questionnaire for New York	275
APPENDIX 7: Questionnaire for Pennsylvania	279
APPENDIX 8: Pennsylvania Court Reporting Network--Client Intake Form	285

LIST OF TABLES

		Page
Table 1:	Chronological Summary of Federal Anti-DWI Initiatives	3
Table 2:	Analysis by States--1983-84 High Interest Alcohol and Driving Legislation	16
Table 3:	Chronological Summary of Texas DWI Legislation	20
Table 4:	Chronological Summary of Texas DWI Penalties	22
Table 5:	Background Information on Visited Texas Counties	89
Table 6:	1983 DWI Statistics on Visited Texas Counties	90
Table 7:	1984 DWI Statistics on Visited Texas Counties	91
Table 8:	List of Responding County and District Attorneys by County	101
Table 9:	Background Information on Visited States	112

LIST OF FIGURES

Figure 1:	A Model DWI System	35
Figure 2:	Agency-to-Agency Interaction--Law Enforcement	49
Figure 3:	Agency-to-Agency Interaction--Prosecution and Adjudication	51
Figure 4:	Agency-to-Agency Interaction--Punishment	54
Figure 5:	Agency-to-Agency Interaction--Treatment	55
Figure 6:	Agency-to-Agency Interaction--Prevention	56

LIST OF EXHIBITS

Exhibit 1:	1983 Fatal Accident-Reporting System (FARS)--Accident Level	66
Exhibit 2:	1983 Fatal Accident-Reporting System (FARS)--Vehicle-Driver Level	67
Exhibit 3:	1983 Fatal Accident-Reporting System (FARS)--Personal Level	68
Exhibit 4:	City of Austin DWI/DUID Traffic Case Report	75
Exhibit 5:	Pennsylvania Uniform Data Collection System--Client Admission Form	156

MAP

Map 1:	Locations of Visited Texas Counties	88

FOREWORD

The Lyndon B. Johnson School of Public Affairs has established interdisciplinary research on policy programs as the core of its educational program. A major part of this program is the nine-month Policy Research Project, in the course of which two or three faculty members from different disciplines direct the research of ten to twenty graduate students of diverse backgrounds on a policy issue of concern to a government agency. This "client orientation" brings the students face to face with administrators, legislators, and other officials active in the policy process, and demonstrates that research in a policy environment demands special talents. It also illumunates the occasional difficulties in relating research findings to the world of political realities.

This report on drunk driving policies in Texas and other states is the product of a Policy Research Project conducted at the LBJ School in the 1984-85 academic year. The publication was funded by the Texas Department of Highways and Public Transportation.

The curriculum of the LBJ School is intended not only to develop effective public servants but also to produce research that will enlighten and inform those already engaged in the policy process. The project that resulted in this report has helped to accomplish the first task; it is our hope and expectation that the report itself will contribute to the second.

Finally, it should be noted that neither the LBJ School nor The University of Texas at Austin necessarily endorses the views or findings of this study.

Max Sherman
Dean

ACKNOWLEDGMENTS

This report on drunk driving policies was made possible by Texas Traffic Safety Program Contract No. (85)02-05-A1-AA between the Texas Department of Highways and Public Transportation and The University of Texas at Austin.

The vehicle of research was a Policy Research Project at the LBJ School of Public Affairs involving two faculty codirectors (Leigh B. Boske, LBJ School, and Robert J. Macdonald, Texas Department of Highways and Public Transportation) and the participation of sixteen graduate students from the LBJ School: Beth Beck; Yvonne M. Brunson; Andrew D. Campbell; William E. Coll; Peter T. Ginsberg; Jo Anne Hawkins; Susan K. Kelly; Sue E. Masica; Cary L. McDougal; Diane Mettenburg; Lisa Norman; Joanie Carson Raff; Ann M. Setterlund; Chris A. Vein; Julie K. Ware; and Terri R. Williams.

The following individuals and specialists from relevant fields visited the LBJ School to share information and ideas with project team members: Captain Kenneth Bertling, Chief, Traffic Law Enforcement, Texas Department of Public Safety; Officer Charley Chipman, S.T.E.P. Coordinator, Traffic Section, Austin Police Department; Claire Dawson-Brown, former Chief, Criminal Trial Section, Travis County Attorney's Office; Marilynn Dierschke, Special Programs Coordinator, Texas Adult Probation Commission; Susan B. Herbel, former Program Analyst, Office of Alcohol Countermeasures, National Highway Traffic Safety Administration; Mary Lauderdale, Statistical Analyst, Statistical Services, Texas Department of Public Safety; Lydia McDaniel, Coordinator, Travis County Anti-DWI Project; John G. McKay, former Alcohol Programs Manager, Traffic Safety Section, Texas Department of Highways and Public Transportation; Jennifer Solter, President, Travis County Chapter, Mothers Against Drunk Drivers; Marinelle Timmons, Texas State Director, Mothers Against Drunk Drivers; and Vernon With, Program Director, Region VI, National Highway Traffic Safety Administration.

This list is not exhaustive and in particular does not include the many persons who provided their time and knowledge to individual members of the project team. Hundreds of people, both in Texas and other states, were consulted, interviewed, and responded to mail-out questionnaires. All are properly cited at the end of each chapter and appendix of this report.

Finally, the project codirectors wish to express their indebtedness to Marilyn Duncan, Director, LBJ School Office of Publications, for ensuring the prompt scheduling and projection of this report, and to Mary Beissner, Office of Publications, for the copy editing of the many drafts of the manuscript.

Leigh B. Boske
Robert J. Macdonald

EXECUTIVE SUMMARY

INTRODUCTION

The purpose of this study is to provide a comprehensive overview and assessment of the Texas DWI system and laws which govern drunk driving. The study also investigates federal DWI policy initiatives and the programs employed by a select group of states to deter drunk drivers.

Information was obtained from a number of different sources: published material on statutes, policies, and programs; class seminars and lectures involving invited experts and specialists from relevant fields; telephone interviews; mail-out questionnaires; and field trips to Texas localities and to other states and their localities.

The first chapter traces drunk driving legislation at both the federal and state level. It begins with a discussion of federal efforts to promote highway safety through the enactment of legislation, the provision of financial support to the states to develop highway safety programs, and the establishment of data collection activities. A recurring theme is the striving for national uniformity in the establishment of minimum state alcohol traffic safety standards.

The second section of the chapter summarizes state DWI legislative activity over the period 1983-84. Key topics examined are sanctions and penalties, minimum legal drinking ages, illegal per se laws, administrative per se laws, and preliminary breath tests.

The final section focuses on Texas. It contains a chronological summary of changes in Texas DWI laws pertaining to penalties, blood and breath tests of blood alcohol concentration (BAC) levels, deferred adjudication, conditions of probation, and the like. Special emphasis is given to highlighting the major provisions of Senate Bill 1, passed by the Sixty-Eighth Legislature in regular session and signed into law by Governor Mark White in June 1983. This legislation profoundly changed DWI laws in the state.

The second chapter presents a detailed description of the DWI system in Texas. The description is based on interviews with state and local officials involved in the DWI process. Travis County is used as a case study. The chapter is divided into three major sections: DWI system components, agency descriptions, and agency-to-agency interactions. This format is used to indicate where each agency is involved in the overall DWI system, and illuminates system "bottlenecks," or areas that could be improved.

The third chapter describes DWI information collection activities at the federal, state, and county levels of government. Federal programs included for discussion are the National Accident Sampling System (NASS), the Federal Accident Reporting System (FARS), the National Driver Register (NDR), and the FBI Uniform Crime Reporting System (UCR). Also discussed are data collection activities performed by three offices within the Texas Department of Public Safety (DPS). The three offices are the Statistical Services Bureau, the Driver and Vehicle Records Division, and the Uniform Crime Reporting Bureau. The final section of the chapter is devoted to describing DWI case administration and information processing performed by county and district clerks, local law enforcement agencies, prosecutors, and the various courts.

The fourth chapter provides an assessment of the DWI systems of eight Texas counties and the views of county officials regarding the effectiveness of reforms in Texas DWI law continued in Senate Bill 1. The findings are intended to supplement those of the second chapter. The eight counties were selected on the basis of geographic dispersion and varying population size. The visited counties are Comal, Dallas, El Paso, Gray, Harris, Harrison, Webb, and Williamson. Information was collected through in-depth interviews with elected officials and employees of county agencies and departments involved in the DWI process. The field trips took place in February and March of 1985.

The results of a survey mailed to all Texas county and district attorneys also are analyzed. The survey, which posed questions about Senate Bill 1 and solicited recommendations for improvements in existing Texas DWI law, is similar to the one used for the county interviews. Of the 316 surveys mailed, 140 were returned. The response rate of 44.3 percent is quite high and probably represents the degree of high interest in the subject of DWI.

The final chapter addresses special programs employed by Florida, Minnesota, New York, and Pennsylvania to deter drunk driving. These four states were selected for study because of the perceived effectiveness of their programs, the development of their programs into national models, and the specific problems addressed by their programs. The intent was to study a variety of state programs that concentrated on different aspects of the DWI system so as to acquire an understanding of the possible range of options available to Texas.

Information was obtained by field trips to the states in February 1985. Questionnaires were developed for each state. A variety of state and local officials were interviewed so as to obtain a balanced perspective for this report. Moreover, interviewed officials were asked to identify any existing problems and to suggest improvements in their programs. Published material also was collected and used for program descriptions. This material is cited, along with those interviewed, at the end of the chapter.

Appendix 1 contains the individual reports and findings of the eight visited Texas counties. A list of all interviewed county officials appears at the end of the appendix. Whenever possible, interviews were arranged with representatives of the sheriff's department, local police department, district court, district attorney's office, district clerk's office, county court, county attorney's office, county clerk's office, Texas Department of Public Safety (DPS), adult probation department, alcohol council, and the local chapter of Mothers Against Drunk Drivers (MADD).

Copies of the questionnaires used for the in-state and out-of-state interviews are found in Appendices 2, 3, 4, 5, 6, and 7.

The Sixty-Ninth Texas legislature raised the minimum legal drinking age to twenty-one (effective September 1, 1986) and enacted a mandatory seat-belt law (effective September 1, 1985) for front-seat passengers of passenger vehicles and light trucks. These two legislative items are not considered in the following pages because they were signed into law after the research for this report was performed.

FINDINGS

The following summary contains selected excerpts of _some_ of the study's salient findings. However, one is strongly advised to consult the appropriate chapters before rendering a final judgment on a particular matter, as it simply is not possible to cover all findings and to develop complex issues within the context of an executive summary. A firmer appreciation and more intimate understanding of the issues can be acquired by reviewing background information and reading the many individual comments, assessments, and recommendations offered by those who actively participate in the DWI process. This is important because no single set of prescriptions exists that is universally appropriate for all localities and all circumstances. Every attempt has been made to fully document the bases of all conclusions.

Texas DWI System

Focus of DWI Program Efforts

The county DWI systems in Texas are characterized by diversity in their anti-DWI program efforts. Officials in Comal, Dallas, Harris, and Webb counties identified law enforcement and adjudication as the primary focus of their efforts to deter drunk driving. Dallas County also concentrates on public information activities. El Paso County stresses prosecution, public information, and education. Harrison County stresses probation, with a secondary interest in rehabilitation and treatment. Gray County did not identify any particular area of the DWI process as being more important than others in focusing its program efforts. The same applies to Williamson County, although county officials take great pride in their treatment and education programs. In spite of these variations, it should be noted that virtually all interviewed county officials acknowledged that public information, education, and treatment ought to be considered integral components of a comprehensive program to combat drunk driving.

Special Programs

The largest of the visited counties--Harris, Dallas, and El Paso--have established special DWI task forces to improve the effectiveness of county DWI activities and to increase public awareness. The county commissioner's task force in Dallas initially organized to disseminate information on the legislative intent of Senate Bill 1 to the Hispanic community, and later expanded its audience to the entire city. Harris County has two task forces operating within the community as special law enforcement programs to apprehend drunk drivers. The county attorney in El Paso heads a special task force of attorneys to strengthen the county's commitment to enhanced prosecution of DWI cases and to upgrade community public information and education programs addressing the problem.

Harris, El Paso, and Harrison counties participate in the Selective Traffic Enforcement Program (STEP), directed at increasing DWI arrests. Police officers patrol areas with high levels of alcohol-related accidents during peak hours. These officers are specially trained to deal with DWI-related cases.

Most counties, large and small, operate some type of alcohol treatment program, whether through private centers and organizations such as Alcoholics Anonymous, or through county alcohol councils or adult probation departments. Some counties support follow-up programs for the problem drinker in an effort to solve the more basic problem of alcohol abuse. Individual counties identified various alcohol/drug awareness programs within their county as an important, but peripheral, part of the county DWI system.

Williamson County's Dial-a-Ride program, El Paso County's Project Graduation, and Dallas County's Holidays Ahead Campaign and Suspect-A-DWI program are useful and worthwhile special programs. These types of special programs--some of which are being used widely in other Texas counties--can be innovative in the way that they disseminate the message to the entire community that drinking often is lethal to the driving public.

Both Harrison and Comal counties maintain successful work release programs which allow the offender, if convicted of a DWI offense, to serve the sentence while earning a living and maintaining self-esteem. Comal County judges, in particular, attempt to take advantage of the offender's talents through community restitution programs that require the offender to make a constructive contribution to society. This action is viewed as the appropriate punishment for the offense. The county's court system successfully uses innovative forms of alternative punishment for DWI offenses that are believed to make a greater impact on the offender than just a simple fine or jail sentence. They benefit the community as well. These alternate sentences also help to alleviate pressure on the crowded jail facilities in Comal County.

Alcohol Councils

Only three of the eight counties visited--Dallas, Harris, and Williamson--have functioning alcohol councils. Although an alcohol council exists in Harrison County, its functions are severely limited by an annual budget of $500 per year. The Mental Health and Mental Retardation (MHMR) facility, therefore, has assumed the rehabilitation functions and Mortimer-Filkins Test referrals normally performed by the council.

The alcohol councils in Dallas, Harris, and Williamson counties all work closely with their respective adult probation departments for the evaluation and treatment of DWI offenders. These councils offer alcohol education classes, provide Mortimer-Filkins Test referrals, and sponsor various public information programs. Each council offers some form of advanced alcohol education program for problem drinkers and gives high priority to DWI cases. Officials at the Houston Regional Council on Alcoholism, Inc., in Harris County, believe that all convicted DWI offenders should be evaluated and that treatment should be required by law whenever an individual is identified as a problem drinker.

The Dallas Council on Alcoholism currently is targeting the Hispanic community with bilingual pamphlets on Senate Bill 1 to help educate local residents on the changes in the DWI law. Council officials pointed out the difficulties involved with posttreatment evaluations due to the mobile nature of the Dallas community.

Adult Probation Departments

The role of adult probation departments varies among the visited counties. Although all of the adult probation departments offer DWI evaluation and counseling or sponsor DWI schools, the scope of these programs differs. Adult probation departments in Comal and El Paso counties have taken an especially active role in treatment and evaluation by developing and coordinating unique programs. The Harris County Adult Probation Department conducts research and planning. In Comal County, the adult probation department maintains an eight-week "Discovery Program," and the West Texas Regional Adult Probation Department in El Paso County has developed "Project Home" and Pre-Trial Intervention.

The other visited counties offer standard evaluation and treatment. Two counties, Williamson and Gray, refer probationers for treatment to the area alcohol council or Mental Health and Mental Retardation (MHMR) facility. Williamson County contracts with the alcohol council for all of its treatment programs, and Harris County works in conjunction with its alcohol council to evaluate and treat DWI offenders.

Problems with the DWI Process

Problems with the DWI process exist in each of the eight counties. One common problem cited in most counties is a lack of personnel and resources necessary to operate the DWI system effectively or to comply with the changes brought about by Senate Bill 1. Webb and Williamson counties have too few certified officers to administer breath tests, causing substantial delays in the processing of DWI arrests. A general lack of resources for evaluation and treatment of DWI offenders in Harrison, Williamson, and Dallas counties also reduces the effectiveness of their DWI systems.

County officials dislike the legislature's propensity to enact laws without providing adequate funding to assist in their enforcement. The provision calling for the purchase of videotape equipment is a noteworthy example. Additional funding was not provided to purchase videotape equipment or to train officers to use the equipment effectively. This lack of funding causes some officers to feel uncomfortable about using the equipment, leading to major processing delays or a reluctance to use videotaping at all. Comal, Harrison, Williamson, Harris, Dallas, and Webb counties all reported these types of negative experiences with videotaping.

Five counties cited the judicial system as an obstacle to an effective DWI system. In one small county, Harrison, some of the interviewed officials indicated that the prosecution of DWI offenders at times can be political, and many borderline cases are not prosecuted. Webb County officials complained of a lack of effort on the part of prosecutors. This is due, in part, to the unique situation which exists in Webb County. The paperwork involved in prosecuting DWI offenders often is a problem for two reasons. First, the large percentage of Hispanics in the population of Webb County makes using names, addresses, and social security numbers inadequate for checking criminal records. Many individuals have the same first and last names, change addresses frequently, and do not have social security numbers. This results in some individuals receiving a misdemeanor charge, when a felony charge is more appropriate. To combat this problem, county officials have begun using the date of birth as a primary source of information. Second, a large number of DWI arrests involve Mexican nationals who post bond and return to Mexico, leaving the county with extra paperwork and no ability to follow up.

In Harris County, the difficulty lies in the use of jail time versus probation. Offenders sometimes opt for jail time rather than for probation because it proves more troublesome to comply with probation requirements and because there is a failure to enforce minimum jail confinement standards. County officials feel that if jail time is viewed only as a minor inconvenience, both the judicial system and the community's understanding of DWI suffer. The Dallas County judicial system is viewed as relatively ineffective due to judges' lack of knowledge about DWI laws and the inconsistency and leniency in sentencing. Problems in El Paso County focus on the requirement that a justice of the peace must be summoned to give the magistrate's warning after arrest before tests of blood alcohol concentration (BAC) levels can be given. This causes substantial delays in the processing of DWI offenders.

The most fundamental problem is associated with DWI data collection activities. No central agency is charged with collecting information on all DWI arrests and convictions. Although DPS maintains records on DWI arrests made by its own personnel, this information is incomplete. It does not include all DWI arrests made by local law enforcement agencies because Texas has no law requiring such reporting. This often creates problems for prosecutors attempting to determine an offender's previous DWI arrests and convictions on record in other Texas counties and attempting to comply with the speedy trial act.

Each county's record-keeping system appears to be operated differently. This diversity may be due to individual personalities, long-time habits and procedures, or to a lack of guidelines from the state. Data collection at the county level also suffers from a lack of computer systems and computer training, and from insufficient staff to operate the existing systems. The district clerk's office in Comal County sometimes fails to provide information on prior convictions, and reports on judgments sometimes are delayed. The office is just beginning to use computers for record keeping. The effectiveness of the district clerk's office in Dallas County is hindered by administrative problems. The office has trouble retaining competent staff. Pay generally is low and career mobility is limited. In Webb County, the county clerk's office suffers from the same types of administrative problems.

The district clerk's office in Harrison County claims that it files all cases with DPS on the appropriate forms, although no log or record of this exists. A duplicate copy of the form apparently is filed in the office, but the number of duplicates is less than the number of felony dispositions. Therefore, either the clerk does not report all cases to DPS or there is a problem in the filing system of the receipts of dispositions sent to DPS. Also, since the county clerk does not have the felony conviction information necessary to complete the forms, the office does not fill out all the forms. Instead, DPS officers follow up on the cases themselves.

Harris County law enforcement officers reveal frustration over being unable to determine the status of an individual's driver's license quickly. Because of the large backlog of license suspensions, DPS has not confiscated all the licenses. County officials believe the delay is at the DPS facility in Austin, because information is not being entered onto the individual's driving record as rapidly as it should be.

Finally, no formal mechanism is available and no individual(s) has ultimate responsibility at either the state or county level for ensuring cooperation among the various departments and agencies involved in the DWI process. County task forces do create an atmosphere for voluntary cooperation, and most interviewed state and county officials voiced satisfaction in their working relationships with other agencies. Yet, instances of friction among law enforcement agencies, prosecutors, judges, and county and district clerks do occur (as noted in the report) and remain unresolved. Friction can lead to morale problems within agencies.

Effectiveness of Senate Bill 1

One part of the county interviews and the survey mailed to all Texas county and district attorney's involved asking questions about the several reforms in DWI law contained in Senate Bill 1. Officials were asked to respond by rating these "reforms" as very effective, somewhat effective, no change, less effective, or much less effective. Responses varied widely, both within and among counties and among attorneys, indicating that the impact of Senate Bill 1 is an important and diverse issue.

The Senate Bill 1 change that visited counties considered most effective was the admission of a BAC test refusal as evidence in court. Eighty-five percent of the attorneys rated this reform as very or somewhat effective.

The change making .10 percent BAC the per se level of legal intoxication drew the second most positive response. This change is regarded as very or somewhat effective by 70.2 percent of responding attorneys. Although most counties agreed that this reform is very or somewhat effective in strengthening the DWI system, several problems were noted. One problem arises when the .10 percent BAC rule is combined with the use of videotaping. Officials suggested that if the videotape is not convincing, the application of .10 percent BAC rule as per se level of legal intoxication will be made less effective. Gray County officials indicated that juries are reluctant to convict an offender on a .10 percent BAC and that prosecutors often look for other extenuating evidence. This becomes a problem in the opposite direction when juries are discouraged from convicting a DWI offender who registered less than a .10 percent BAC level. The viewpoints of the responding attorneys regarding this and other changes are too numerous to summarize here.

The prohibition of deferred adjudication in DWI cases received a variety of responses. El Paso County considers this an effective change and feels that this will result in more offenders being given probation, which (because it is considered a final conviction) will be used effectively for enhancement (upgrading a penalty) and prosecution. Several counties believe this is an important change but indicated that they had not used deferred adjudication before and, therefore, were not likely to see any change from this reform. In contrast, Gray and Harris counties consider deferred adjudication an effective tool and feel that its removal has made their DWI systems much less effective. Comal County represented a "middle of the road" view. Although officials support an end to the abuse of deferred adjudication by legislative prohibition, they believe a modified system could be effective in certain circumstances. In regard to the prohibition, 31.8 percent of the attorneys rated this change as less or much less effective; 36.7 percent of the county attorneys rated it as less or much less effective; and 35.0 percent of the district attorneys are inclined to view it as producing no change or having little impact.

The provision giving police officers the authority to order alcohol blood and breath tests is given a positive response by most counties, but counties also indicate that this provision would rarely be used. In addition, many counties are not aware this authority exists and do not know how it is to be used. Several counties note that some hospital and medical personnel are reluctant to take blood samples, when requested or ordered to do so by the police, because they feel the limited immunity to civil suit given to them in the law does not afford sufficient protection. Article 67011, section 3(c) of Vernon's Annotated Texas Civil Statutes, as amended in 1983 by the Sixty-Eighth Legislature, provides that registered nurses, qualified technicians, and vocational nurses under the supervision of a physician may take a blood specimen at the direction of a peace officer using "recognized medical procedures . . . provided further that the foregoing shall not relieve any such person from liability for negligence in the withdrawing of any blood specimen." Quite apart from the issue of who can draw the sample, and under what conditions, the point is that negligence is the basis of medical malpractice law. Both physicians and medical paraprofessionals are sensitive to exposing themselves to possible personal involvement in a separate civil suit arising from their cooperation with a law enforcement agency.

The implementation of new procedures for reporting convictions or probations to DPS is considered to have very little impact in most counties. Several counties were complying properly with reporting procedures before the new law, and they consider these changes to be additional paperwork. In Harrison County, the changes have had no impact because the county clerk's office is not complying with the new procedures. Instead, the DPS comes to them periodically to collect data. Attorneys also view this change as having very little impact. District attorneys, however, consider it to be more effective than do county attorneys.

Changes in the implied consent license revocation procedures also drew a mixed response. Comal County believes there has been a substantial reduction in BAC test refusals as a result of this change, but El Paso County believes it is effective because it has shifted the burden of requesting a hearing to the offender. Negative responses focused on the judicial discretion that allows this to be circumvented and the perception that it is being used mostly on low-income offenders. Harrison and Gray counties believe that the poor are at a disadvantage because they are more likely to need a license and are less likely to be in a position to afford counsel to obtain an occupational driver's license.

Attorneys generally are more positive about implied consent license revocation procedures. This change is rated as very or somewhat effective by 65.4 percent of the respondents; attorneys of larger counties--those over twenty-five thousand--rate it as more effective than those of smaller counties.

Responses to the stiffer penalties mandated in Senate Bill 1 vary widely. While Harris and Dallas counties indicated that penalties and fines are not stiff enough, Webb County believes that fines and penalties are too stiff. In Gray County, the majority of low-income offenders could not pay the fines assessed before the Senate Bill 1 changes, making the new fines less effective. Comal and El Paso counties rated the new fines and penalties as an effective change in the system.

Stiffened penalties are considered to be very or somewhat effective by 66.1 percent of the responding attorneys; however, 72.3 percent of those in larger counties versus 59.7 percent of the attorneys in smaller counties view this change as very or somewhat effective. It is interesting to note that 70.9 percent of the county attorneys, who are more likely to be involved with misdemeanor cases, consider stiffened penalties to be very or somewhat effective, whereas only 58.9 percent of the district attorneys responded in kind.

The provision concerning the purchase of videotaping equipment received both negative and positive responses. Every county cited the "skilled or experienced drunk" as a major flaw in the use of videotaping. The procedure has become a "double-edged sword" because it aids in prosecution in some cases and destroys the prosecution's case in others. When the videotape is incriminating, it is an extremely useful tool that seems to elicit guilty pleas in most cases. In contrast, the "skilled drunk," even with a BAC level of .10 percent or greater, may be acquitted because of a jury's interpretation of his/her behavior on videotape. Several counties indicated that the lack of funding has made it difficult to acquire high quality equipment and to train officers to use the equipment effectively. If fact, Gray County has not complied with this provision because officials feel that cheap equipment, which is all they can afford, is worse than no equipment at all.

The videotaping of suspects is seen by 42.7 percent of the attorneys as producing no change; 37.3 percent view it as very or somewhat effective; and 20.0 percent regard it as less or much less effective. The size of a county is directly related to the particular response. This finding is logical since the provision requiring the purchase of videotaping equipment only applies to counties having twenty-five thousand residents or more. Thus, smaller counties are inclined to view this provision as producing no change in their DWI efforts. In larger counties, 46.8 percent of the attorneys consider it to be very or somewhat effective; 19.0 percent as producing no change; and the remainder as less or much less effective. More district attorneys consider this provision to be very or somewhat effective than do county attorneys.

In summary, the change adjudged to be the most effective in reducing drunk driving is the provision allowing admission of BAC test refusal in court. The redefining of legal intoxication as .10 percent BAC or more also is rated as an effective step. To a lesser degree, changes in license revocation procedures and stiffened penalties also are ranked positively. Ambivalence is revealed toward the changes in the authority of police officers to order blood and breath tests of BAC levels and new procedures for reporting convictions. Finally, the prohibition of deferred adjudication and the provision concerning videotaping equipment are rated as the least effective of the changes.

Programs in Other States

In addressing the DWI problem, the four visited states take different means to deter drinking and driving. In two Florida counties, law enforcement, public information, and education are stressed. The state of Minnesota chooses to emphasize administrative procedures to ensure that their DWI system provides certainty of punishment. New York believes in a community-based approach to the problem. Pennsylvania, within a health and legal context, provides for a statewide management information system.

Florida

Two Florida counties, Orange and Pinellas, provide examples of effective DWI activities at the local level. While operating under Florida laws, the counties took the initiative in developing their programs. Both counties created programs that emphasize enforcement, public information, and education.

In Orange County, the sheriff's department's Breath Alcohol Testing Mobile Units (Batmobiles) are the primary feature, used for both enforcement and public information and education. In terms of enforcement, the Batmobiles function most effectively as fixed testing sites while being rotated among high visibility locations. Each Batmobile includes the equipment and paperwork necessary for testing and prosecuting DWI offenders. With closer access to a testing site, offenders are tested soon after being apprehended. With trained personnel in the Batmobile to perform the tests and videotape the offender, the officers' average arrest processing times decreased from five hours to thirty to forty-five minutes.

The Batmobiles are also used to inform and educate the public. The units are taken to junior and senior high school demonstrations. The deputies are also active in showing movies and making presentations as a part of their public education and information activities.

In Pinellas County, the "Arrest Drunk Driving" campaign focuses on officer training, enforcement, and public information and education. Police officers associated with the campaign received extensive enforcement training. As a part of the enforcement efforts, the use of roadblocks was increased. Altogether, only twelve checkpoints have been set up. The media publicized them to such an extent, however, that it appears to the public that there are many more than twelve checkpoints. Public information and education activities have centered on the "we will catch you" theme. The philosophy behind such publicity is that an enforcement campaign cannot survive without proper public information and education, and that public information and education is the most effective tool for changing societal attitudes regarding drinking and driving.

In both Orange and Pinellas counties, the use of videotaping is highly touted. Officials in both counties consider it to be the main reason behind their increased conviction rates (which went from 67 to 92 percent in Orange County, and from 65 to 96 percent in Pinellas County). In regard to the increases in the conviction rates, several things must be considered. Other factors, such as the national awareness of DWI, occurred at the same time these two counties began using videotaping. This could account for some of the increase. Both counties emphasize close proximity to a test site; with the offender videotaped soon after arrest, there is less time for the driver to sober up.

Videotaping is not currently mandated by Florida law, and some local officials strongly support the discretion left to the individual counties. They believe that law enforcement officers are generally more enthusiastic over voluntary practices initiated to satisfy local needs. Officials in Florida feel that the fixed testing sites are best in urban areas. Sharing of these testing resources has been another important factor in the success of the Florida DWI system. The four cities involved in the "Arrest Drunk Driving" campaign have demonstrated that much more can be accomplished through a cooperative effort than by municipalities acting autonomously. Orange County officials have shown that private groups often are willing to contribute additional resources to aid in purchasing new equipment.

One other public education effort in Florida that deserves to be mentioned is one directed at college students. Through the BACCHUS program, an attempt is being made to provide peer support and education for making responsible decisions about drinking and driving. Also, the Florida Department of Health and Rehabilitative Services is providing help to students at Florida state universities who have been convicted of DWI.

The programs in Orange and Pinellas counties are specific examples of what can be accomplished through local initiatives in a short period of time. The examples also lend support to the idea that local levels of government should be allowed the freedom to design programs that will most efficiently and effectively meet their needs. Finally, without the latitude given them by the state, and the generous support from the private sector, the programs in the two counties would not have achieved the same measure of success.

Minnesota

The most prominent feature of Minnesota's DWI system is its two-track method for handling DWI offenders. In the administrative track, a driver automatically loses his license for one year for refusing to take an alcohol concentration test, or for six months for testing at or above the .10 percent level. The officer is authorized to take the license from the driver and issue a seven-day permit. The revocation is not stayed pending the outcome of a hearing, if one is requested by the driver. The administrative revocation is automatic, regardless of the outcome of any criminal charges. Because they have the ability to take the driver's license and know that the offender will receive some form of punishment, officers have dramatically increased the number of DWI arrests made in the state.

In the criminal track, the offender faces additional penalties if convicted. In the Twin Cities metropolitan area, first-time DWI offenders are generally sentenced to two days in jail and fined $200 to $300. Even if the sentence is plea bargained down, the driver's history contains a record of an alcohol-related offense due to the administrative revocation.

Minnesota was the first state to require that all convicted DWI offenders undergo an alcohol problem assessment. The assessment includes alcohol-related questions as well as questions about family situation and financial status. The assessment report includes information on the driver's traffic record, prior alcohol problems, and amenability to rehabilitation. The assessment is used to assign a level of alcohol problem and level of probation. It is used as an aid by the judge when sentencing.

A recent report by the Minnesota House Research Department recommended that to maintain a long-term reduction in alcohol-related accidents, DWI laws must continually be reviewed and amended. Also, social disapproval of drinking and driving and moral commitment to upholding the laws must be encouraged. Encouragement can be in the form of public information and education. Several catalysts have helped in the continuous development of the DWI laws, including tragic examples of the damage drunk drivers can incur, heavy media attention, the governor and attorney general's working together, the efforts of citizen groups, expert testimony before the legislature, and favorable rulings by the state's courts.

Minnesota's strongest DWI efforts are at the state level, in areas that are the state's traditional functions, such as driver licensing and legislation. Changes to help the state's DWI control system have also facilitated local level DWI efforts. Also, along with increasing local enforcement efforts, the administrative license revocation automatically and immediately removes DWI offenders from the state's roadways.

New York

New York, interested in retaining a community focus on the DWI problem, developed the Special Traffic Options Program for Driving While Intoxicated, or STOP-DWI. Counties that develop STOP-DWI programs and budgets receive all of the fine money from DWI offenders in that county. While the state did not mandate participation, most counties have developed their own STOP-DWI program. Participating counties are required to appoint a coordinator who has the responsibility of developing the DWI program and budget. Otherwise, state requirements are minimal.

There are several benefits to the STOP-DWI program. The county governments are granted the autonomy to develop DWI programs that are appropriate for that locale, while the state government still remains as the overall coordinator and overseer. The county programs are funded by those who abuse the DWI laws; as more offenders are convicted, county funding increases. The counties do not have to fear that their funding will be cut off nor priorities changed unexpectedly. And the STOP-DWI program is compatible with the existing criminal justice system.

Each county has a STOP-DWI program designed by and for its citizens and facilitated by the county coordinator. Soon after STOP-DWI was initiated, the county coordinators formed an association. This has resulted in an additional benefit--the STOP-DWI Coordinators Association provides a forum for the exchange of ideas and information among the counties. In sum, STOP-DWI has provided New York with a state-coordinated, locally implemented, self-financing approach to the DWI problem.

Pennsylvania

Within the context of its health and legal approach, the Commonwealth of Pennsylvania has developed several programs for addressing the drinking driver problem. The three programs that would be most applicable to Texas are the Court Reporting Network (CRN), the Accelerated Rehabilitative Disposition (ARD), and the use of county coordinators to facilitate interaction between the criminal justice system and the alcohol education and treatment agencies.

The CRN gives the commonwealth the capability to combine information on an offender's driving history, alcohol use, prior alcohol-related treatment, license and insurance status, income source, and an alcohol-highway safety evaluation. This information is generated into a Client Profile Form (CPF) which also recommends appropriate treatment, including diversion into the ARD program. The CRN also provides vital information to the county coordinators through aggregated county data and access to statewide information. Because of the CRN, the commonwealth has centralized and standardized statewide information on drinking drivers.

The ARD program is a pretrial diversion mechanism used throughout the commonwealth. In order to qualify for the ARD, certain basic criteria must be met. Participants in ARD must agree to pay restitution, attend an alcohol highway safety school, go through probation, have their licenses suspended for one to twelve months, and, in some cases, undergo alcohol treatment. ARD is not considered a first conviction for enhancement purposes unless another alcohol-related conviction occurs within seven years. The program saves time and money in the adjudication process and relieves crowding in jails.

While the commonwealth provides oversight and direction for drunk driving activities, the counties are responsible for carrying out the programs. Pennsylvania law requires each county to have a DUI coordinator. Therefore, like Florida and New York, local government activities for attacking the drinking and driving problem are emphasized. The coordinator may be located in the county's probation office or health department or the county may contract with a private consultant.

The county coordinators are responsible for planning, implementing, and monitoring the county alcohol highway safety program. While the county must implement state programs, they may also develop additional programs of their own. Funding for county activities comes from federal highway safety funds dispersed by the commonwealth and from a combination of fines and fees. Through the county coordinators, the commonwealth ensures that counties adopt a minimum level of DWI activity, while at the same time allowing the counties the autonomy to develop additional programs.

CONCLUSIONS

The approaches reviewed in this report to deter drunk driving are varied, yet a few common themes are obvious. Most of the programs were either locally initiated or facilitated local activity. DWI is a problem within each locality; the evidence suggests that local programs, supported or encouraged by the state, are the most effective. Encouragement can be in the form of financial incentives, access to statewide DWI information, or even authorization to take the offender's driver's license. This focus on local programs suggests that programs should not be mandated for each local government; instead, localities should be granted the latitude to develop their own programs to meet their individual needs.

The state does have an important role to play, however. Local government programs need to meet minimum requirements, and some state supervision is desirable. Some of the DWI control functions belong at the state level, such as legislation and driver licensing. Other functions require close state supervision, such as adjudication, probation, and treatment. Any action taken by the state should be sure not to hinder local efforts.

Such general observations, nevertheless, can be carried too far. While localities are in the best position to know their individual needs, friction and differences of opinion over policy matters can and do exist among local officials, and no one has ultimate responsibility for resolving differences or coordinating DWI activities. Moreover, localities often are not aware of the great variety of options available elsewhere for combating DWI; a few local officials are not even fully aware of the existing provisions of the law.

It seems to us that a compelling case can be made for the need to establish some type of formal mechanism to address these and other DWI-related problems in Texas, but we recognize that in the context of the existing judicial and administrative structures of the state such reforms may not be possible. Texas lacks the centralized executive structure of many other states. At the top, the executive function is diffused among dozens of boards and commissions, each with extensive and independent authority in its particular area of responsibility. The governor's ability to influence the day-to-day management of most state agencies is legally and politically circumscribed.

The diffusion of executive authority at the state level is mirrored in the structure of county government, where there is no central executive authority. There is no general ordinance-making authority at the county level. Texas county government is essentially a congeries of competing elected officials, each with constitutionally established areas of responsibility over which the Commissioner's Court (its members are also members of the congeries) exercises little control except through the budgetary process. Although county governments perform many ministerial and administrative functions for the state, the state exercises very little direct executive authority over county officials.

There seems to be little possibility that many of the concepts and ideas involving special forms of executive control over the DWI problem at the state or county level which have worked well in other states can be achieved in Texas. The whole "systems approach" touted by the National Highway Traffic Safety Administration (NHTSA) is predicated on the assumption that sufficient central executive authority exists to mandate the necessary coordination at the state and local levels.

We do think that much can be achieved in Texas through voluntary efforts at the local level. Many Texas communities organized DWI task forces in response to the findings of the recent Governor's Task Force on Traffic Safety, which focused public attention on administration of the DWI problem at the local level. The efforts of volunteer public interest groups such as Mothers Against Drunk Driving, Remove Intoxicated Drivers (RID), and Students Against Driving Drunk (SADD) were of crucial importance in the successful passage of Senate Bill 1.

Finally, the same general needs and deficiencies are also reflected in the judicial system. Many people do not realize that the attorney general, nominally the state's attorney and its chief law enforcement officer, exercises no direct hierarchical authority over the conduct of district and county attorneys in criminal matters. As a practical matter, these prosecutors, like other county officials, perform without executive oversight. The basic reason that records of previous DWI offenses are difficult to obtain is that Texas lacks a central reporting system for serious misdemeanors. The deficiencies affecting DWI prosecutions are encountered in prosecutions of other comparable offenses. County clerks can fail to do their duty in reporting DWI case dispositions to the DPS for inclusion in the driver's license history because there is no state level oversight of their activities and no legal structure beyond the constitutional provisions defining their duties or the organization of their offices.

In the preceding paragraphs, we have attempted to provide a context in which the needs and recommendations which follow can be evaluated by policymakers and public interest groups. The obstacles are formidable but not insurmountable. The best chance for eventual success rests on the development of long-term planning to provide the legislature with a comprehensive, fully documented, and practical program for achieving these ends.

In reading this report, one will encounter many useful insights offered by officials working within the DWI system on a daily basis. Among these insights, a few surface as being overridingly important:

DWI systems consist of several interrelated components--legislation, law enforcement, prosecution and adjudication, case administration and information processing, punishment, treatment, and prevention (public information and education programs). Each component is partially dependent upon and contributes to the performance of the other components. The need for close and continuous interaction requires that all components have balanced roles to play in the functioning of the DWI system. Insufficient funding, crowded jail facilities, growing backlogs of pending judicial cases, and many other credible reasons can be given as to why localities adopt certain strategies; and localities ought to be given flexibility to develop anti-DWI programs in accordance with their individual needs. However, all the evidence suggests that excessive reliance on law enforcement without accompanying changes in societal attitudes toward drunk driving, or excessive use of probation without effective treatment programs, or stiffened penalties without certain and swift punishment, ultimately leads to a DWI system failure in attempts to properly address the drunk driving problem.

The state of Texas needs both a centralized statewide DWI reporting system and consistent, accurate, and accessible county record-keeping systems. It makes absolutely no sense to enact stiffer penalties for first and second offenses and new penalties for third and subsequent offenses unless prosecutors are able to determine prior arrests, convictions, and other relevant legal information. Ideally, Texas should have a comprehensive management information system which is capable of tracking an offender throughout the entire DWI process. Such a system would facilitate communication and coordination and would provide the requisite factual information for program evaluation and planning.

The Travis County Anti-DWI Project, a three-year effort to end March 31, 1987, is attempting to address this problem. One of the most significant aspects of the project is the development of an automated countywide management information system. A number of data elements including statistics on enforcement, prosecution, adjudication, probation, rehabilitation and treatment, and public information and education are being collected and reported by participating agencies to the program coordinator. A parallel effort should be initiated on an automated statewide management information system.

A special concern voiced by county officials is that a lack of funding has limited the effectiveness of county DWI systems and has hindered compliance with the changes brought about by Senate Bill 1. The areas of probation, treatment, county record keeping, and videotaping of suspects are particularly susceptible to fiscal restraints. While complaints of inadequate funding by all state and local agencies are a common refrain these days, careful thought should be given to instituting a self-financing DWI system, funded by alcohol-impaired drivers. Since this is the equivalent of a highway user (abuser) fee, it hardly constitutes a radical proposal. Fees collected within a county would go to supporting county anti-DWI activities.

Finally, we are particularly impressed with Minnesota's administrative per se law. It has dramatically increased the certainty of punishment; reduced requests for license suspension hearings, plea bargaining of cases, and delay tactics; restricted the issuance of occupational driver's licenses to those who truly need them; and has not proved to be costly in its implementation. Minnesota was a pioneer in administrative per se law and, therefore, has had the most time to work out problems. An extensive discussion of the relative merits of Minnesota's administrative per se law appears in Chapter 5.

CHAPTER 1

LEGISLATIVE HISTORY OF FEDERAL AND STATE DWI POLICY INITIATIVES

INTRODUCTION

This chapter provides a comprehensive overview of public policy initiatives to combat the problem of drunk driving at the state and federal levels. The first two sections consist of legislative actions taken by the federal government and various states, and the third section deals specifically with driving while intoxicated (DWI) public policies in the state of Texas.

Federal activities have been cyclical in nature. The early years (1920-65) were characterized by an emphasis on driver behavior and precautions he could take to protect himself. The middle stage (1965-80) emphasized the regulatory mechanism and actions that could be taken to protect the driver and occupants of a motor vehicle. The current focus (1980-present) has returned to the driver, and public policy decisions on drunk driving again emphasize the implications of driver actions.

Ongoing state legislative activity will be examined in terms of the major changes that new legislation makes in existing DWI statutes. The key topics to be explored include sanctions and penalties, minimum drinking age legislation, illegal per se laws, administrative per se laws, and preliminary breath tests.

The examination of drunk driving legislation in Texas will focus on three major areas. Penalties comprise the first and most expansive area, as their history can be traced to 1923. The second area involves the taking of specimens: for example, the use of blood and breath tests and refusal to submit to the tests. And the third area of legislation concerns deferred adjudication and probation. Also highlighted in this section are novel changes in DWI legislation, including "aggravated DWI"--allowing an intoxicated driver to borrow a motor vehicle--and using forfeiture of the offender's motor vehicle as a punitive measure.

FEDERAL DWI PROGRAM ACTIVITIES

The extent to which alcohol-related highway safety concerns evoke public policy actions reflects the degree of public awareness and concern for the issue. Although the problem of drunk driving has been in existence for decades, the issue did not gain widespread awareness until the early 1980s. The purpose of this historical analysis is to examine not only vital legislative actions, but also the social and political conditions contributing to the success or failure of different anti-DWI initiatives.

Early Concerns: 1920-46

Prior to World War II, highway traffic safety programs in the United States focused on general safety and roadway conditions. The national conferences conducted during the 1920s and 1930s emphasized the need for uniformity among state laws and requirements. The absence of a role for the federal government went unquestioned. Federal officials accepted the desire of individual states to develop their own traffic safety programs and laws, rarely stopping to consider whether the federal government should be involved.

The minimal federal presence and low priority given to highway traffic safety continued through the war years. By 1946, however, President Truman saw the need for a more aggressive approach by the government in propelling the states to develop effective traffic safety programs (see Table 1). Although state compliance was voluntary, the President's Highway Safety Conference of 1946 reported several key areas where action was required to combat ever-increasing problems. The resulting "Action Programs" called for states to initiate efforts to: facilitate laws and ordinances; modernize traffic accident records; strengthen education; improve engineering; expedite motor vehicle administration; foster police traffic supervision; aid traffic courts; increase public information; supplement research; provide health, medical care, and transportation for the injured; and encourage organized citizen support.[1] However, in these early efforts, drunk driving was not yet recognized as a problem in and of itself. Rather, an acknowledgment of the potential dangers of drinking and driving came in the form of an educational approach. Public Information programs to warn of the risks were encouraged, but assistance in developing and sustaining such programs failed to reach the states, resulting in a continued failure to address the problem effectively.

Growing Awareness: 1954-59

State compliance with the Action Programs remained voluntary. As can be expected when participation is optional, most states chose not to act. By 1954, an increasing awareness of state autonomy in implementing traffic safety programs led President Eisenhower to chair the White House Conference on Highway Safety. Conference organizers sought to push the states toward adoption of the Action Programs. A realization surfaced, however, that more forceful steps would be necessary if the United States was ever to have a comprehensive traffic safety program. The Federal-Aid Highway Act of 1956 authorized the Secretary of Commerce to investigate the issue of highway safety and to determine whether the federal government had an appropriate role in furthering safety goals.

The Secretary's report, issued in 1959, concurred with the contention that increased federal involvement would benefit the public. Specifically, the findings of the Department of Commerce urged participation and oversight by the federal government in the areas of traffic enforcement,

Table 1
Chronological Summary of Federal Anti-DWI Initiatives

Year	Action Taken	Results and Provisions
1946	President's Highway Safety Conference	Initiated Action Programs covering eleven areas of highway safety. Drunk driving under auspices of educational programs.
1954	White House Conference on Highway Safety	Pushed for state adoption of 1946 Action Programs.
1956	Federal-Aid Highway Act of 1956	Directed Congress to study what actions should be taken at federal level to improve highway safety.
1960	Driver's Licenses—Record of Revocations Act of 1960	Created National Driver Register to act as a clearinghouse for central compilation and review of driver's licenses.
1965	Baldwin Amendment	Required each state to establish an approved highway safety program.
1966	Highway Safety Act of 1966	Provided guidance and funding for state highway safety programs and special projects.
1967	Alcohol Safety Standard No. 8	Established guidelines for state anti-DWI activity.
1970	Alcohol Safety Action Program (ASAP)	Established a systems approach to combat drinking driver in selected cities.
1974	NHTSA Countermeasure Programs	Contained efforts to improve identification and apprehension of drunk drivers.
1979	*Delaware* v. *Prouse*	U.S. Supreme Court upheld constitutionality of vehicle roadblocks to check for DWI.
1982	Presidential Commission on Drunk Driving	Created task force to thoroughly study DWI problems and make recommendations to combat the growing problem.
1982	Alcohol Traffic Safety and National Driver Register Act of 1982	Created financial incentives for states to enact stricter drunk driving programs.
1984	National Minimum Drinking Age Act of 1984	Required states to raise drinking age to twenty-one or face the withholding of federal highway construction funds.

laws, vehicles, education, highways, and driver records. As with the Action Programs, alcohol-related driving fell under the broad category of education.[2]

The National Driver Register: 1960

The first real federal effort to combat drunk driving through a noneducational format came in 1960. Pursuant to the Secretary of Commerce's recommended areas for national action, Congress passed the Driver's Licenses--Record of Revocations Act (PL 86-660), thereby creating the National Driver Register (NDR). Designed to act as a clearinghouse for central compilation and review of driver's licenses, the NDR faced several restrictive limitations from its beginning. First, it included records of those with a license revocation or refusal due to either of two reasons: driving while intoxicated or conviction of a violation of a highway safety code which involved loss of life. The concern for individual rights, combined with a hesitation to allow extensive federal intrusions into state records, led Congress to narrowly define the jurisdiction of the National Driver Register. Additionally, a technicality regarding the term "driving while intoxicated" adversely affected the integrity of the data compiled in the NDR. States choosing not to participate could argue that their revocations were not for "driving while intoxicated" but rather for "drinking while driving" or "driving under the influence."[3]

The Baldwin Amendment of 1965

In the 1960s, the federal responsibility for traffic safety came to fruition. Acting on the guidelines established by the 1946 Action Programs, the Congress began to pass the requisite legislation for an assertive federal role in traffic safety. The Baldwin Amendment of 1965 (PL 89-139) called for uniformity among the states in their traffic safety programs. The Secretary of Commerce issued standards to the states for developing their traffic safety programs. The Baldwin Amendment was perceived to be a step toward greater uniformity and cooperation, and it did lay the groundwork for the landmark legislation passed in 1966. However, its effectiveness was limited because it failed to include any enforcement provisions in the event a state refused to develop a traffic safety program.

The Highway Safety Act of 1966

The Highway Safety Act of 1966 (PL 89-564) and the National Traffic and Motor Vehicle Act of 1966 (PL 89-563) shifted the emphasis of traffic safety from the driver to the automobile. The federal government undertook an active role in regulatory rulemaking for motor vehicles. Propelled in part by Ralph Nader's book <u>Unsafe</u> <u>at</u> <u>Any</u> <u>Speed</u> and by the traffic fatality statistics of the early 1960s--approximately forty-nine thousand deaths in 1965--Congress took the necessary steps to strengthen the Baldwin Amendment and to firmly implant the federal government's role in traffic safety and its related aspects. The primary importance of the Highway Safety Act is section 402 and the requirement that states base their traffic safety programs on certain uniform standards or face the imposition of sanctions and the loss of federal highway funds. The standards, later issued by the Secretary of Transportation, express the goals of a state traffic safety program in terms of performance criteria. The state programs must be approved by the Secretary of Transportation.[4] Also, section 403 provided for research and development. It concentrated on preventing accidents, minimizing the adverse affects of an accident, improving accident investigation procedures, and developing comprehensive data collection and analysis procedures.

Work began immediately thereafter on developing the first set of standards. The Department of Transportation (DOT) walked a fine line in accommodating both the intentions of Congress and the capabilities of the states. The rival aspirations of a mandate for uniformity and a quest for flexibility forced the Department of Transportation to develop standards emphasizing broad goals beneficial to society. The mode of implementation was delegated to the state, a policy which remains in effect to this day.[5] So long as states, as determined by the Secretary, exert efforts to achieve full compliance, sanction proceedings remain a superficial threat.

In any case, the standards remain as the guideline for state traffic safety programs. The initial standards, issued in 1967, address those areas felt to be most in need of immediate attention, as determined by the Department of Transportation in cooperation with the states. They include motor vehicle registration, motorcycle safety, driver education, driver licensing, codes and laws, traffic courts, alcohol in relation to highway safety, and traffic records.[6] The Secretary is to report to Congress annually on the progress made in addressing the standards.

The Alcohol Safety Standard

The alcohol safety standard, issued as Standard No. 8 by the Department of Transportation, provides a key example of the conflict inherent in striving for uniformity while retaining flexibility. Congress acknowledged this dilemma in the formulation of the Highway Safety Act of 1966. Instead of ordering a specific standard for alcohol safety, Congress required the Department of Transportation to conduct a thorough study of the issues involved in drunk driving. Issued in 1968, this report--1968 Alcohol and Highway Safety Report--contained the first major comprehensive study of alcohol and its role in highway safety.[7]

Recognizing the seriousness of the problem proved to be only the first step in developing a standard acceptable to all fifty states. The Department of Transportation differentiates the alcohol-safety program from others for three key reasons: (1) drunk driving covers a problem area in which responsibilities are delegated to numerous agencies, whose jurisdictions often overlap; (2) drunk driving is but a part of the broader problem of social drinking in the United States; and, (3) alcohol is "the single biggest traffic safety problem," accounting for one-half of the fatalities in traffic accidents across the country.[8]

The initial Standard No. 8 cited three criteria that states should strive for in the development of their highway safety plan. First, chemical testing should be used to determine the amount of alcohol in a person's body at the time of apprehension. Second, the establishment of a blood alcohol concentration (BAC) level of .10 percent (or more) is to be presumptive evidence of intoxication. Third, laws should confirm the implied consent of a motorist to submit to a chemical test.[9] The National Safety Council's (NSC) Committee on Alcohol and Drugs played the major role in developing these guidelines, as the Department of Transportation acknowledged the prominence of the NSC in the field of chemical testing.

Decade of Challenge: The 1970s

The 1970s brought many challenges to the actions occurring in the highway safety arena. The Department of Transportation's efforts to initiate mandatory activities for state program development encountered stiff resistance in the Congress. In 1972, the Department of Transportation sought to force states to pass two controversial laws--mandatory helmet usage for motorcyclists and blood alcohol concentration level of .10 percent or more to be per se evidence of intoxication. Congress responded in 1973 by passing legislation prohibiting the Secretary of Transportation from "issuing or changing standards without the express consent of Congress."[10]

In 1974, the group Public Citizen filed a lawsuit charging the DOT with failure to comply with the intent of Congress by not stringently enforcing the safety standards. The United States District Court for the District of Columbia ruled, however, that as long as states were making "reasonable progress" in attaining the standards, the Secretary of Transportation would be in compliance with the Highway Safety Act of 1966. If the states were not making such progress, it was incumbent upon the Secretary to invoke the sanctions.[11]

The rules of procedure in applying sanctions appeared in the Federal Register. Shortly thereafter, proceedings began against Maryland and Puerto Rico for their failure to comply with the Alcohol in Relation to Highway Safety Standard. By 1975, both states strengthened their statutes to comply with federal regulations. These events taught both parties the value of coordination and cooperation, but the sanction process severely strained the balance of federal-state relations.[12] In the future, efforts to increase federal involvement would take into account state interests, and the states would recognize the statutory responsibilities of the Department of Transportation to implement congressional mandates.

The Department of Transportation program initiatives constituted the primary achievements in combatting drunk driving during these early years. In recognition of the limited ability of Standard No. 8 to bring about a comprehensive national DWI program, the National Highway Traffic Safety Administration (NHTSA)--an administration within the Department of Transportation created by the Highway Safety Act of 1966--began funding special programs in various localities. The most far-reaching of these programs began in 1970 during the Nixon Administration. Formally known as the Alcohol Safety Action Program (ASAP), its projects targeted $78 million in grants to thirty-five cities across the country.[13] The unique approach taken by the ASAP reflected the view presented in the 1968 Report on Alcohol and Highway Safety, namely, the importance of a systems approach to combat the drinking driver. Thus, agencies responsible for detection, apprehension, prosecution, treatment, rehabilitation, and public information came together under the auspices of ASAP to evaluate the DWI system in each community. Funded for three years, these projects sought to establish effective measures for detection and prosecution, and to address the need for decisive action to put those measures into effect.[14] Additionally, the social drinker became the target of massive public information and education efforts warning of the dangers of drinking and driving.

As noted, the ASAP projects received funding for a limited period of time. When the funds expired, the programs either were dissolved or were assimilated into the city's budget. Meanwhile, NHTSA continued sponsoring numerous research projects designed to provide "a better definition of the extent and nature of the alcohol safety problem." In 1971, the Mortimer-Filkins Test was developed. This test, widely used across the United States, categorizes alcohol-impaired drivers according to the severity of their drinking problem so as to facilitate referral to the appropriate treatment agency.[15]

Ongoing Efforts: 1974-77

By 1974, NHTSA had shifted its emphasis from alcohol safety to the implementation of effective countermeasure programs. Drawing upon the systems approach of the ASAP projects, these countermeasures focused on improving the identification and apprehension of drunk drivers. Federal funds not only allowed for greater training in law enforcement techniques, but also went toward ensuring that court decisions regarding punishment and treatment were implemented and followed.[16] This three-pronged approach of identification, decision, and action was intended to spur greater initiatives by states and communities in enforcing existing DWI statutes.

As the decade drew to a close, however, it became evident that the concerned parties were dragging their feet. A 1977 effort by Rep. James Oberstar (D-Minn.) to upgrade the National Driver Register to facilitate comprehensive records of repeat traffic offenders encountered difficulty in Congress. Instead of increasing funding and passing a new law, Congress requested a thorough study of the NDR and the legitimacy of Oberstar's request. The results of the study would not be known until 1981.

Delaware v. Prouse

Not all states avoided their responsibility in combatting the drunk driver. Some had initiated programs of roadblocks and searches designed to detect alcohol-impaired drivers during the high-risk weekend night hours. Some of the drivers who were stopped claimed the search methods were in violation of their Fourth Amendment rights. A case went before the Supreme Court, and in Delaware v. Prouse (1979) Justice Byron White held that arbitrarily stopping a vehicle to check for driver's license and registration is unreasonable, and thus illegal, unless "there is at least articuable and reasonable suspicion . . . or that either the vehicle or an occupant is otherwise subject to seizure for violation of law."[17] Justice White went on, however, to uphold practices of roadblocks where all vehicles are stopped. In a concurring opinion, Justice Harry Blackman assumed random spot checks involving other less obtrusive stops--for example, every tenth car to pass a given point--to be likewise protected by the Court.

The Carter Years: 1977-80

One additional aspect of traffic and alcohol safety during the later 1970s should be noted. During the Carter Administration, NHTSA was headed by Joan Claybrook. A firm believer in the primacy of federal regulations to protect drivers and passengers in motor vehicles, Claybrook oversaw many regulatory initiatives designed to further protect motor vehicle occupants, including passive restraint requirements, bumper and windshield standards, and tire specifications.[18] And although most would agree with the basic intent of these actions, the focus on motor vehicle improvements, rather than on the driver, may have been to the detriment of DWI program efforts. This is evidenced by the fact that no major alcohol safety initiatives can be traced to NHTSA during the late 1970s.

Heightened Interest: The 1980s

Upon taking office in 1981, President Reagan pledged to do away with many regulations determined to be "burdensome." The Administration's budget proposals targeted many safety programs as unnecessary or overly burdensome to the distressed automotive industry. In June 1981, the Department of Transportation favored abolishing the National Driver Register. The DOT support would be restored only upon the issuance of the congressional report supporting Rep. Oberstar's efforts to upgrade it.[19] Despite these factors, major legislation regarding drunk driving was passed during the early years of the Reagan Administration.

Citizen Involvement

The return to emphasizing driver behavior in traffic safety programs is not the sole impetus to the recent reforms and initiatives regarding drunk driving. Rather, the growth of citizen participation and organized movements, particularly Candy Lightner's Mothers Against Drunk Drivers (MADD), has contributed more than any government-sponsored study ever could. In addition, combatting drunk driving is an issue that few people oppose. As more and more accounts surfaced of the victims killed or seriously injured by drunken drivers, a public outcry arose demanding immediate action.

Presidential Commission on Drunk Driving

President Reagan, responsive to the political popularity of the drunk driving movement and under pressure from public interest groups, created the Presidential Commission on Drunk Driving in April 1982.[20] Charged with the task of encouraging state and local governments to implement new programs to reduce the damages caused by drunk drivers, the Commission conducted public hearings and briefings throughout the country. While promoting public awareness of the problem, the Commission also issued numerous recommendations covering all aspects of the DWI system. The recommendations were designed to foster state and local action.[21] In terms of prevention, the Commission stressed the need for alcohol-impaired driving to be recognized as socially unacceptable behavior and suggested a variety of public information and education campaigns to heighten public awareness. Community efforts play a key role in stimulating local concern for drunk driving. The Commission made specific recommendations regarding alcoholic beverage regulation, including support for making twenty-one the minimum legal purchasing age, dramshop laws--laws concerned with third-party liability in the serving and/or selling of alcoholic beverages--and improved systems support through program financing. Improvements in prosecution and adjudication to strengthen the penalties and to discourage drunk driving gained the support of the Commission.

Congressional Activity: The Alcohol Traffic Safety and National Driver Register Act of 1982

Also during 1982, hearings held before congressional subcommittees reflected the need to reduce the number of highway fatalities attributable to alcohol. Approximately one-half of fatal traffic accidents were alcohol related in 1982. This is the near equivalent of experiencing every day for an entire year the tragedy of the January 1982 Air Florida crash in which seventy-eight people died.[22]

Largely through the dedicated support and sponsorship of Rep. James Howard (D-N.J.) and Rep. Michael Barnes (D-Md.), Congress enacted the first major federal drunk driving law in October 1982. The Alcohol Traffic

Safety and National Driver Register Act of 1982 (PL 97-364) amended Title 23 of the U.S. Code to encouraged states to establish effective alcohol traffic safety programs.[23] In keeping with the ever-pressing demands for flexibility, the Barnes-Howard Bill, as it is known, does not require state participation in the program, nor does it specifically guide them in their actions. Rather, the act creates financial incentives in the form of grants from the Highway Trust Fund for states enacting stricter drunk driving programs. For a state to receive a share of the $125 million appropriation contained in the bill--up to a maximum of 30 percent of its 1983 section 402 highway funds--its alcohol traffic safety program must meet these criteria:

1. Establishment of .10 percent blood alcohol concentration (BAC) as the per se level of intoxication;

2. Prompt suspension or revocation of a driver's license for at least ninety days for the first drunk driving offense and at least one year for a subsequent offense;

3. Mandatory jail sentence of forty-eight consecutive hours or at least ten days community service for any offender convicted of drunk driving more than once in five years; and,

4. Increased enforcement of state drunk driving laws supported by increased public information programs.

In addition, a state may qualify for a supplemental grant of 20 percent of its 1983 section 402 highway funds if it implements at least eight of the twenty-one supplemental criteria issued by the Secretary of Transportation (see List of Eligibility Criteria below).[24]

States adopting a minimum of four of these supplemental criteria also can qualify for 10 percent of their section 402 apportionment. In order to be eligible for the supplemental grant a second and third year, states must continue to adopt two or more additional criteria each year and demonstrate improved performance in criteria previously adopted. A state is not required to adopt more than fifteen of the supplemental criteria, but must demonstrate higher levels of achievement in all criteria that were adopted in prior years.[25]

List of Eligibility Criteria
Section 402 Supplemental Grant Provision
1982 Alcohol Traffic Safety Act

1. Establishment of twenty-one as the minimum age for drinking any alcoholic beverage.

2. Designation of a single state official as the coordinator for the alcohol safety program in the state.

3. Establishment of minimum standards for rehabilitation and treatment programs for those convicted of alcohol-related traffic offenses.

4. Establishment of a state task force to combat drunk driving. County, city, or regional task forces are encouraged, but not required; however, if they are not used, the state task force must be able to demonstrate that local community interests are represented.

5. Establishment of a statewide driver record system readily accessible to the courts and to the public which identifies drivers who are repeatedly convicted of drunk driving.

6. Establishment of a locally coordinated alcohol traffic safety program in each major political subdivision. Communities themselves are to decide the specific geographic area to be involved in the program.

7. Establishment of prevention and education programs aimed at changing societal attitudes toward drunk driving. These programs are to include a kindergarten though twelfth grade education program and involve the private sector.

8. Establishment of a pre- or postscreening process for convicted drunk drivers (based on BAC level at time of arrest, prior alcohol-related convictions, and a self-administered questionnaire) in order to classify the offenders according to their drinking habits.

9. Development and implementation of a statewide evaluation system to ensure program quality and effectiveness.

10. Establishment of a plan for achieving self-sufficiency for the state's total alcohol traffic safety program.

11. Use of roadside sobriety checks as a part of a comprehensive enforcement program.

12. Establishment of citizen reporting programs, with compliance demonstrated by information regarding the degree of participation (e.g., number of citizen reports).

13. Enactment of a BAC level of .08 percent as presumptive evidence of driving while under the influence of alcohol.

14. Adoption of the one-license/one-record policy, as well as full participation in the National Driver Register and the Driver's License Compact.

15. Authorization of preliminary breath testing where there is probable cause to suspect that a driver is under the influence of alcohol.

16. Adoption of a requirement that no alcohol-related charge be reduced to a non-alcohol-related offense or probation without declaration that the judgment is in the interest of justice. The law adopted must also provide that if a charge is reduced, the reduced charge is alcohol related.

17. Provision of victim assistance and victim restitution programs and requirement that victim impact statements be used prior to sentencing in all cases where death or serious injury results from an alcohol-related offense.

18. Mandatory impoundment or confiscation of license plate/tags of any vehicle operated by an individual whose license has been suspended or revoked for an alcohol-related offense.

19. Enactment of legislation or regulation authorizing the arresting officer to determine the type of chemical test to be used to measure intoxication.

20. Enactment of dramshop liability laws or upholding common-law dramshop liability in the state's highest court.

21. Adoption of new, unique, and innovative alcohol traffic safety programs.[26]

As of October 1984, only sixteen states had qualified for the basic incentive grant and no states had qualified for the supplemental grants.[27] NHTSA originally had estimated that thirty states would qualify by 1985 for at least the basic grant; they now believe their estimate may have been too high.[28] States that have qualified for the basic grants include Alabama, Alaska, Arizona, Delaware, Indiana, Louisiana, Maine, Mississippi, Montana, Nevada, New Hampshire, New Jersey, New Mexico, North Dakota, Rhode Island, and Utah.[29]

Public concern over the alcohol-impaired driver continued to grow in 1982 and 1983. Other lobbying groups, such as Students Against Driving Drunk (SADD) and Remove Intoxicated Drivers (RID), in concert with MADD, pressured Congress to pass legislation creating "National Drunk and Drugged Driving Awareness Week" (December 12-18, 1982; PL 97-343), and "DWI Awareness Week" (December 11-17, 1983; PL 98-103).[30]

The National Minimum Drinking Age Act of 1984

This heightened awareness of drunk driving as a national problem continued into 1984. Numerous bills introduced to the Congress were designed to require states to raise the minimum legal drinking age to twenty-one. President Reagan and the Presidential Commission on Drunk Driving endorsed the proposal. Members of Congress, again lobbied heavily by the anti-drunk-driving groups, rejected the opposition of student groups, restaurant owners, and liquor manufacturers. In resorting to the threat of withholding highway funds, Congress fought state opposition by reminding states that the supplemental criteria of the 1982 Barnes-Howard Bill provided financial incentives for states to pass twenty-one as the minimum legal drinking age. Only a few states raised their drinking age to twenty-one subsequent to the passage of the 1982 law. They were Alaska, Arizona, Delaware, Nebraska (effective July 1, 1985), New Jersey, Oklahoma, and Rhode Island.[31]

The 1984 drunk driving legislation, initially sponsored by Senator Frank Lautenberg (D-N.J.), passed the House as a set of amendments added to a Child Safety Restraint Act (H.R. 4616). The National Minimum Drinking Age Act (PL 98-363) requires states to raise their legal drinking age to twenty-one or face withholding of federal highway construction funds. If states fail to pass the legislation by September 30, 1986, they will lose 5 percent of their highway construction funds in fiscal year 1987, and if this legislation is not passed by September 30, 1987, the government will withhold an additional 10 percent of those funds. These funds can be restored if states raise their legal drinking age to twenty-one in subsequent fiscal years.[32]

The 1984 legislation does contain some financial incentives for states to strengthen their DWI programs. A state qualifies for an additional 5-percent grant of its 1984 highway safety funds if it enacts mandatory minimum sentences for persons convicted of drunk driving such that:

1. Persons convicted of a first offense of driving under the influence of alcohol shall receive a mandatory ninety-day license suspension and either an assignment of one hundred hours of community service or a minimum jail sentence of two days;

2. Persons convicted of a second offense of driving while under the influence of alcohol shall receive a mandatory one-year license revocation and a minimum sentence of imprisonment of ten days;

3. Persons convicted of a third or subsequent offense of driving while under the influence of alcohol within five years of a prior conviction for the same offense shall receive a license revocation of at least three years and a mandatory minimum sentence of imprisonment for one hundred and twenty days; and,

4. Persons convicted of driving with a suspended or revoked license due to driving under the influence of alcohol shall receive a mandatory sentence of imprisonment of at least thirty days.[33]

STATE LEGISLATIVE ACTIVITY: 1983-84

State legislative activity regarding the drinking and driving issue continues throughout the United States, due in part to the National Minimum Drinking Age Act (PL 98-363), the criteria established under section 402 of the Alcohol Traffic Safety Act of 1982 (PL 97-362), and ongoing public awareness of the problem (see Table 2). Forty-nine states and the District of Columbia introduced a total of 776 pieces of legislation in 1983, and 129 of those bills were enacted into law; the only two jurisdictions not introducing alcohol and driving legislation that year were Puerto Rico and Kentucky (Kentucky's legislature was not in session in 1983).[34] Through the end of August 1984, approximately thirty states reported successful passage of alcohol and driving bills over the course of that legislative year.[35] Several states reported major revisions in their laws during 1983 and 1984. Connecticut, Nevada, North Carolina, Oregon, and Texas, among others, significantly updated laws in their states in 1983. Iowa, Kentucky, and Vermont successfully strengthened a major portion of their drunk driving laws during the 1984 legislative year. Hawaii, attempting to qualify for the supplemental grants available under section 402, fine-tuned several of its requirements as well.

Other states simply made specific changes in their laws, focusing on what they perceived as the weaker aspects or problem spots. Major areas of legislative activity included sanctions and penalties, minimum legal drinking age legislation, illegal per se laws, administrative per se laws, and preliminary breath test provisions.

Sanctions and Penalties

Sanctions and penalties proved to be the most concentrated area of legislative activity in 1983.[36] A total of twenty-six states enacted mandatory jail statutes for drunk driving convictions: seven for first-offense convictions, and nineteen for second-offense convictions. Besides the states having major revisions in 1984, Colorado, New Jersey, and Oklahoma stiffened their levels of punishment. This brought the total number of states requiring first-offense mandatory jailings to sixteen; forty-one states now require mandatory jail sentences for second convictions. In addition, thirty states currently have community service sentencing options.

Drinking Age Legislation

Seven states enacted drinking age legislation in 1983. As previously stated, Alaska, Delaware, and Oklahoma established twenty-one as the minimum legal drinking age for all alcoholic beverages. Connecticut raised its drinking age to twenty, while Virginia and North Carolina raised the age for beer purchases from eighteen to nineteen, leaving twenty-one as the drinking age for all other alcoholic beverages. West Virginia made a novel change in its drinking age during 1983. It established nineteen as the minimum legal drinking age for state residents and twenty-one as the age for out-of-state residents, apparently attempting to target college students.[37] Given the amount of money involved for each state, it is clear that most states eventually will comply with the new age requirement contained in the National Minimum Drinking Age Act.

Twenty states introduced drinking age legislation during 1984, but only five states reported successful passage of these bills. South Dakota raised its drinking age for 3.2 percent beer to nineteen, and Arizona, Nebraska, Rhode Island, and Tennessee raised their drinking ages to twenty-one. This brought the number of states with a legal drinking age of twenty-one to twenty-three states.[38]

Illegal Per Se Laws

An illegal per se law makes it a criminal offense for a person with a particular BAC level to operate a motor vehicle. Fifteen states added such provisions in 1983 and Virginia adopted a .15 percent per se law in 1984, becoming the forty-third state--forty-fourth jurisdiction overall, including Washington, D.C.--to add an illegal per se law to its drinking and driving laws.

Most states have the conventional .10 percent per se level, while two states--Oregon and Utah--have a more stringent .08 percent level. Four states, including Virginia, use more liberal levels (Georgia, .12; Iowa, .13; Colorado, .15). Minnesota includes a unique stipulation in its per se law. If a driver is stopped and registers a BAC level of .07 percent or higher, it is recorded on his/her license; a second test of .07 percent within two years may require the driver to undergo an alcohol assessment.[39]

Table 2
Analysis by States — 1983-84
High Interest Alcohol and Driving Legislation

State	Drinking Age	Preliminary Breath Test	Illegal Per Se and Level (%)	Presumptive and Level (%)	Administrative Per Se	Dramshop	Open Container	Community Service	Mandatory Jail - 1st Offense	Mandatory Jail - 2nd Offense
Alabama	19		0.10	0.10		Statute				
Alaska	21	X	0.10		X	Statute[1]		X	X	X
Arizona	21		0.10	0.10		Case law	X[8]	X	X	X
Arkansas	21		0.10	0.10		No		X		
California	21		0.10	0.10		Statute[5]	X			X
Colorado	21	X	0.15	0.05 0.10[6]	X	Statute			X	X
Connecticut	20		0.10;0.07-0.10[4]	0.10[7]	X	Statute		X		X
Delaware	21	X	0.10	0.10[7]	X	Case law				X[11]
Dist. of Columbia	18[2], 21[3]		0.10	0.05[7]	X	Case law[5]				
Florida	19	X	0.10	0.10		Statute		X		X
Georgia	19		0.12	0.10		Case law		X		X
Hawaii	18		0.10	0.10		Case law				
Idaho	19		0.10	0.08		Statute				X
Illinois	21		0.10	0.10		Case law	X	X		X
Indiana	21	X[9]	0.10	0.10[7]	X	Statute	X	X	X[9]	X
Iowa	19		0.13	0.10	X	No		X	X	X
Kansas	18[2], 21[3]		0.10	0.10[9]		Case law	X	X	X	X
Kentucky	21	X		0.10		No	X	X		X
Louisiana	18		0.10	0.10		No				X
Maine	20		0.10		X[10]	Statute	X			X
Maryland	21	X		0.08, 0.13[6,7]		No	X	X		X[11]
Massachusetts	20			0.10		Case law	X	X		X
Michigan	21	X	0.10	0.07,0.10[6]	X[12]	Statute	X	X		X
Minnesota	19	X	0.10		X[13]	Statute		X		
Mississippi	18[2], 21[3]		0.10			Case law		X		X
Missouri	21		0.10	0.10[7]		Case law				X
Montana	19		0.10	0.10		No			X	
Nebraska	21	X	0.10		X	No	X[8]	X		X
Nevada	21	X	0.10	0.10		No	X[14]			X
New Hampshire	20	X	0.10	0.10[7]		No	X			X
New Jersey	21		0.10			Case law		X		X

Table 2 (cont.)
Analysis by States — 1983-84
High Interest Alcohol and Driving Legislation

State	Drinking Age	Preliminary Breath Test	Illegal Per Se and Level (%)	Presumptive and Level (%)	Administrative Per Se	Dramshop	Open Container	Community Service	Mandatory Jail - 1st Offense	Mandatory Jail - 2nd Offense
New Mexico	21			0.10	X	Case law	X			X
New York	19	X[15]	0.10	0.06-0.10[7]		Statute	X			X
North Carolina	19[2], 21[3]	X	0.10		X	Statute	X	X	X	X
North Dakota	21	X	0.10		X	Statute	X	X		X
Ohio	19[2], 21[3]		0.10		X[12]	Statute			X	X
Oklahoma	21		0.10	0.10[7]	X	No	X			X
Oregon	21		0.08		X	Statute	X	X	X	X
Pennsylvania	21	X	0.10	0.10		Statute	X	X		X
Puerto Rico[16]	18	X		0.10		No				
Rhode Island	21	X	0.10	0.10		Statute[12]		X		X
South Carolina	20[2], 21[3]			0.10		No	X	X		X
South Dakota	19[2], 21[3]	X	0.10			Case law	X			X
Tennessee	21			0.10		Case law		X	X	X
Texas	19		0.10			No		X		X
Utah	21		0.08		X	Statute	X	X		
Vermont	18	X	0.10	0.10		Statute	X			
Virginia	19[2], 21[3]	X	0.15	0.10		No				
Washington	21		0.10	0.10	X (effective 1-1-86)	Case law	X		X	X
West Virginia	19, 21[17]	X		0.10[18]	X	No	X	X	X	X
Wisconsin	19	X	0.10			Statute[12]	X			
Wyoming	19			0.10[7]	X	Statute			X	X

Sources: U.S. Department of Transportation, National Highway Traffic Safety Administration, *State and Community Program Area Report: Alcohol Counter Measures 1983-84* (Washington, D.C., August 1984), pp. A-4 - A-7; National Safety Council, "Policy Update: 1984 Drunk Driving Legislative Update" (Washington, D.C., September 1984), pp. 3-58.

1. Applies to businesses only.
2. Beer (alcohol content limitations range from 3.2 percent to 4 percent by weight to 6 percent by volume) and unfortified wine.
3. Fortified wine and distilled spirits.
4. Infraction if BAC level is between these levels.
5. Applies only to intoxicated minors.
6. Lower of two numbers is driving while impaired (DWI); higher is driving under the influence (DUI).
7. BAC level or levels which indicate prima facie evidence.
8. Partial; illegal to drink while driving.
9. Applies only when there has been an injury or death involved in accident.
10. Youth offender with BAC .02.
11. Law appears to require a mandatory imprisonment saction via indirect language.
12. Limited.
13. Cannot be imposed if arrest occurred at roadblock/checkpoint stop in which there was no probable cause for stop.
14. Applies only if under twenty years old and traveling without parent or legal guardian.
15. Limited to drivers involved in accidents.
16. Statistics as of December 31, 1983.
17. Lower age is for residents; higher age is for nonresidents.
18. Both prima facie and presumptive evidence laws with this BAC level.

Administrative Per Se Laws

Administrative per se laws enable the arresting officers to suspend a driver's license immediately upon recording an illegal blood alcohol concentration reading from the driver. Since administrative per se laws allow prompt action and on-site license revocation, they save time and money and immediately remove dangerous drivers from the roadway. Fourteen states adopted administrative per se laws in 1983; Nebraska, New Mexico, and Wyoming added this provision during 1984.

Preliminary Breath Tests (PBTs)

Preliminary breath tests allow police officers to give a field breath test to a driver they have reasonable cause to believe is driving under the influence. These tests are made to confirm the officer's belief that he ought to make a drunk driving arrest.[40] Nevada, New Hampshire, Colorado, and Kentucky (as part of its major revision policy) all passed provisions during 1983 and 1984 allowing the use of PBTs, although none of these states allows PBTs to be admissible as evidence in a trial.[41]

Other Areas of Legislation

Additional areas of drunk driving legislation that did not experience particularly high levels of activity were dramshop laws and laws relating to roadblocks. Dramshop laws are concerned with third-party liability in the serving and/or selling of alcoholic beverages. They allow recovery of civil damages against a person who sells, dispenses, and in many cases, gives away liquor to a person who later is injured or causes an injury. Currently, twenty-two states have dramshop laws, and sixteen states have case law histories supporting dramshop claims; this represents an increase of two in the statute category and four in the case law category over approximately the past two years.

Many states introduced bills relating to police roadblocks, apparently in response to arguments from civil liberties groups about the constitutionality of this law enforcement method. Only two of these bills passed, however. Missouri now prohibits the use of administrative license revocations when the arrest is made without probable cause at a roadblock or checkpoint. Hawaii legislation set up procedures for police to conduct roadblocks: either all vehicles or vehicles in a specific numbered sequence can be stopped; a sufficient number of uniformed police officers must be present to ensure that the stops are speedy and comply with established procedure; and minimum safety precautions must be met.[42]

Major legislation still is pending in three states at the time of this writing. Michigan and New Jersey both have bills pending that would strengthen certain sanctions already contained in their laws.

Massachusetts currently has eleven bills pending, including measures to raise the minimum legal drinking age to twenty-one, establish a .10 percent per se level, increase or clarify certain penalties for repeat offenders, and eliminate the ability for DWI offenders to serve jail sentences on weekends, evenings, or holidays. Massachusetts also recently became the first state to formally outlaw "happy hours" and other drink promotions by bars.

LEGISLATIVE HISTORY OF TEXAS DWI LAWS

Driving while intoxicated (DWI) was first declared illegal in Texas in 1917 by a one-sentence provision, which outlawed the operation of a motor vehicle or any other vehicle on any public highway in the state by an intoxicated driver.[43] A complete chronological summary of Texas anti-DWI laws appears in Table 3. Since 1917, the laws in Texas regarding DWI have increased in complexity and most recently culminated in the passage of Senate Bill 1 (S.B. 1). Senate Bill 1 was passed by the Sixty-Eighth Legislature in regular session and signed by Governor Mark White in June 1983. Effective on January 1, 1984, this legislation profoundly changed DWI laws in the state.

The following pages provide a discussion of the development of laws within major categories. Beginning first with modifications, the development of three major areas is addressed. Penalties incorporate the most expansive area, as their history can be traced to 1923. The second major area involves the taking of specimens: use of material tests and refusal to submit to the tests. Finally, deferred adjudication and probation are explored. Novel provisions in DWI legislation also are examined, including "aggravated DWI," allowing a dangerous driver to borrow a motor vehicle, and forfeiture of a motor vehicle.

This overview does not deal with all aspects of DWI legislation in Texas. Instead, it focuses on these major provisions and their precursors, if any. The laws discussed in this section are found in Vernon's Revised Civil Statutes of the State of Texas (Vernon 1983), Articles 6701l-1, 6701l-4, and 6701l-7; Adult Probation Parole and Mandatory Supervision Law, Texas Code of Criminal Procedure (Vernon 1983), Article 42.12; and Involuntary Manslaughter, Texas Penal Code (Vernon 1983), Article 19.05.

Penalties

Penalties for DWI in Texas have undergone many changes in this century. The detailed progression of these alterations can be seen in Table 4. Trends and major changes will be addressed.

Table 3
Chronological Summary of Texas DWI Legislation

Year	Legislation	Provisions
1917	Regulating Operation of Motor Vehicles H.B. 37, Ch. 207	No intoxicated person shall operate or drive a motor or any vehicle upon any public highway in Texas.
1923	Penalty for Driving Motor Vehicle While Driving Intoxicated H.B. 33, Ch. 23	Felony offense to drive a motor vehicle upon streets of incorporated city, town, village, or public highway while under influence of liquor. Set penalties for violation.
1935	Penalty for Operation of Motor Vehicles While Intoxicated H.B. 93, Ch. 424	Set minimum penalties for driving while intoxicated.
1937	Providing a Penalty for Driving While Intoxicated H.B. 120, Ch. 60	Decreased minimum county jail time.
1941	Drunken Drivers H.B. 73, Ch. 507	First offense decreased to a misdemeanor. Decreased penalties. Second offense a felony; set penalties. Penalty for felony offense committed while intoxicated shall be levied.
1941	Driver's License Law H.B. 20, Ch. 173	Automatic suspension of license for six months upon conviction of DWI.
1949	Motor Vehicles - Driving on Beaches - Speed H.B. 212, Ch. 430	Unlawful to drive motor vehicle on any beach in the state while intoxicated. Penalties established.
1951	Motor Vehicles - Minors H.B. 581, Ch. 436	Unlawful for minors between 14 and 17 to drive under influence. Misdemeanor punishable by $1-50 fine or 90-day probation.
1951	Driving While Intoxicated - Second Offenders S.B. 153, Ch. 457	Increased penalties for second offense.
1953	Motor Vehicles - Driving While Intoxicated S.B. 59, Ch. 167	Allowed probation to commute jail sentence for first offense.
1955	Driving While Under Influence of Narcotic Drug	Driving under influence of narcotic drug made a felony offense. Set penalty.
1957	Minors - Driving While Intoxicated - Traffic S.B. 45, Ch. 302	Misdemeanor for males 14-17 and females 14-18 to drive while under influence. Punishable by fine of no more than $100.
1969	Driving While Intoxicated Chemical Tests - Consent S.B. 74, Ch. 434	Authorized use of chemical tests. Provided for suspension or denial of license for refusal, hearing and judicial review, admissibility of test results as evidence, and severability clause.

Table 3 (cont.)
Chronological Summary of Texas DWI Legislation

Year	Legislation	Provisions
1971	Motor Vehicles - Traffic Regulations S.B. 183, Ch. 83	Unlawful to drive while under influence of any narcotic drug or any other drug which renders driver incapable of driving safely. Established penalties.
1971	Driving While Intoxicated Chemical Tests - Presumptive Limits H.B. 261, Ch. 709	Established presumptive limit of .10 of blood alcohol for intoxication.
1973	Penal Code S.B. 34, Ch. 399	Transferred article 802 from Texas Penal Code, 1925, to new Penal Code, arts. 6701l-1, 6701l-3, and 6701l-5.
1979	Public Beaches - Traffic Regulation - Speed and Driving While Intoxicated S.B. 1071, Ch. 682	Driving while intoxicated on a "public beach" unlawful. Increased maximum penalties.
1981	Probation - Misdemeanors - Conditions S.B. 368, Ch. 142	Educational program condition of probation for DWI. After successful completion of program, DWI conviction would not appear on driver's record.
1983	Driving While Intoxicated S.B. 1, Ch. 303	Increased penalties for first, second, and third offenses. Made involuntary manslaughter involving motor vehicle criminally negligent homicide. Provided for visual recording of a person arrested in certain counties. Described test and trial procedures, and criminal and civil consequences of a conviction, including suspension of license, insurance consequences, and forfeiture of or prohibition of sale of motor vehicles. Redefined DWI to include influence of drugs and alcohol.

Sources: Texas General and Special Laws 1917, 1923, 1935, 1937, 1941, 1949, 1951, 1953, 1955, 1957, 1969, 1971, 1973, 1981, and 1983.

Table 4
Chronological Summary of Texas DWI Penalties

	H.B. 33 Acts 1923 37th Leg. 2nd Called Session Ch. 23	H.B. 93 Acts 1935 44th Leg. Ch. 424	H.B. 120 Acts 1937 45th Leg. Ch. 60
First Offense			
Classification	Felony	Felony	Felony
Fine	No $500	$50 - $500	$50 - $500
	or	or	or
Time in county jail	No 90 days	30 - 90 days	5-90 days
	or	or	or
Time in penitentiary	No 2 years	Same	Same
	or	or	or
	Fine and imprisonment	Fine and imprisonment	Fine and imprisonment
Probation	Not mentioned	Not mentioned	Not mentioned
Second Offense			
Classification			
Fine			
Time in county jail	Not Mentioned	Not mentioned	Not mentioned
Time in penitentiary			
Probation			
Third Offense			
Classification			
Fine	Not mentioned	Not mentioned	Not mentioned
Time in county jail			
Time in penitentiary			
Probation			
Notes	First penalties for DWI in Texas		Reduced county jail time

Table 4 (cont.)
Chronological Summary of Texas DWI Penalties

H.B. 73 Acts 1941 47th Leg. Ch. 507	S.B. 153 Acts 1951 52nd Leg. Ch. 457	S.B. 73 Acts 1953 53d Leg. Ch. 167	S.B. 1 Acts 1983 58th Leg. Ch. 303
Misdemeanor $50 - $500 or 10 days - 2 years	Misdemeanor $50 - $500 3 days - 2 years	Misdemeanor $50 - $500 3 days - 2 years	Misdemeanor $100 - $2,000 3 days - 2 years
None	None	None or	None
Not mentioned	Not mentioned	Judge may commute jail sentence to no 6 months probation	DWI education course as condition for probation
Felony None None 1 - 5 years	Felony $100 - $5,000 10 days - 2 years 5 years or County jail time and fine	Not mentioned	Felony $300 - $2,000 15 days - 2 years (mandatory 3 days) None
Not mentioned	Not mentioned		Alcohol or drug dependency testing and mandatory 3 days minimum jail time as condition for probation
Not mentioned	Not mentioned	Not mentioned	Felony $500 - $2,000 30 days - 2 years 60 days - 5 years Mandatory 10 days minimum jail time as condition for probation
If felony crime is committed while DWI, shall be punished for felony committed		First introduction of probation for DWI offense	**License Suspension** First offense: 90 - 365 days or DWI education course Second offense: 180 days - 2 years Third or subsequent offense: 180 days - 2 years Involuntary manslaughter: 180 days **Involuntary Manslaughter** Felony of third degree fine $5,000 2 - 10 years in penitentiary

Penalties for DWI were first established in 1923 (H.B. 33).[44] It was declared a felony offense for any person to drive or operate a vehicle within the limits of a city, town, or village or upon a public road or highway in Texas while intoxicated or in any degree under the influence of intoxicating liquor. Maximum penalties were assessed involving fines and/or imprisonment.

Modified in 1935 (H.B. 93) to include minimum penalties, an intoxicated person would serve no less that thirty days in county jail and/or pay less than a fifty-dollar fine, or serve less than two years in a penitentiary. The 1937 act (H.B. 120) reinstituted the condition that the person be intoxicated or in any degree under the influence of liquor and reduced the minimum county jail sentence.

First offenders no longer were charged with committing a felony as of 1941 (H.B. 73). Misdemeanor charges were filed, and penalties included only county jail time and/or fines. A second offense constituted a felony punishable by one to five years in a penitentiary. Moreover, if one committed a felony crime while driving while intoxicated, this act allowed the penalty for the felony to be assessed. Expansion of penalties associated with second offenses occurred in 1951 (S.B. 153). A fine, time in county jail, or time in the penitentiary were the available options for punishment.

Probation was introduced as an option for a judge in sentencing in 1953 (S.B. 73). A probationary period of not less than six months could be used to commute the jail sentence. Also, in the same year, the Legislature reduced the minimum time in the county jail from ten to three days.

In 1973, the new Texas Penal Code was enacted (S.B. 34), and legislation dealing with DWI was categorized under Traffic Regulations in the Civil Statutes. No changes were made in first- or second-offense penalties.

Ten years later, in 1983, sweeping changes in penalties were made. Senate Bill 1 (S.B. 1) provided increased punishments for first and second offenses, and created new penalties for third and subsequent offenses. Provisions for license suspension, aggravated DWI, and a redefinition of DWI were added. Moreover, terms of the offense were more narrowly defined. The offense must have been committed in a public place--as defined by sec. 1.07(a)(29) of the Texas Penal Code--by a person intoxicated while driving a motor vehicle.

Thus, the latest legislation was built on a foundation set decades ago, although the penalties have varied and not always increased in strength. The culmination of these amendments appears in Senate Bill 1 with the strictest and most explicit penalties ever established for DWI in Texas.

Taking of Specimens: Use of Material Tests and Refusal to Submit

Before a penalty can be assessed, intoxication must be proved. The development and subsequent legalization of tests to determine the level of alcohol concentration in a person's blood greatly enhanced the ability of police officers to prove intoxication.

In 1969, Senate Bill 74 authorized the use of tests as evidence of the amount of alcohol contained in the person's blood at the time of the alleged act. Chemical analysis of blood, breath, urine, or any other bodily substance was deemed admissible as evidence. Moreover, the person administering the test or the hospital could not be held liable for damages arising from the taking of a specimen upon request of a law enforcement officer unless negligence could be shown. Most important, Senate Bill 74 decreed that any person who operated a motor vehicle upon the public highways of Texas was deemed to have given consent to such chemical tests. Failure to submit to a breath test was cause for the Texas Department of Public Safety to set a hearing to suspend the offender's driver's license. If probable cause existed that the person was intoxicated, then that person's license could be suspended up to one year. The authorization of chemical tests increased the probability of conviction and allowed for administrative punishment for refusal to submit.

In 1971 (H.B. 261), the Texas Legislature amended this provision by including the .10 percent blood alcohol concentration (BAC) rule. The existence of a concentration level of .10 percent or more by weight of alcohol in the persons's blood constituted a presumption that the person was under the influence of intoxicating liquor. Chemical analysis of blood, breath, urine, or any other bodily substance was to be used to determine this blood/alcohol ratio. Also, the person tested could request an additional test to be conducted by a physician, qualified technician, chemist, or professional nurse of his/her own choosing within a two-hour period after arrest. House Bill 261 stiffened the conditions for license suspension, requiring that in addition to showing probable cause, it must be shown that the person had the opportunity to be tested, but refused to submit.

Senate Bill 1 made additional modifications to this provision of DWI laws in Texas. The definition of intoxication was extended to include not having the normal use of mental or physical faculties due to alcohol and/or a controlled substance or having a BAC level of .10 percent or more. Moreover, implied consent was maintained, and the procedure for license suspension was altered. Under Senate Bill 1, the license of a person who refused a test would be automatically suspended for a period of ninety days without a hearing unless the person requested one. The fact that the person refused to give a specimen of breath or blood was deemed to be admissible as evidence in court. Also, further strengthening this provision, any person who was dead, unconscious, or otherwise incapable of refusal would be deemed not to have withdrawn consent. Senate Bill 1 additionally outlined grounds which gave broad authority to peace officers requiring tests. Even if the person refused to voluntarily give a specimen, a test could be required if he or she were arrested for involuntary manslaughter, or were involved in an accident which the officer reasonably believed occurred as a result of the offense, or if a person had died or would die as a direct result of the accident.

Deferred Adjudication and Probation

The third major modification dealt with the areas of deferred adjudication and probation. Persons charged with a misdemeanor DWI no longer are eligible for deferred adjudication. However, it is afforded to a "defendant who pleads guilty to a first-offense felony that does not involve bodily injury or the threat of bodily injury to any person and for which the maximum punishment assessed against the defendant does not exceed ten years' imprisonment." Deferred adjudication allows the defendant to be eligible for community restitution probation.[45] Thus, those convicted of DWI may not have their punishment reduced to community restitution. Participation in a community service work program, however, may be a part of the penalties assessed for DWI.

Changes in laws regulating probation call for mandatory detention in jail as a condition for probation for those who are convicted of a felony offense.[46] The length of detention is dependent on whether the person has been convicted of one, two, three, or more previous DWI offenses. A second condition for probation of these offenders is an evaluation for prescribing a course of conduct necessary for rehabilitation. Finally, the third condition for probation applies to those convicted of involuntary manslaughter.[47] These persons must spend no less than a 120-day period in a penal institution as a condition of probation.

In sum, Senate Bill 1 modified three major areas of DWI legislation: penalties were stiffened; use of specimen tests was expanded; and deferred adjudication was eliminated, while stricter terms of probation were established. Additionally, provisions in Senate Bill 1 created the novel concept of enhancement, punishment for allowing a dangerous driver to borrow a motor vehicle, and rules regarding forfeiture of a motor vehicle.

Novel Additions

"Aggravated DWI" is an enhancement provision, which is a new concept in Texas DWI law. Penalties for DWI are enhanced if another person suffers serious bodily injury as a result of the offender's driving while intoxicated. A $500 increase to the minimum and maximum fines is made and minimum confinement is increased by sixty days.[48]

Senate Bill 1 also created a new Class C misdemeanor. It is now illegal for a vehicle owner knowingly or intentionally to allow a person whose license has been suspended for DWI or for refusal to submit to give a specimen to drive that vehicle.[49]

Moreover, in the area of new provisions, Senate Bill 1 outlined the rules regarding forfeiture of a motor vehicle.[50] Basically, the motor vehicle owned and operated by a person who is arrested for DWI and currently is on probation for DWI or has been finally convicted three or more times of DWI is subject to forfeiture to the county in which the offense occurred.

CONCLUSIONS

Federal and state anti-DWI efforts to combat drunk driving represent an ongoing process. Recent federal involvement in the fight against drunk driving focuses on the driver and programs to punish those who drink and drive. The federal government has created both incentives and mandates for states to follow in strengthening their DWI systems. The moves by various states to enact stricter sanctions and penalties, illegal per se laws, and administrative per se laws; to raise the minimum legal drinking age; and to more widely use preliminary breath tests should be viewed as honest efforts to address the problem.

Senate Bill 1 dictates the current status of DWI legislation in Texas. The reforms brought about by this bill advanced and strengthened laws dealing with intoxicated drivers. Although progress has been made, Texas laws still do not meet the minimum requirements for receiving any of the grant monies authorized by the Barnes-Howard Bill.

NOTES

[1] U.S. Department of Transportation (DOT), National Highway Traffic Safety Administration (NHTSA), *An Evaluation of the Highway Safety Program: A Report to the Congress from the Secretary of Transportation* (Washington, D.C., July 1977), pp. I-4-I-6.

[2] Ibid., p. I-6.

[3] *Driver's Licenses - Record of Revocations Act, U.S. Code Congressional and Administrative News*, vol. 2, 86th Cong., 2d sess., 1960 (St. Paul, Minn.: West Publishing Co., 1960), pp. 3189-94.

[4] Migdon R. Segal, *Auto Safety and Related Issues* (Washington, D.C.: Congressional Research Service, April 12, 1983), p. 10.

[5] U.S. DOT, NHTSA, *Evaluation*, p. I-10.

[6] U.S. Department of Transportation, Federal Highway Administration, National Highway Safety Bureau, *Highway Safety Program Manual: Planning and Administration* (Washington, D.C., January 1969), p. i.

[7] U.S. Congress, House Committee on Public Works, *1968 Alcohol and Highway Safety Report: A Study Transmitted by the Secretary of the Department of Transportation to the Congress, in Accordance with the Requirements of Section 204 of the Highway Safety Act of 1966, Public Law 89-564*, 90th Cong., 2d sess., 1968.

[8] U.S. DOT, NHTSA, *Evaluation*, p. III-33.

[9] U.S. Department of Transportation, National Highway Traffic Safety Administration, *Highway Safety Program Manual No. 8: Alcohol in Relation to Highway Safety* (Washington, D.C., March 1975), p. I-2.

[10] U.S. DOT, NHTSA, *Evaluation*, p. I-10.

[11] Ibid., p. I-15.

[12] Ibid.

[13] Segal, *Auto Safety*, p. 52.

[14] U.S. Department of Transportation (DOT), National Highway Traffic Safety Administration (NHTSA), Guidelines for Planning and Developing State and Community Alcohol Safety Programs (Washington, D.C., November 1973), p. 1.

[15] U.S. DOT, NHTSA, Evaluation, p. III-36.

[16] U.S. DOT, NHTSA, Guidelines, p. 4.

[17] Delaware v. Prouse, 99 S. Ct. 1391 (1979).

[18] Segal, Auto Safety, pp. 14-15.

[19] Migdon R. Segal, Drunk Driving and the National Driver Register (Washington, D.C.: Congressional Research Service, June 18, 1984), p. 4.

[20] "Presidential Commission on Drunk Driving," Weekly Compilation of Presidential Documents 18, no. 15 (April 19, 1982): 457-93.

[21] Presidential Commission on Drunk Driving, Final Report (Washington, D.C., November 1983).

[22] U.S. Congress, Senate Committee on Commerce, Science, and Transportation, Federal Legislation to Combat Drunk Driving including National Driver Register: Hearings before the Subcommittee on Surface Transportation, 97th Cong., 2d sess., March 3, 1982, p. 46.

[23] Alcohol Traffic Safety - National Driver Register Act of 1982, 23 U.S.C. 408, PL 97-364 (October 25, 1982), pp. 922-23.

[24] "Drunk Driving Bill Passed," Congressional Quarterly Weekly Report, October 2, 1982, p. 2444.

[25] Alcohol Traffic Safety - National Driver Register Act of 1982.

[26] U.S. Department of Transportation (DOT), National Highway Traffic Safety Administration (NHTSA), State and Community Program Area Report: Alcohol Countermeasures, 1983-1984 (Washington, D.C., August 1984), pp. A-2, A-3.

[27] Compilation list from Vernon With, Manager, Alcohol Programs, Region

VI, National Highway Traffic Safety Administration, Dallas, Texas, October 1984.

[28]Segal, Drunk Driving, p. 3.

[29]Compilation list from Vernon With.

[30]Segal, Drunk Driving, p. 5.

[31]Ibid., p. 7.

[32]Stephen Gettinger, "Congress Clears Drunk Driving Legislation," Congressional Quarterly Weekly Report, June 30, 1984, p. 1557.

[33]National Minimum Drinking Age Act, PL 98-363, 98 Stat. 435 (1984).

[34]U.S. DOT, NHTSA, Program Area Report, p. 3.

[35]National Safety Council (NSC), Policy Update: 1984 Drunk Driving Legislative Update (Washington, D.C., September 1984), pp. A-2, A-3.

[36]U.S. DOT, NHTSA, Program Area Report, p. 3.

[37]Ibid., p. 4.

[38]NSC, Policy Update, p. 2.

[39]Ibid. p. 28.

[40]U.S. DOT, NHTSA, Program Area Report, p. 4.

[41]U.S. Department of Transportation (DOT), National Highway Traffic Safety Administration (NHTSA), Alcohol-Highway Safety: A Digest of State Alcohol-Highway Safety-Related Legislation, 1983, 2d ed. (Washington D.C., August 1983); and NSC, Policy Update, pp. 33, 34, 9, 21.

[42]Ibid., p. 15.

[43]Tex. H.B. 37, 35th Leg. (1917).

[44]Tex. H.B. 33, 37th Leg. (1923). Hereafter referred to in text by House or Senate bill number.

[45]Tex. Crim. Proc. Code Ann., art. 42.12, sec. 10A(a) (Vernon 1983).

[46]Ibid., sec.6(b).

[47]Tex. Penal Code Ann., art. 19.05 (Vernon 1983).

[48]Tex. Rev. Civ. Stat. Ann., art. 67011-1 (Vernon 1983).

[49]Ibid., art. 60711-6.

[50]Ibid., art. 60711-7.

CHAPTER 2

DESCRIPTION OF THE TEXAS DWI SYSTEM

INTRODUCTION

This chapter contains a detailed description of the driving while intoxicated (DWI) system in Texas. This description is based on interviews with state and local officials involved in the DWI process. The chapter is divided into three major sections: DWI system components, agency descriptions, and agency-to-agency interactions. This format will indicate where each agency is involved in the overall DWI system, and will illuminate system "bottlenecks," or areas that could be improved.

The first section, DWI system components, contains a description of a model DWI system for Texas which breaks the DWI process down into seven broad system components. These components are legislation, law enforcement, case administration and information processing, prosecution and adjudication, punishment, treatment, and prevention. This particular delineation is based on similar system components that the Presidential Commission on Drunk Driving recommended at the national level for states to use as a guide in designing a DWI system. The model DWI system presented in this chapter is neither an ideal construct nor a representative picture of the current DWI system in Texas. Rather, it is a compromise between the two.

In the second section, agency descriptions, selected agencies within the DWI system in Texas are described in detail. The purpose of this section is to acquaint the reader with the responsibilities and activities of the various agencies as they relate to DWI so that the agency-to-agency interactions can be understood. Staffing and workload levels are provided whenever possible in order to present a clear understanding of the constraints placed on agencies in dealing with the DWI problem. The detailed information should convey the magnitude of the DWI problem in Texas. For explanatory purposes, Travis County is used as a case study. The DWI systems of eight other Texas counties are examined in Chapter 4 and Appendix 1. These eight counties differ in terms of size of population and geographic location.

In the third and final section, agency-to-agency interactions, a subsystem is described, detailing the agency-to-agency interactions within the overall DWI system. It is imperative to remember that not all agencies around the state will have the same interactive patterns, but in most cases they will be similar. The purpose of this section is to show the complexity of the DWI system. The agency-to-agency subsystem shows the interactions which take place.

Depictions of both the model DWI system components (see Figure 1) and the agency-to-agency interactions (see Figures 2-6) are provided to give a clear illustration of the system. This chapter is intended to be descriptive in nature. An evaluation of the DWI system in Texas will be provided in Chapter 4.

DWI SYSTEM COMPONENTS

The following system description represents a theoretical model of one possible way to view the DWI system in Texas. The seven system components described below are designed to be of equal importance. For example, a well-balanced DWI system would place the same emphasis on treatment as it would on legislation. Each component is briefly defined in terms of its responsibilities as they relate to subsequent components.

Legislation

DWI legislation is handled at both the federal and state levels. The federal government encourages compliance with its DWI guidelines through supplemental grant programs and the occasional threat of withholding highway safety funds. At the state level, Texas passed a new DWI law in 1983. Senate Bill 1 (S.B. 1) materially strengthened penalties and sanctions for driving while intoxicated. Both federal and state laws pertaining to DWI are detailed in Chapter 1. As a component in the DWI system, legislation is important because it reflects the concern which society feels for the DWI problem. The strength of existing legislation indicates that solving the DWI problem is a high priority in Texas. Legislation directly affects the enforcement component because law enforcement agencies need strong legislation to remove the drinking driver from public roadways. To be effective, legislation must provide clear guidance to the law enforcement officer and stiff penalties for the DWI offender.

Enforcement

Enforcement is one of the most critical components in the DWI system. Because of the inherent difficulties in identifying all intoxicated drivers, relatively few people are actually arrested for driving while intoxicated. Law enforcement agencies must therefore enhance their effectiveness through increasing the public's perception of the possibility of being arrested. This is accomplished through special high-visibility programs such as roadblocks and selective traffic enforcement programs. Staffing levels and priority given to DWI determine to a large degree the effectiveness of enforcement. Enforcement practices, such as writing a clear offense report, provide the basis for the next component in the DWI system, case administration and information processing.

FIGURE 1
A Model DWI System

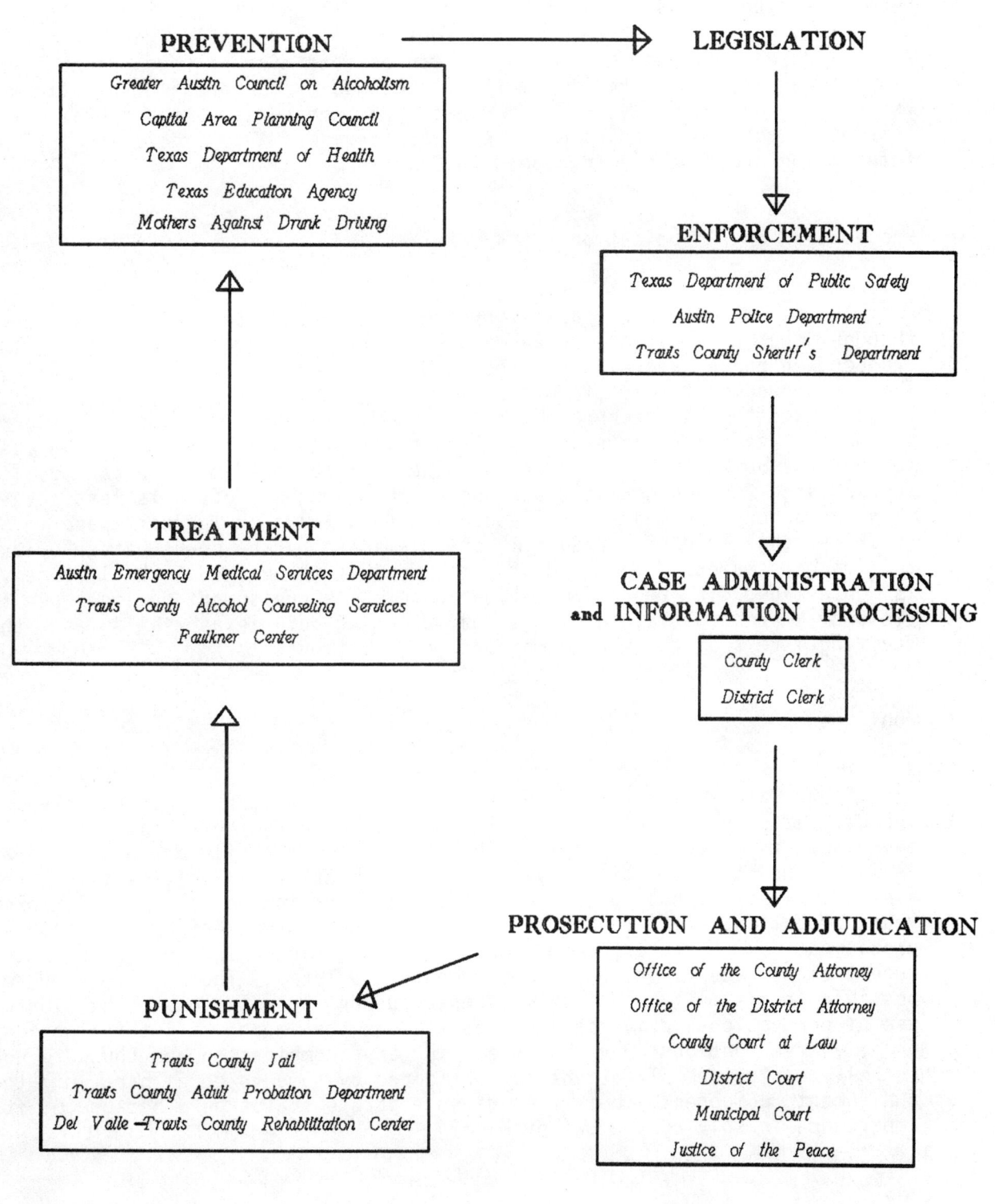

Case Administration and Information Processing

Information about the DWI defendant consists of the offense report filed by the law enforcement agency, complaints, affidavits, the driving record, and the previous arrest record of the defendant. This component also includes information on the defendant's psychological health and alcohol dependency level. The latter can be determined through established testing procedures. Records must be accessed by the prosecuting attorney for use in the court system. Unless these records are accurate and complete, the court system cannot do its job. A more detailed look at information processing is provided in Chapter 3.

Prosecution and Adjudication

As the DWI defendant passes through the court system, he first goes through the prosecution phase and then the adjudication phase. The prosecution phase determines whether the defendant is innocent or guilty. This pronouncement may involve plea bargaining or a jury trial. Plea bargaining often is preferred by attorneys due to the crowding of the court system. When the prosecuting attorney feels that he has a strong case against the defendant, the defendant usually is persuaded to plead guilty in exchange for a negotiated sentence. This sentence often is less severe than one a jury would assess. Cases lacking a thorough arrest report or other strong evidence frequently are dismissed by the county attorney due to time constraints. The type of sentence that the defendant will receive is determined in the adjudication phase. The punishment options open to the courts are constrained by the overcrowding of Texas jails and the staffing levels of the various probation departments.

Punishment

There are at least three possible punishments which may be given to the DWI defendant in Texas. First is the option of going to jail. This may include a couple of days in the city or county jail, or up to several years in the state penitentiary. The district attorney's office cites the average first-offense penalties as thirty days in the county jail, three years probation, and a $300.00 fine. The second type of punishment is probation. Stricter conditions for probation, including increased supervision, recently have been implemented in Texas. The third type of possible punishment is driver's license suspension. In Texas, the liberal use of occupational driver's licenses weakens the impact of this option. These three options may be used in any combination and thus are not mutually exclusive. Treatment is considered by some to be a part of the punishment component, but it is given separate status here because of its importance in solving the DWI problem.

Treatment

Treatment programs may be as simple as a few educational or training classes or as intensive as a residential alcohol rehabilitation program, depending upon the severity of the drinking problem. There are both private and public treatment programs in Texas. It is generally the responsibility of the offender to pay for the treatment. However, if this is financially impossible, a state-run, no- or low-cost treatment can be provided. Treatment usually involves counseling (individual, group, and/or family) to assist the problem drinker in coming to terms with his or her illness. The primary goals of alcohol treatment programs are to instill a responsible attitude toward drinking and driving and to prevent future incidents of driving while intoxicated. Effectiveness of treatment depends entirely on the individual. Treatment programs have reported cases in which the problem drinker has gone through the program numerous times without successful results; finally, for some reason, the message of responsible driving is instilled.

Prevention

Prevention is the key to solving the DWI problem in the long run. A major health objective for the nation by the year 1990 is a reduction of the adverse health consequences associated with alcohol abuse, which includes injury and death to others as well as to the individual who misuses alcohol. Local efforts include the Dial-a-Ride program, undertaken during the Christmas holidays. Individuals who believe they have had too much to drink can call for a free ride home. Additionally, various public information programs highlight the drinking and driving problem. Once societal attitudes toward the acceptability of drinking and driving are modified, the problem can be averted. DWI prevention involves several aspects—public information and education programs, coordination and evaluation efforts, and program development. All the system components described above contribute to the prevention of DWI, but the prevention component is unique in that it emphasizes the public awareness factor. Data are not available to adequately assess the impact of such prevention programs to the mutual exclusion of the other DWI system components.

Overview

Each component is partially dependent on the proper functioning of the other system components. Therefore, no single component in the DWI system should be emphasized to the point of excluding another. Sometimes there is a tendency to believe that the DWI problem can be solved through one factor alone, such as stricter legislation or massive public information programs. One purpose of the above section is to demonstrate the importance and interrelated nature of each component in the system. This brief overview allows the system to be seen in a skeletal form. What follows is a detailed description of principal agencies (actors), organized according to the system components.

AGENCY DESCRIPTIONS

Legislation

The Texas Legislature convenes biennially in odd-numbered years for a period of 160 days. Proposed bills are submitted by legislators, and then are referred to committee for consideration. The Lieutenant Governor assigns Senate DWI-related bills to the state affairs committee. The House Speaker assigns House DWI-related bills to at least two committees. Bills with criminal penalties are referred to the criminal jurisprudence committee. Other types of action may be referred to the liquor regulation or transportation committee. Bills are reported and a vote taken in each legislative chamber; a majority is needed for passage. Unless the bill specifies otherwise, legislation becomes effective ninety days after the end of the regular session.

Law Enforcement

Texas Department of Public Safety

The Texas Department of Public Safety (DPS) deploys approximately eighteen hundred highway patrol officers throughout the state. These troopers further are subdivided into various regions covering the entire state. A Captain is assigned to each region command. Depending on population, the region may be divided into subregions. A Lieutenant is assigned to each of these subregional commands and reports directly to the Captain. In general, one or two Sergeants are assigned to each subregion.

One of the primary responsibilities of a trooper is to patrol and make arrests of those driving while intoxicated. Apprehension of a suspect occurs when an officer perceives that the suspect may be under the influence of alcohol or other drugs. The officer is careful to watch for any abnormalities in driving or in the suspect's behavior once apprehended. The arrest procedure continues after apprehension and detainment with an effort by the officer to reinforce "probable cause" for the apprehension. Additional field sobriety tests provide evaluation of coordination and mental astuteness to substantiate a more concrete probable cause. Following the officer's determination of the possible intoxication of a suspect, the officer may arrest the suspect and request that he take a breath test. The suspect has the right to refuse this test, but if he refuses, he is informed that his license will be suspended. This refusal must be documented in the form of a certificate of refusal which the suspect signs acknowledging such refusal.

The entire process of apprehension and detainment is compiled in the arrest report. The officer documents in detail the circumstances surrounding the arrest and the factors which led him to make the arrest.

In this report, the officer explains the probable cause for the arrest, accounting for the time from the moment of detection to the subsequent transfer to jail. The detail and accuracy of the arrest reports are critical to the establishment of a strong and viable prosecution. Additionally, a trooper compiles the driving record of the accused for presentation in court.

All DPS troopers are trained extensively in the apprehension of DWI offenders. Each patrol officer is trained to identify various indicators of alcohol influence such as weaving, speeding, extremely slow driving, and any other erratic or abnormal occurrences. They also are trained to apprehend the suspect in accordance with due process of law, and to perform duties such as administering the breath test.

Austin Police Department

The Austin Police Department (APD) has an average of 126 officers for day patrol and 96 for night patrol. Approximately 300 DWI arrests currently are made each month, with the number increasing annually. Each of these officers participates in the apprehension and arrest of individuals driving while intoxicated.

The responsibility of the APD is illustrative of many other local police departments. It begins with the detection and apprehension of a suspected DWI violator. The offender is then informed of his rights and that he will be requested to take an breath test. If the test is refused, the offender is informed that his license will be suspended. The arrest continues with transportation to the city jail where the report is filed. The report, in essence, is a story of exactly what occurred from the moment of detection to the jailing of the defendant. It includes any photographs taken at the scene, any evidence which may aid in establishing probable cause for the arrest, and the arrest procedure. Probable cause is enhanced with certain physical observations of the offender such as the odor of alcohol, blood shot eyes, or slurred speech. The offender is videotaped if he has refused a breath test. Only those refusing the breath test are required to be videotaped. The offender may not refuse to be videotaped; however, he may refuse to answer any questions or to perform coordination tests while being filmed.

Once completed, the report is then given to data entry clerks, who enter data from the report into the department's computer system. A copy of that same report is then routed to the Traffic Division, where a determination is made regarding the severity of offense (misdemeanor or felony). Finally, the report is filed in the Austin Police Department and a copy given to the court liaison officer in the county or district attorney's office.

All APD officers receive DWI detection training, but many have not yet received training on the new Texas DWI law, Senate Bill 1. While literature on all new laws is sent to all officers, only about 75 percent of the officers have received formal training on the new law. Approximately 8 percent of APD officers receive training in the administration of the breath test.

Travis County Sheriff's Department

The Travis County Sheriff's Department is a law enforcement agency with jurisdiction throughout Travis County and with a concentration outside the city limits of Austin. While the sheriff's department has many functions, it is involved in DWI activities through the enforcement of DWI laws and the treatment of certain offenders at the Del Valle Rehabilitation Center. A more extensive explanation of the center's treatment responsibilities will be found under the punishment section of this report. These responsibilities are carried out through the Patrol Division of the department.

Prosecution and Adjudication

Office of the County Attorney

The responsibility of the county attorney's office is to prosecute misdemeanor cases. Of these, approximately 60 percent are DWI related. The county attorney's office is composed of seven attorneys. For purposes of DWI, the county attorney's office is divided into a trial court branch and an intake branch. The intake office screens approximately 330 DWI cases per month. Once cases are brought to the office, the intake attorney creates a file on the defendant consisting of the officer's report, the complaint, and various other affidavits. All information is edited to eliminate any technical deficiencies. Following this preparation, the cases are set on the docket, a specific trial date is obtained, and the cases finally are disposed of in one of the three trial courts.

The county attorney's office participates in the Travis County Comprehensive Anti-DWI Project aimed at coordinating and centralizing the DWI system in Travis County. This state-funded program is described in more detail in Chapter 3. To facilitate in this coordination effort, the county attorney's office forwards information regarding arrest, preparation of the prosecution's case, and disposition of the case to the Travis County Comprehensive Anti-DWI Project. Centralizing the DWI system is of primary importance to the county attorney's office, and the staff cooperates fully with the task force.

Office of the District Attorney

The Travis County District Attorney's (DA) Office prosecutes all felony DWI cases committed within the county. The process begins with the arrest report filed by the law enforcement agency. The report then comes to the DA's office for intake, where the reports are evaluated and validated. The officer differentiates the cases according to "jail cases" or "nonjail cases." In general, jail cases receive priority because individuals are not able to make personal bond. It takes approximately one week for a jail case to be presented to the grand jury if this is necessary. Presentation to the grand jury usually involves only jail cases where the DWI offense resulted in a fatality. Nonjail cases involve those individuals who meet the requirements of personal bond. These cases are readied for trial within ninety days.

The second phase is the determination of whether the case meets the evidence criteria necessary to validate for prior arrests. A final conviction packet is secured from the county courts involved. The packet includes certification from the court clerk that the defendant actually was convicted of a prior DWI. This is the instrument by which a felony DWI is proven and is crucial to a strong prosecution. Approximately 4 percent of the cases do not meet the evidence criteria for prior arrests. Many times this phase is lengthy due to the difficulty of compiling evidence of prior DWI convictions. For instance, a defendant may have been convicted of three DWI offenses in another county, but once arrested in Travis County the office must search for each prior conviction and then certify that conviction. This lengthy process is a liability in prosecution due to the speedy trial rule: 90 days for a Class A misdemeanor and 120 days for a felony.

When all information is prepared and evaluated, the case proceeds to the grand jury if the individual does not plead guilty or plea bargain. However, in 95 percent of the cases, a guilty plea is entered and plea bargained.

Plea bargaining cannot be used in cases where the DWI offense resulted in a fatality. Instead, the defendant is automatically indicted and subsequently is tried in court. Such cases are the top priority of the district attorney's office. Because of a lack of staff, the office attempts to plea bargain cases in which no death occurred while heavily prosecuting fatality DWIs.

Justice of the Peace and Municipal Courts

These two courts serve nearly identical functions in the DWI system, the justice of the peace (JP) court at the county level and the municipal court (sometimes called corporation court) at the city level. A justice of the peace is elected for each of the four precincts in the county, while almost all municipal judges are appointed by city councils. This difference in the source of incumbency can have important consequences for DWI and implied consent enforcement.

Both courts try only Class C misdemeanors, those involving fines of two hundred dollars or less, usually without incarceration. Most traffic offenses fall into this category. DWI is a Class A misdemeanor offense. The JP courts normally hear cases brought by county authorities and the Department of Public Safety, although the latter has the technical authority to file cases in a municipal court as well. With the noted exception, municipal courts hear cases brought by city police except in cities too small to have a court where the JP courts serve them as well.

In the DWI system, JP and municipal courts perform only magisterial or administrative functions. They arraign the DWI offender, ensuring that his or her civil rights have been protected, and initiate the documents on which prosecution will be based, the Order of Commitment and the Order of Complaint. The latter can comprise fourteen different forms depending on the nature of the DWI offense charged. In implied consent cases, these courts act as administrative tribunals for the Department of Public Safety by hearing appeals of driver license suspensions imposed for refusing to submit to BAC tests after arrest for DWI. In this role, both courts are restricted to ruling on a narrowly defined set of procedural criteria concerning the probable cause for the DWI arrest and related issues of due process.

County Court at Law

Travis County has four county courts, three of which routinely handle DWI cases. Each judge has a coordinator, a court reporter, and a bailiff. The court coordinator handles settings which establish trial dates and are entered on the docket. If a defendant's attorney requests a continuance, a motion for continuance is filed; if the continuance is granted by the judge, the coordinator resets the trial to a subsequent date. The court system in Travis County is extremely understaffed in each department, which causes delays. Three additional clerks recently have been hired to handle data collection.

The county courts at law hear misdemeanor cases arising in Travis County. The adjudication process begins when the accused goes before the judge to have his bond set. The county clerk then obtains all documents from the county attorney's office and assigns the case a unique number. The individual then is released and given a new date to appear in court in approximately two weeks. At this next appearance, called the first setting, the defendant is informed of his right to an attorney and is given a new setting. At this final setting, the defense enters a plea, and the case finally is disposed of either through a guilty plea or through a trial. If tried, the defendant has the option of being tried in a "trial by the court," wherein the judge determines guilt or innocence, or by a jury trial. In general, the rate of conviction and severity of punishment is greater in trials by a judge than by jury trial.

District Court

There are eleven state district courts in Travis County, four of which are criminal courts. Each of the four criminal courts hears DWI cases. Each judge has a court reporter who transcribes all of the proceedings for the official record. A bailiff also is provided for each judge; generally, the bailiff regulates the docket for the judge. These courts are understaffed and the dockets are continually full.

The state district courts in Travis County deal only in felony cases. Following arrest, a complaint is filed by the state detailing the charge, and arraignment is held. The judge then sets the bond, and a date for trial is assessed. The defendant enters his plea and a trial subsequently is held. A suspected felony offender generally is incarcerated in the county jail under the supervision of the sheriff's office pending disposition.

Punishment

Travis County Jail

The Travis County Sheriff's Department is responsible for operating and maintaining two jails. The main jail, located in central Austin, has maximum security capability. All presons arrested for DWI in the county, except those arrested by the Austin Police Department, initially are detained at this facility. The Del Valle-Travis County Rehabilitation Center is a minimum security facility located in rural southeast Travis County.

Most DWI offenders who are given jail sentences serve their time at the Del Valle facility. All inmates must be nonviolent and have committed crimes against property, not persons. Most of the DWI population participate in the work release program. Inmates go to their regular place of employment during the day and return to the facility at night. If an inmate is unemployed when entering the program, the person is given ten working days to find a job. The facility does have an informal job bank. Some employers call the facility when they need help. At times, inmates are placed on county work crews. Officers randomly monitor the inmates and keep close contact with the employers. The program provides a mechanism for inmates to meet their financial responsibilities to support their families. Although treatment is voluntary, the facility provides the atmosphere, incentive, and opportunity for therapy.

The facility is administered by a superintendent. Eighteen officers are split evenly among three shifts for continuous twenty-four hour supervision. Due to vacation and illness, the average per shift is four officers. At the present time, the daily number of inmates is 140. This ratio meets the state standard of no more than forty-eight inmates per officer.

Two additional officers are responsible for the work release program. These officers are funded through the Travis County Comprehensive Anti-DWI Project. Approximately seventy inmates participate in this program. The officers screen prospective candidates for the program and monitor their performance.

Travis County Adult Probation Department

The primary functions of the Travis County Adult Probation Department are to monitor and counsel offenders placed on probation. The agency has four probation officers who deal exclusively with DWIs. Two positions are funded by the Travis County Comprehensive Anti-DWI Project. Caseloads are limited to fifty probationers per officer, and each officer handles an average caseload of thirty-five individuals.

Treatment

Austin's Emergency Medical Services

The City of Austin Emergency Medical Services Department (EMS) is responsible for providing emergency medical treatment to those individuals who have sustained injuries resulting from motor vehicle accidents, including alcohol-related accidents, within Travis County. The EMS department maintains a field staff of one hundred technicians, who respond to an average of five hundred motor vehicle accidents per month. Approximately 40 percent of those accidents are DWI related.

Travis County Alcohol Counseling Services

Travis County Alcohol Counseling Services (TACS) is primarily an education and evaluation agency. All individuals arrested for DWI in Travis County are required to be screened by TACS. The primary tool used in screening is the Mortimer-Filkins Test. Additionally, all those convicted of DWI and placed on probation must complete an eight-hour DWI class. Based on the screening test results, the staff recommends an individual counseling program. Offenders are referred to both private and public treatment programs depending on the client's ability to pay.

Counseling services are provided at TACS. Besides the DWI class, supplemental sessions can include individual and/or group counseling. The length of the process varies with the individual, but the average program lasts one to three months.

TACS has twelve full-time counselors and fifteen part-time counselor/therapists. The program is administered by an executive director and two support staff secretaries. Since the beginning of 1984, 1,251 individuals have been screened using the Mortimer-Filkins Test. During fiscal year 1984, 3,031 people completed at least one counseling program.

Faulkner Center

The Faulkner Center is a private sector organization providing a variety of services for total family recovery from chemical dependency. Most of the clients of the center are multiple drug abusers. Patients initially are evaluated by a medical doctor and then detoxified. After detoxification, the patient is admitted to a therapy group. There is no specific program intended solely for alcohol abusers or individuals who have been charged with or convicted of DWI.

The Faulkner Center employs approximately fifty full-time staff members, with support from a small part-time consulting staff. The center supports a capacity of seventy beds while attempting not to exceed a self-imposed fifty-five patient limit.

Prevention

Greater Austin Council on Alcoholism

The Greater Austin Council on Alcoholism serves as a clearinghouse for information regarding alcohol and alcoholism and the associated agencies that exist in the Travis County area. The staff provides information and training on a formal and informal basis to public and private groups. The agency does some assessment intervention and referrals for people with drinking problems. In addition, the council produces a newsletter and coordinates monthly meetings of service providers for alcohol-related programs. The council has a five-person staff including an executive director, three program directors, and a secretary. It is estimated that fifteen thousand persons are assisted annually by the council through its programs.

Capital Area Planning Council

The Capital Area Planning Council (CAPCO) is one of twenty-four regional councils formed in 1971 by the Texas Legislature. The council provides assistance to city and county governments in response to requests or through legislative mandates. CAPCO provides technical and intergovernmental assistance, comprehensive planning, growth assessment, training, and information management. Alcohol abuse is an area mandated to be administered at the regional level. CAPCO has three functions related to DWI, all coordinated by one alcohol planner. First, educational and prevention programs are undertaken several times a year. Programs are tailored to the specific needs of groups or agencies. An effort also is made to plan programs that allow for collaboration with organizations on associated issues and projects. The second function involves monitoring existing DWI projects and programs. CAPCO monitors all programs within its ten-county jurisdiction in order to evaluate their effectiveness. The final function is to obtain sources of funding for regional programs. The major focus is to finance more programs in junior and senior high schools.

Texas Department of Health

The Texas Department of Health develops health promotion programs for health behavioral risk areas. The Behavioral Risk Factor Surveys were initiated by the federal government in 1981 to help states obtain estimates concerning the prevalence of health behaviors that have been associated with risk of chronic disease. These behaviors include seatbelt use, hypertension control, smoking, and alcohol use. Three risk questions involve alcohol usage. One specifically relates to drinking and driving. Information is collected using a telephone survey that is statistically valid, random, and cross-sectional.

The collected information identifies particular high-risk groups, defines baseline prevalence estimates for the risk factors, and traces temporal trends in rates. These efforts enhance the development and ability to monitor prevention programs in the future.

Texas Education Agency

The Texas Education Agency (TEA) deals with prevention of DWI through driver education programs which are made available in high schools. Driver education is not a mandatory course for high school students, but for minors it is a prerequisite for obtaining a driver's license. At the present time, four of the thirty-two instructional hours focus on alcohol and its effects on the human body. Additionally, the health education curriculum addresses alcohol abuse and treatment. The subject is presented to classes from kindergarten through grade twelve. Health education is a required course for graduation.

Mothers Against Drunk Drivers

The primary function of the Austin chapter of Mothers Against Drunk Drivers (MADD) is lobbying for legislation. Additional functions include sponsoring community awareness programs, monitoring the courts, and providing victim support. MADD lobbies against plea bargaining, probation, light sentences, and low fines. Information is provided to the community through education and awareness programs. The organization provides victim assistance through support groups. Information and referral assistance also are provided during the adjudication process. Individual and family counseling is provided as well. The Austin chapter of MADD is operated by volunteers and is funded through contributions. Because of inadequate staffing, individuals have a very heavy workload and assist on more than one project.

A system description has been presented that utilizes Travis County as a case study. Principal agencies involved in the DWI process were explained, with emphasis placed on responsibilities, staffing, and workloads.

AGENCY-TO-AGENCY INTERACTIONS

In order for any system to be effective, interaction--communication and cooperation--among the key elements of that system is essential. This is especially true for the DWI system, where there are so many different agencies, organizations, and personalities that must interact for anti-DWI programs to work effectively.

The following figures (see Figures 2-6) illustrate the interactions among agencies. They are divided into areas of responsibility such as law enforcement, prosecution and adjudication, and treatment. Interaction is divided into three types--regular, occasional, and problematic. The interaction is categorized according to information gleaned from interviews. It may be helpful to use the figures in addition to the narrative description. Not every party involved in the DWI system is mentioned below; direct forms of contact could not be established in all instances.

Law Enforcement

All enforcement agencies stated that they were in contact with other enforcement agencies in the county--the Travis County Sheriff's Department, the Texas Department of Public Safety (DPS), and the Austin Police Department (APD). This interaction takes place at various levels and to various degrees. There generally is very good cooperation among these agencies, and all expressed a commitment to fighting drunk driving.

Travis County Sheriff's Department

The enforcement arm of the sheriff's department interacts with the district court, and to a lesser extent with the county court. It also is in contact with the adult probation department in tracking persons who have been charged with driving while intoxicated. Along these same lines, the department also maintains contact with the county and district attorneys.

Texas Department of Public Safety

The Texas Department of Public Safety (DPS) is in contact with the justice of the peace daily, the county court weekly, and the municipal court occasionally through the filing of cases. It also deals with the attorney general's office on an occasional basis. Contact with the county attorney is on a daily basis when officers present the driving record to the county court. For example, if a breath test is refused, officers present the affidavit that the arresting officer wrote at the time of refusal. Relations with the district attorney (DA) are more strained. Some DPS officers feel that the district attorney is slow to prosecute cases or does not prosecute cases at all. Contact is only occasional and not very good. A desire was expressed for cooperation with Mothers Against Drunk Driving (MADD) in order to prod county and district attorneys into prosecuting more cases.

Austin Police Department

The Austin Police Department (APD) deals with the county attorney's office daily. Either agency initiates the contact, most often by phone. Arrest reports are given to the county attorney from APD. APD also provides arrest reports to the district attorney, but there is little communication from the DA to the APD. APD occasionally requests legal opinions from the attorney general via the APD legal adviser. The frequency of this contact depends on the relationship with the DA at the time. If communication with the DA is fairly open, the APD will not turn to the attorney general's office.

APD provides arrest reports to the district, county, municipal, and justice of the peace courts. This communication generally occurs on a daily basis. APD deals occasionally with the adult probation department and the DPS Driver's License Section. There also is contact with the Texas Department of Highways and Public Transportation in coordinating the Selective Traffic Enforcement Program (STEP) and its funding. APD also has an official, but informal, liaison with MADD. One officer maintains contact with the local MADD chapter. Arrest reports may only be released when a case is disposed of, but information about various aspects of DWI cases are informally relayed to MADD.

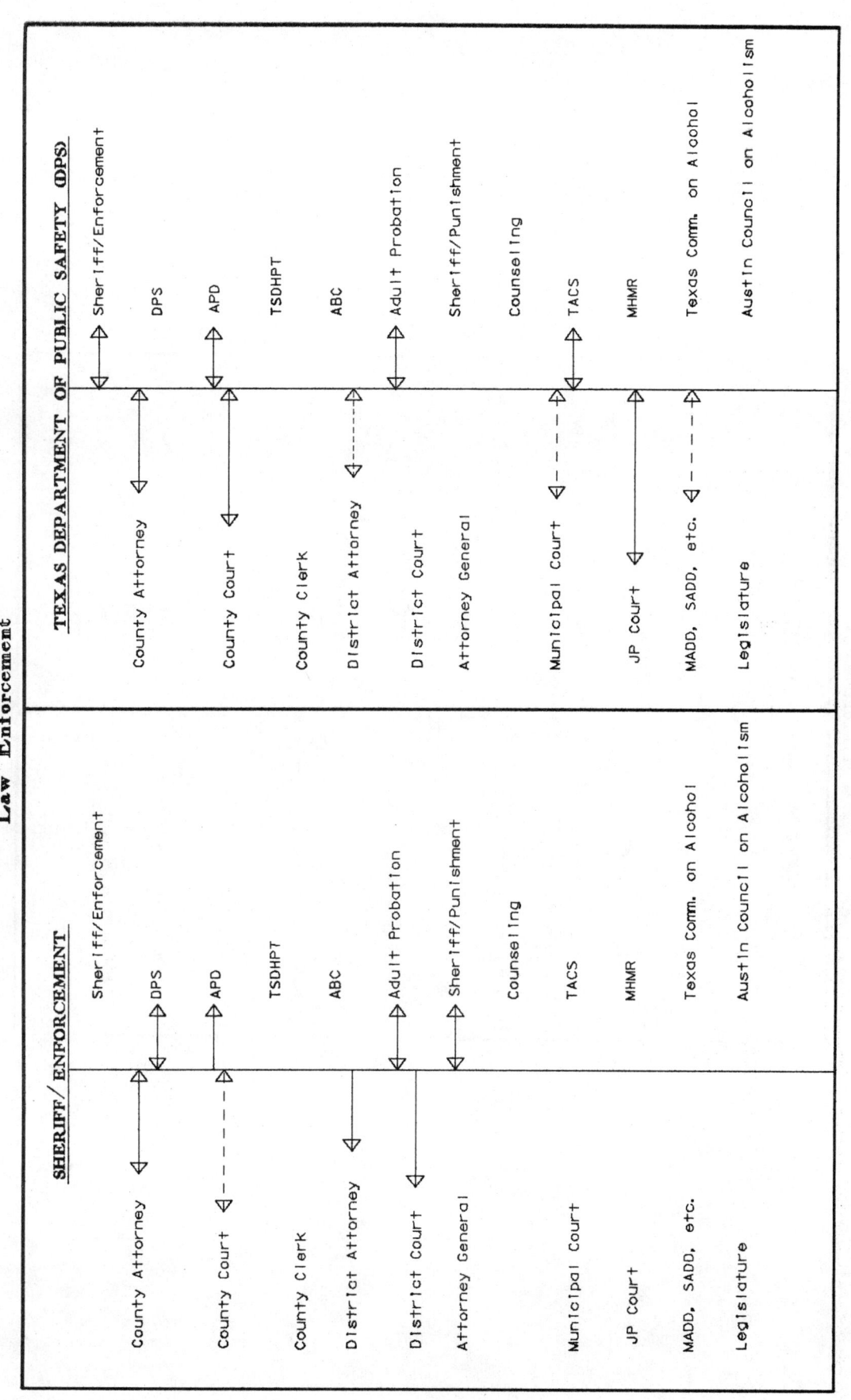

FIGURE 2

FIGURE 2 (cont.)

Agency-to-Agency Interaction
Law Enforcement

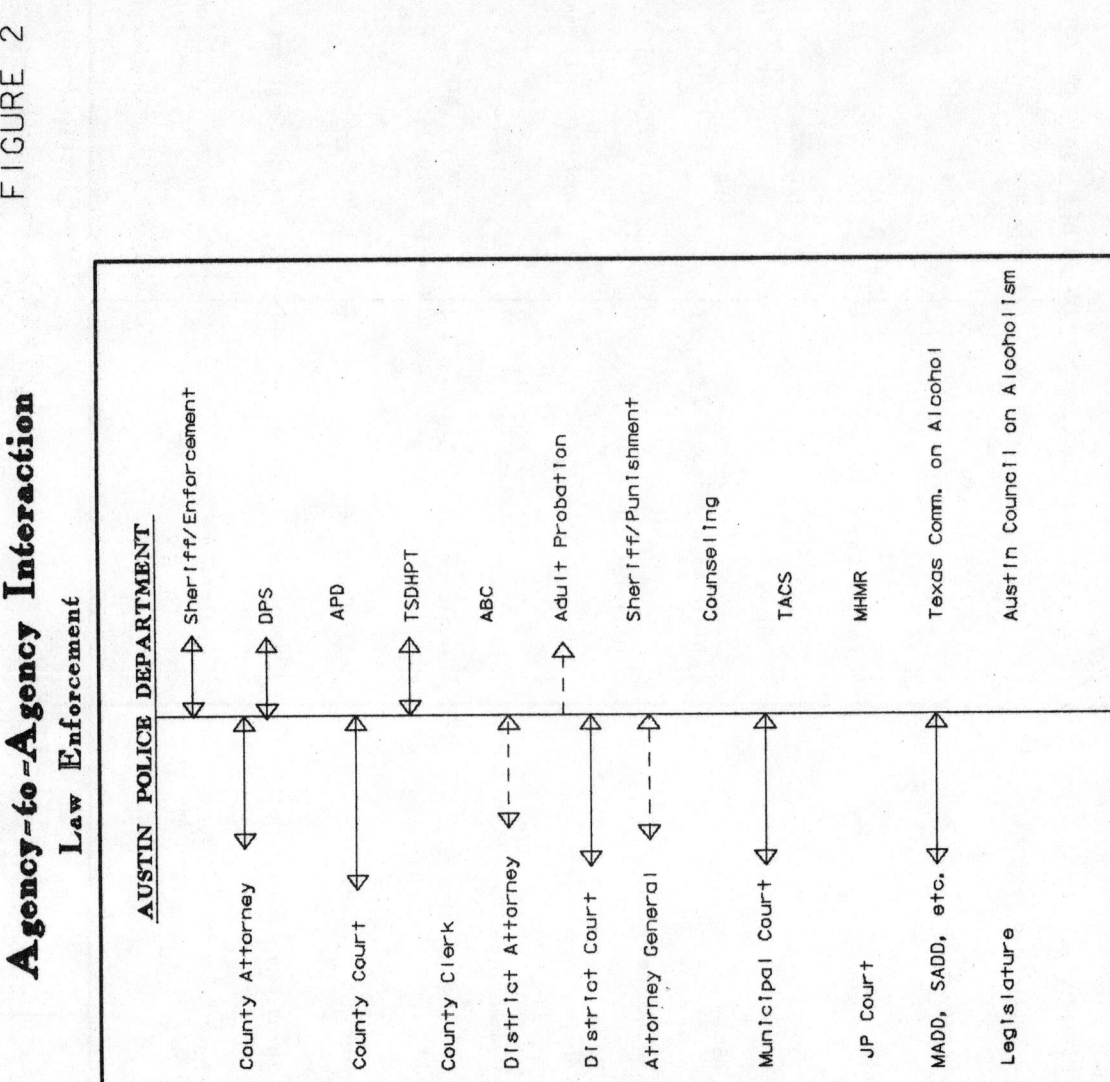

LEGEND

Regular ⇦——— Occasional ⇦ - - - Problematic ⇦ · · · · ·

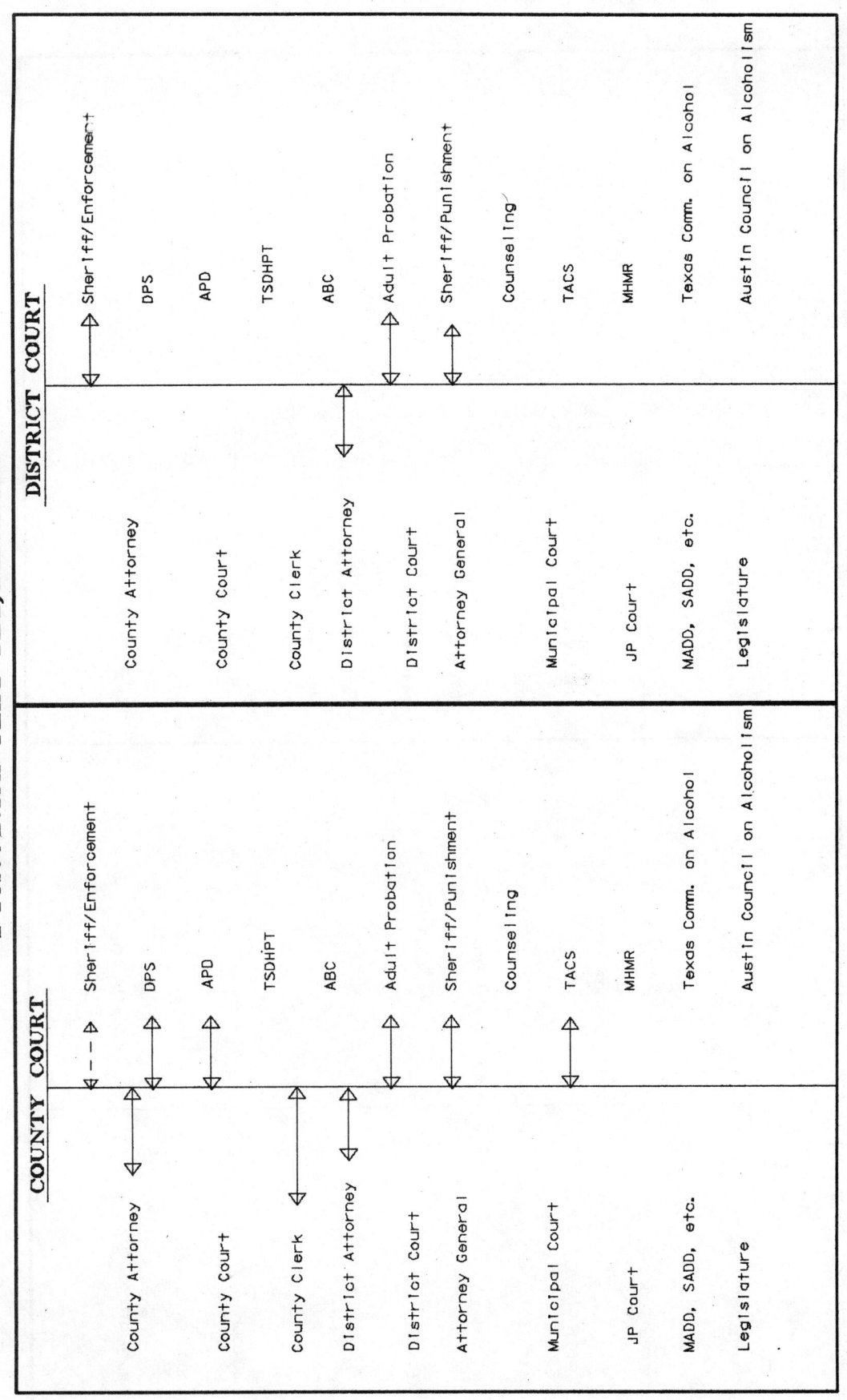

FIGURE 3

Agency-to-Agency Interaction
Prosecution And Adjudication

Agency-to-Agency Interaction
Prosecution and Adjudication

FIGURE 3 (cont.)

MUNICIPAL COURT

Left	Right
County Attorney	Sheriff/Enforcement
County Court	⇠--⇢ DPS
County Clerk	⇕ APD
District Attorney	TSDHPT
District Court	ABC
Attorney General	⇕ Adult Probation
Municipal Court	Sheriff/Punishment
JP Court	Counseling
MADD, SADD, etc.	⇕ TACS
Legislature	MHMR
	Texas Comm. on Alcohol
	Austin Council on Alcoholism

COUNTY ATTORNEY

Left	Right
County Attorney	⇕ Sheriff/Enforcement
County Court	⇕ DPS
County Clerk	⇕ APD
District Attorney	⇕ TSDHPT
District Court	ABC
Attorney General	⇕ Adult Probation
Municipal Court	Sheriff/Punishment
JP Court	Counseling
MADD, SADD, etc.	⇕ TACS
Legislature	MHMR
	Texas Comm. on Alcohol
	Austin Council on Alcoholism

LEGEND

Regular ⇕   Occasional ⇠-----   Problematic ⇠········

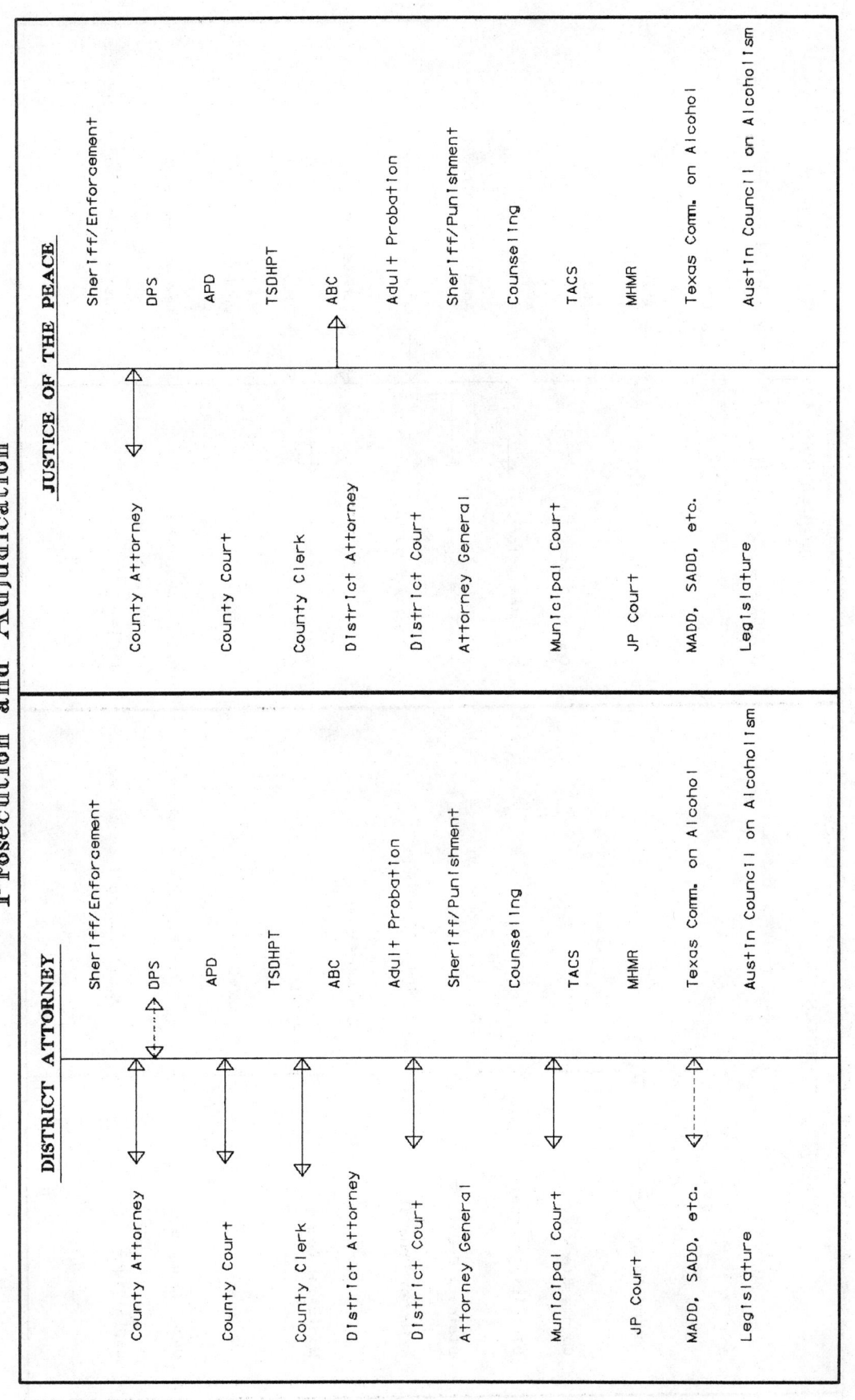

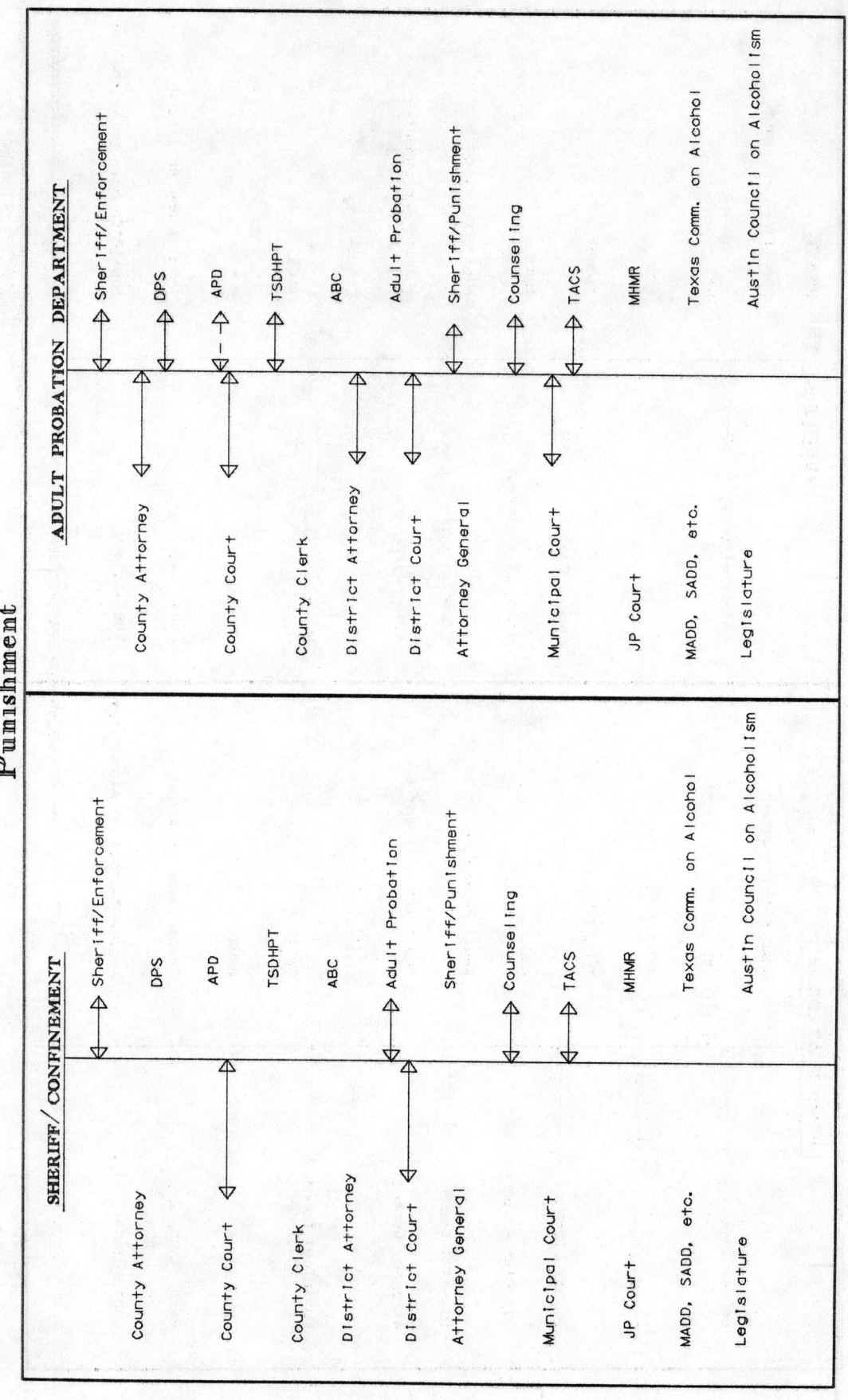

FIGURE 4
Agency-to-Agency Interaction
Punishment

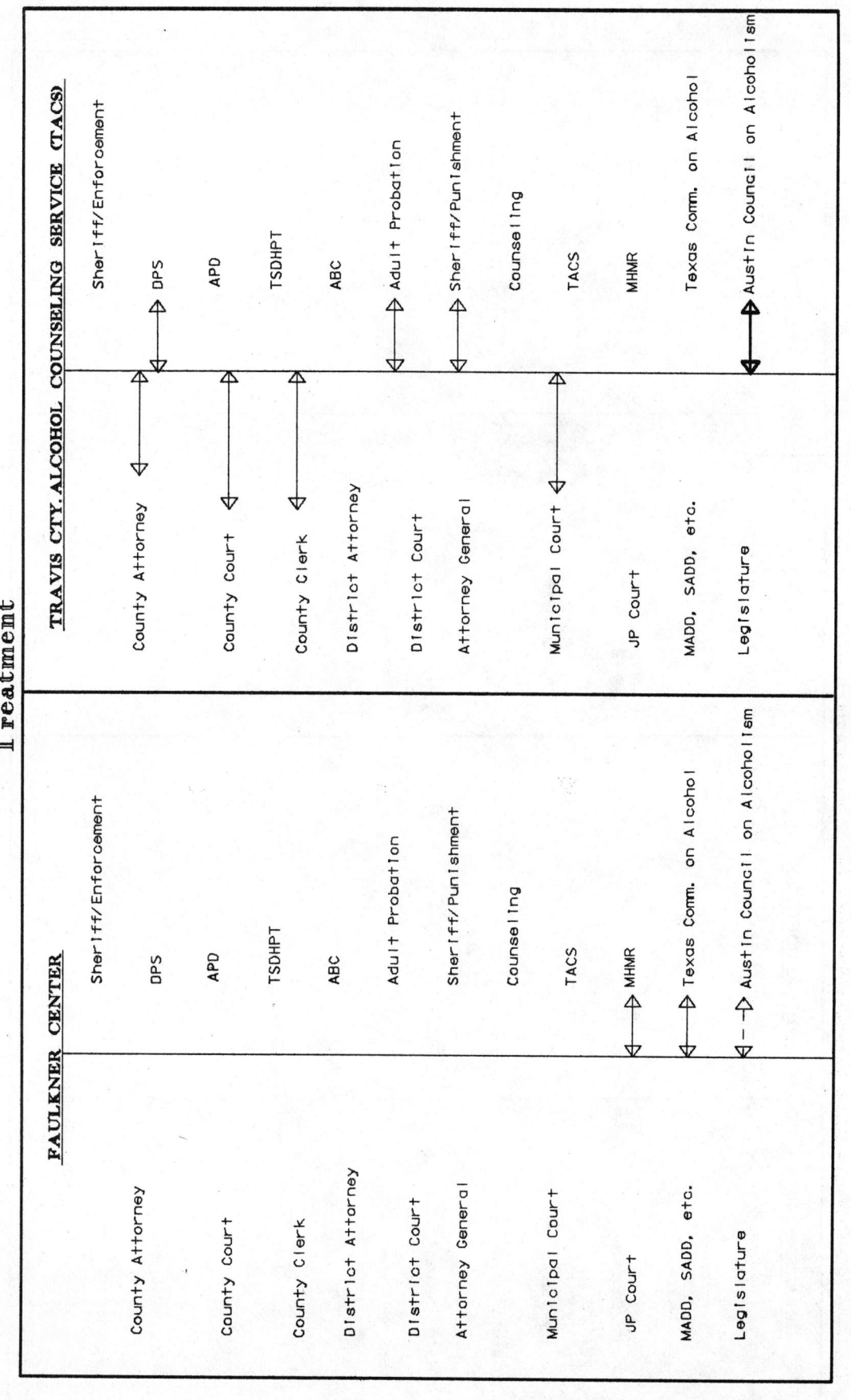

FIGURE 5

Agency-to-Agency Interaction
Treatment

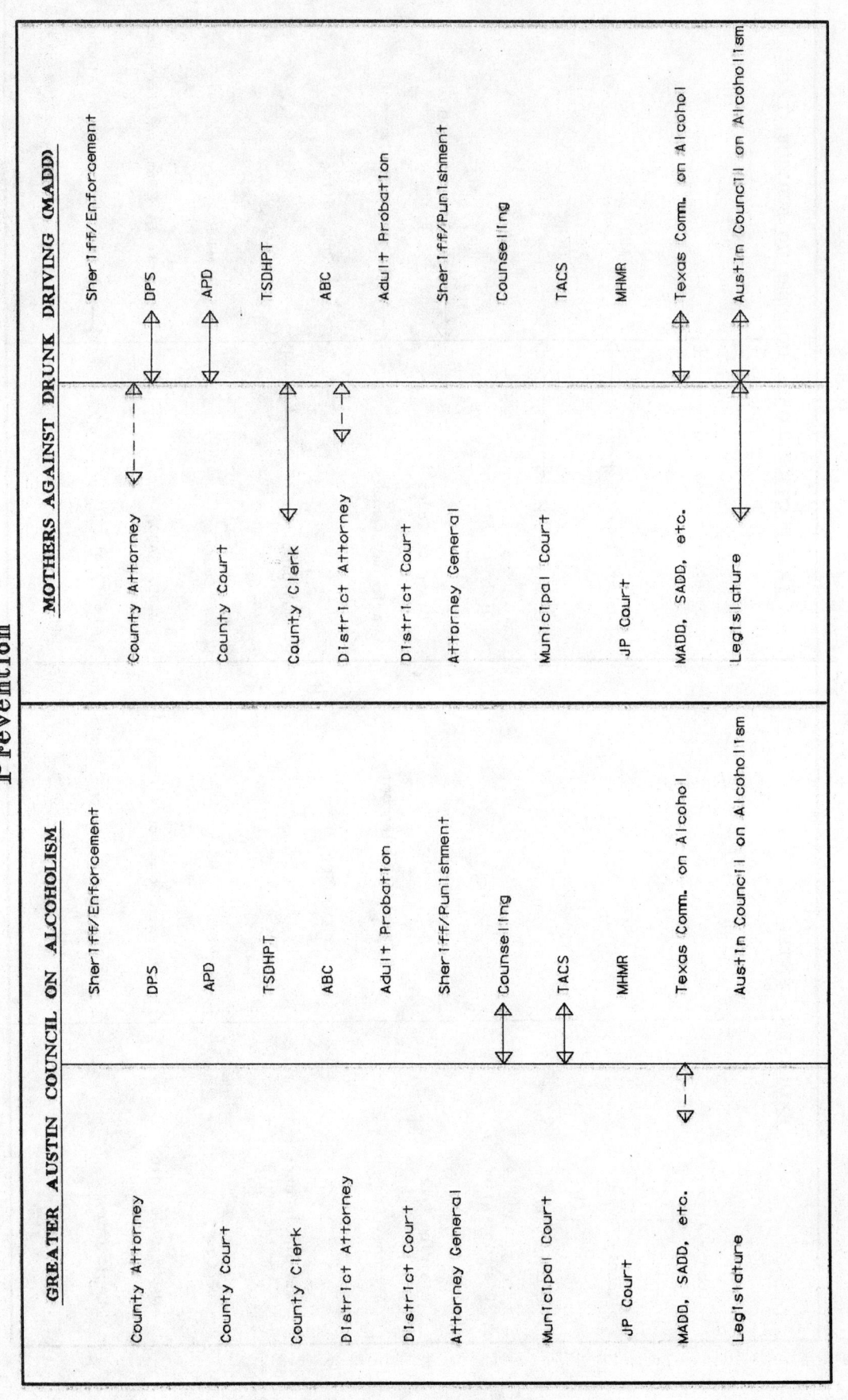

FIGURE 6

Agency-to-Agency Interaction
Prevention

Prosecution and Adjudication

Office of the County Attorney

The county attorney maintains contact with all county law enforcement agencies. The intake department receives reports, affidavits, and complaints from these agencies.

The county attorney also receives information from local hospitals regarding the extent of injuries in a given accident. This information is received by request only and occasionally is difficult to obtain. The attorney uses this information to determine if serious bodily injury is a factor in the case.

All information regarding cases is given to the alcohol task force for study. The county attorney also shares information with the county court. The county attorney's intake office delivers the files containing information gathered on the defendant, including the offense report, complaint, affidavits, and valid prior arrests. The county attorney's office also manages the Travis County Comprehensive Anti-DWI Project.

Office of the District Attorney

The district attorney's office maintains contact with all law enforcement agencies. Information regarding cases is sent from the original arresting agency to the DA. The DA also shares information with the county attorney regarding cases and individual defendants, as well as with the court clerk of origin. Following disposition of a case, disposition data are sent to the original arresting agency.

Municipal Court

The municipal court interacts with the Austin Police Department in sharing of information regarding specific cases and their eventual outcomes. The court naturally is involved with defense attorneys, prosecuting attorneys, and defendants, as well as with personal bond officers.

County Court at Law

The county court interacts primarily with the county attorney's office and the county clerk's office, sharing information on specific cases. The court also is involved with the Travis County Alcohol Counseling Service and the adult probation department. Their interaction involves testing of the defendant for a level of alcohol dependency, advice on terms of probation and/or treatment, monitoring of probation and/or treatment, and so forth. The county court is involved to a lesser extent with the Austin Police Department, the Travis County Sheriff's Department, and the Texas Department of Public Safety regarding cases and their outcomes, as well as general information regarding DWI.

District Court

The district court deals primarily with the district attorney's office and the district clerk regarding specific cases. The district court also maintains contact with the Travis County Adult Probation Department, the Austin Police Department, and the Travis County Sheriff's Department in exchanging information pertaining to specific cases, disposition of cases, possible terms of probation, and monitoring probation.

Justice of the Peace

The justices of the peace maintain contact with the Department of Public Safety and the county attorney's office regarding specific cases and individuals. They also are in contact with the Alcoholic Beverage Commission and community service restitution regarding laws and possible punishments for DWI offenders.

Punishment

Travis County Adult Probation Department

The Travis County Adult Probation Department is involved with all law enforcement agencies, the county and district attorneys' offices, the Travis County Alcohol Counseling Service, and other counseling programs under contract. They also are in contact with all courts in the county. This interaction to a large extent is based on advice given to other agencies regarding possible terms of probation, treatment alternatives, and the like. The department also is involved with these agencies on a case-by-case basis regarding progress of the probationer, follow-up, and so forth.

Del Valle-Travis County Rehabilitation Center

The center is a branch of the Travis County Sheriff's Department, and as such maintains close contact with that department. The facility also works closely with the adult probation department and the district and county courts (mostly county). There also is close contact with all alcohol treatment agencies and centers and some involvement with the Texas

Department of Public Safety when inmates apply for occupational driver's licenses.

Treatment

The Faulkner Center

The Faulkner Center maintains contact with few agencies and departments in the DWI system. What contact does occur generally is in the form of referrals to the center. The main liaison is with the state Department of Mental Health and Mental Retardation. The Texas Commission on Alcoholism also provides the center with a great deal of information and general training. The center also has limited contact with the Greater Austin Council on Alcoholism.

Travis County Alcohol Counseling Services

Travis County Alcohol Counseling Services (TACS) interacts with the county and municipal courts, the county attorney, the county clerk's office, the Austin Police Department, the Travis County Adult Probation Department, the Travis County Sheriff's Department, and the Texas Department of Public Safety.

Prevention

Greater Austin Council on Alcoholism

The council interacts with various counseling and treatment programs by providing information. It also is in contact with the Travis County Alcohol Counseling Service and various citizen action groups such as MADD and Students Against Driving Drunk (SADD). Currently, there is no chapter of SADD within the Austin area. SADD chapters have existed in the past and are likely to regroup in the future.

Mothers Against Drunk Drivers

The Austin chapter of Mothers Against Drunk Drivers (MADD) enjoys a good working relationship with the Austin Police Department. MADD also works with the county clerk's office when gathering information on the status of a case. Often, once a case is scheduled for pretrial, MADD inquires as to which attorney is representing the defense. MADD maintains contact with the Greater Austin Council on Alcoholism, the Texas Legislature, the Texas Department of Public Safety, the Texas Commission on Alcoholism, the Texas Education Agency (occasionally), and various other citizen action and information groups.

CONCLUSIONS

The Texas DWI system has been presented from two perspectives. First, a model systems approach explained the major system components. Second, a case study of Travis County was presented to describe the principal agencies within the component system. This description detailed responsibilities, staffing, and workloads. Finally, the various interactions among these agencies were presented. It is understood that there is a complex combination of working relationships among the various components as well as the agencies.

The extensive interaction among agencies involved in the DWI system requires that the components have balanced roles in the functioning of the system. No one component should exert excessive domination over the other components. Because of the need for close and continuous interaction, no component can operate to the mutual exclusion of the others.

Interviews with the agencies identified the areas of information management, agency cooperation and communication, and overall coordination as needing improvements. All of these areas are very closely related. Improvement in one area could result in systemwide enhancement.

A comprehensive management information system is essential to ensure that the integrated DWI system will function effectively. A lack of adequate information prevents proper prosecution and treatment from being initiated in some cases. Inefficient information collection and dissemination have further resulted in instances of poor communication and cooperation between interacting agencies. Design and implementation of an effective management information system can result in improved agency interaction. Additionally, repeat offenders may face tougher adjudication and punishment as a result of an improved management information system.

The need for overall coordination of the DWI system was very evident during many of the interviews conducted. The Travis County Comprehensive Anti-DWI Project has resolved some coordination difficulties, but more work in this area needs to be undertaken. In some cases, informal coordination has been taken up by nongovernmental agencies such as MADD. Regardless of the source of the coordination, the agency should be familiar with all components. This will permit effective identification of problems and solutions which will assist the DWI agencies in dealing with the drunk driver.

INTERVIEWS

Interview by Marie Setterlund and Bill Coll with Sue Berkel, Assistant County Attorney, County Attorney's Office, Austin, Texas, November 2, 1984.

Interview by Marie Setterlund and Bill Coll with David Boatright, Assistant District Attorney, District Attorney's Office, Austin, Texas, October 26, 1984.

Interview by Marie Setterlund and Jo Anne Hawkins with Officer Charles Chipman, STEP Coordinator, Austin Police Department, Austin, Texas, October 17, 1984.

Interview by Chris Vein with William E. Coll, Senior Paramedic, City of Austin Emergency Medical Services Department, Austin, Texas, October 20, 1984.

Telephone interview by Bill Coll with Dr. Julie Fellows, Health Education Specialist, Texas Department of Health, Austin Texas, November 6, 1984.

Telephone interview by Joanie Raff with Manuel Fernandez, Alcohol Planner, Capital Area Planning Council, Austin, Texas, October 30, 1984.

Interview by Marie Setterlund and Jo Anne Hawkins with Trooper Frank Fisher, Hearing Officer, Texas Department of Public Safety, Austin, Texas, October 18, 1984.

Interview by Joanie Raff and Lisa Norman with Mary Guttery, Director, Prevention Program, Greater Austin Council on Alcoholism, Austin, Texas, October, 11, 1984.

Interview by Julie Ware with Patsy Johnson, Administrative Secretary, Travis County Adult Probation Department, Austin, Texas, November 1, 1984.

Interview by Bill Coll and Julie Ware with Captain E.A. Knowles, Superintendent, Travis County Rehabilitation Center, Austin, Texas, October 18, 1984.

Interview by Cary McDougal with Carol Lawson, Administrative Assistant, Travis County Court, Austin, Texas, November 6, 1984.

Interview by Julie Ware with Patti Littleton, Deputy Sheriff, Travis County Sheriff's Department, Austin, Texas, October 26, 1984.

Interview by Lisa Norman and Bill Coll with Gil Ortiz, Executive Director, Travis County Alcohol Counseling Services, Austin, Texas, November 7, 1984.

Telephone interview by William Coll with Liza Ossenfort, Special Assistant for Research and Policy Development, Office of the Speaker of the House, Austin, Texas, February 7, 1985.

Interview by Beth Beck and Chris Vein with David Phillips, Judge, Austin Municipal Court, Austin, Texas, October 24, 1984.

Interview by Joanie Raff and Julie Ware with Willie Pribble, District Supervisor, Texas Alcoholic Beverage Commission, Austin, Texas, October 25, 1984.

Interview by Joanie Raff and Lisa Norman with Debra Ravel, Justice of the Peace, Justice of the Peace Court, Austin, Texas, October 17, 1984.

Interview by Cary McDougal with Charles Siepert, District Clerk Court Coordinator, District Court, Austin, Texas, November 12, 1984.

Interview by Beth Beck and Cary McDougal with Jennifer Solter, Director, Mothers Against Drunk Drivers, Austin, Texas, October 16, 1984.

Telephone interview by Lisa Norman with Jim Spearley, Coordinator, Texas Senate State Affairs Committee, Austin, Texas, November 5, 1984.

Telephone interview by Bill Coll with Jim Spearley, Coordinator, Texas Senate State Affairs Committee, Austin, Texas, February 7, 1985.

Interview by Jo Anne Hawkins and Cary McDougal with Don Wegscheider, Community Services Director, Faulkner Center, Austin, Texas, October 17, 1985.

Interview by Beth Beck with Gene Wilkins, Curriculum Director, Texas Education Agency, Austin, Texas, October 30, 1984.

Telephone interview by William Coll with Gene Wilkins, Curriculum Director, Austin, Texas, February 20, 1985.

CHAPTER 3

DWI INFORMATION COLLECTION SYSTEMS

INTRODUCTION

This chapter contains a description of DWI information collection activities at the federal, state, and county levels of government. Federal programs included for discussion are the National Accident Sampling System (NASS), the Fatal Accident Reporting System (FARS), and the National Driver Register (NDR). These programs are administered by the National Highway Traffic Safety Administration (NHTSA) of the U.S. Department of Transportation (DOT). Also discussed is the Federal Bureau of Investigation's Uniform Crime Report (UCR).

Currently in Texas, no procedure exists to enable prosecutors to obtain a complete criminal and legal history of a DWI offender. State officials increasingly are becoming aware that the collection of data on individuals arrested for DWI is an important factor in reducing the amount of property damage and the number of lives lost in DWI-related accidents. In response to this data collection need, the Texas Department of Highways and Public Transportation is developing and testing an automated countywide data collection system in four Texas counties. This chapter contains a case study of this prototype data collection project in Travis County. Three similar projects are soon to be established in Bell, Cass, and El Paso counties. These projects are designed for possible statewide use in Texas to track DWI offenders.

FEDERAL DATA COLLECTION SYSTEMS

In 1979, the National Center for Statistics and Analysis (NCSA), an agency of the National Highway Traffic Safety Administration, implemented the National Accident Sampling System and the Fatal Accident Reporting System. These information systems were created to meet the federal government's need to substantiate national accident trends. Data from the NASS and FARS are used to give direction to the research, development, and evaluation of highway accident countermeasures. Both systems compile their data from local law enforcement accident reports.

Fatal Accident Reporting System

The Fatal Accident Reporting System gathers data on state highway traffic accidents that result in loss of life. An accident recorded on FARS must have involved a motor vehicle on a public roadway resulting in a fatality. This includes both occupants and nonoccupants of the vehicle. FARS statistics include only those deaths which occur within thirty days after an accident takes place.[1]

In Texas, the Department of Public Safety (DPS) collects FARS data. Two FARS code clerks are employed at DPS to gather, translate, and transmit the data. Although employed at DPS, the clerks are paid by the National Center for Statistics and Analysis.[2] Information is obtained from source documents and then is encoded onto standard FARS forms. Sources of information include the Driver's Confidential Accident Report (ST-2) and Texas Peace Officer's Accident Report (ST-3), state driver's license files, Texas Department of Highways and Public Transportation files, death certificates, coroners/medical examiner reports, and emergency medical reports.[3] Clerks enter data into a computerized, central data file, and the information is checked on line to maintain quality control.[4]

The system contains a standard format for accident description. Approximately ninety data elements are encoded to describe each accident, vehicle, and person involved. Data elements which provide information on the role of alcohol in an accident include any previous DWI convictions of the driver, the investigating officer's opinion as to whether alcohol was involved in the accident, and whether an alcohol test was performed. If a test was performed, there is a data element for the actual level of blood alcohol concentration found.

The three standard FARS forms which are used to record data elements are:

1. Accident Level Form--records characteristics of an accident such as time and location of accident, "hit and run" status, number of vehicles and persons involved, and weather conditions (see Exhibit 1).

2. Vehicle-Driver Level Form--records data on each accident, involved vehicle, and driver; includes vehicle type, initial and principal impact points, the most harmful event, and the record and license status of each driver (see Exhibit 2).

3. Person Level Form--records data on each person involved in the accident, such as age, sex, alcohol involvement, injury severity, and whether the person was driver, passenger, or pedestrian (see Exhibit 3).

Because all states report accident and related data through a single system with written guidelines, data generally are consistent. Differences due to variations in data collection procedures usually are minor, but the variations occasionally may be large enough to obscure or exaggerate real differences among the states.[5]

National Accident Sampling System

The basic goal of the National Accident Sampling System is to provide valid estimates of national highway accident trends by investigating and analyzing a statistically valid sample of nationwide accidents. The primary objectives of NASS are to estimate and to disseminate timely information on the causes and consequences of accidents, to evaluate existing countermeasures, to provide a data base suitable for assisting in the design of future countermeasures, and to monitor changes and trends in the safety environments.[6] When in full operation, the system will be capable of analyzing close to fifteen thousand accidents.

The Continuous Sampling System (CSS) is NASS's general purpose accident data collection program. The system consists of fifty small teams of trained investigators under contract with NHTSA who work in Primary Sampling Unit (PSU) areas. These units are counties or groups of counties, which are selected on a probability basis. Within each PSU area, the investigators study a probability sample of accidents and collect data on each accident within that sample. These data, which constitute the CSS, provide nationwide accident statistics, which include the number of persons involved in accidents by extent of injury, age, sex, and vehicle type. The data also are used in evaluating factors related to the severity of injury.

NASS also has a Special Studies Subsystem, which contains a separate sample. It uses supplemental data collection procedures designed to meet the needs of various special studies which have a more narrowly defined emphasis than the CSS.[7]

NASS data concerning drivers in alcohol-involved accidents include the age and sex of the driver, the driver's license status, and any prior convictions for driving under the influence or any related offense. The system also provides information on where and when alcohol-related accidents occur and on the types of vehicles involved in such accidents.[8]

In both NASS and FARS, an accident is considered to be alcohol related if either police statements allege or tests reveal alcohol in the driver's or pedestrian's blood. Alcohol-related accidents include any accident where a driver or pedestrian involved has a blood alcohol concentration (BAC) level of .10 percent or more when test results are known; where any driver is cited for driving while intoxicated or driving under the influence when test results are not known; where there is an indication on the police report that alcohol was present or involved; or where the driver or pedestrian had been drinking, even though test results were not available. NASS also considers accidents to be alcohol related if the driver's BAC level was less than .10 percent, but the reporting officer considered alcohol to be a contributing factor.[9]

According to these criteria, about 11 percent of all accidents in the

Exhibit 1
1983 Fatal Accident-Reporting System (FARS) — Accident Level

Exhibit 2
1983 Fatal Accident-Reporting System (FARS) — Vehicle/Driver Level

U.S. Department of Transportation
National Highway Traffic Safety Administration

Form Approved thru 12/31/83
O.M.B. No. 2127-0006
CODED BY: _____
DATE CODED: _____
STATE CASE NO: _____

1983 Fatal Accident Reporting System (FARS)
VEHICLE/DRIVER LEVEL

CASE NUMBER STATE (GSA CODES) [1,2]
CONSECUTIVE NUMBER [3-6]
TRANSACTION CODE [7,8]
- 21 — Original Submission
- 22 — Update or Change

CARD NO. [9] — 1
VEHICLE NUMBER (Assigned by Analyst) [10,11]

VEHICLE MAKE [14,15]
(See Instruction Manual)

VEHICLE MODEL [16,17]
(See Instruction Manual)

BODY TYPE [18,19]
(See Instruction Manual)

MODEL YEAR [20,21]
Actual Value except 99 — Unknown

VEHICLE IDENTIFICATION NO. [22-32]
Actual Value except:
- Zero Fill if no VIN
- Nine Fill if Unknown

REGISTRATION STATE [39,40]
GSA CODES Except:
- 00 — Not Applicable
- 92 — No Registration
- 93 — Multiple State Reg. In-State
- 94 — Multiple State Reg., Out-of-State
- 95 — U.S. Government Tags
- 96 — Military Vehicle
- 97 — Foreign Countries
- 99 — Unknown

ROLLOVER [41]
- 0 — No Rollover
- 1 — First Event
- 2 — Subsequent Event

JACKKNIFE [42]
- 0 — Not an Articulated Vehicle
- 1 — No
- 2 — First Event
- 3 — Subsequent Event

TRAVEL SPEED [43,44]
Actual Miles Per Hour Except:
- 00 — Stopped Vehicle
- 97 — Ninety-seven MPH or Greater
- 99 — Unknown

HAZARDOUS CARGO [45]
- 0 — No
- 1 — Yes
- 9 — Unknown

VEHICLE TRAILERING [46]
- 0 — No
- 1 — Yes, One Trailing Unit
- 2 — Yes, Two or more Trailing Units
- 3 — Yes, Number of Trailing Units Unknown
- 9 — Unknown

SPECIAL USE [47]
- 0 — No Special Use
- 1 — Taxi
- 2 — Vehicle Used as School Bus
- 3 — Vehicle Used as other Bus
- 4 — Military
- 5 — Police
- 6 — Ambulance
- 7 — Firetruck
- 9 — Unknown

EMERGENCY USE [48]
- 0 — No
- 1 — Yes

IMPACT POINT — INITIAL [49,50]
- 00 — Non-Collision
- 01-12 — Clock Points
- 13 — Top
- 14 — Undercarriage
- 15 — Under Ride
- 16 — Override
- 99 — Unknown

IMPACT POINT — PRINCIPAL [51,52]
- 00 — Non-Collision
- 01-12 — Clock Points
- 13 — Top
- 14 — Undercarriage
- 15 — Under Ride
- 16 — Override
- 99 — Unknown

EXTENT OF DEFORMATION [53]
- 0 — None
- 2 — Other (Minor)
- 4 — Functional (Moderate)
- 6 — Disabling (Severe)
- 9 — Unknown

VEHICLE ROLE [54]
- 0 — Non-Collision
- 1 — Striking
- 2 — Struck
- 3 — Both
- 9 — Unknown

MANNER OF LEAVING SCENE [55]
- 1 — Driven
- 2 — Towed Away
- 3 — Abandoned
- 9 — Unknown

FIRE OCCURRENCE [56]
- 0 — No Fire
- 1 — Fire Occurred in Vehicle During Accident

NUMBER OF OCCUPANTS [57,58]
Actual Value if Total Known
- 96 — 96 or more
- 97 — Unknown — Only Injured Reported
- 99 — Unknown

RELATED FACTORS [59-62]
See Instruction Manual "Related Factors — VEHICLE LEVEL"

VEHICLE MANEUVER [63]
(See Instruction Manual)

MOST HARMFUL EVENT [65,66]
(See Instruction Manual)

Card No. [9] — 2

DRIVER PRESENCE [14]
- 1 — Driver Operated Vehicle
- 2 — Driverless
- 3 — Driver Left Scene
- 9 — Unknown

LICENSE STATE GSA CODES [15,16]
Except:
- 94 — Military
- 95 — Canada
- 96 — Mexico
- 97 — Other Foreign Countries
- 99 — Unknown

LICENSE/CLASS VEHICLE COMPLIANCE [17]
- 0 — No License Required
- 1 — No License, License Required
- 2 — Valid License for This Class Vehicle Only
- 3 — One Valid License, but Not for This Class Vehicle
- 4 — Multiple Class Licenses, Valid License for This Class Vehicle
- 5 — Multiple Class Licenses, No Valid License for This Class Vehicle
- 9 — Unknown

LICENSE STATUS [18]
- 0 — None Required
- 1 — None
- 2 — Valid
- 3 — Suspended
- 4 — Revoked
- 5 — Expired
- 6 — Cancelled or Denied
- 7 — Learner's Permit
- 8 — Temporary
- 9 — Unknown

COMPLIANCE WITH LICENSE RESTRICTIONS [19]
- 0 — No Restrictions
- 1 — Restrictions Complied With
- 2 — Restrictions Not Complied With
- 3 — Restrictions, Compliance Unknown
- 9 — Unknown

DRIVER TRAINING [20]
- 0 — None
- 1 — High School
- 2 — Commercial
- 3 — School Bus
- 4 — Traffic School
- 5 — Two or more Types
- 6 — Training, Type Unknown
- 9 — Unknown

VIOLATIONS CHARGED [21]
- 0 — None
- 1 — Alcohol or Drugs
- 2 — Speeding
- 3 — Alcohol or Drugs and Speeding
- 4 — Reckless Driving
- 5 — Driving with a Suspended or Revoked License
- 6 — Other Moving Violation
- 7 — Non-Moving Violation
- 8 — Violation, Type Unknown or Other Violation
- 9 — Unknown

PREVIOUS RECORDED ACCIDENTS [22,23]
Actual Value Except:
- 00 — None
- 99 — Unknown

PREVIOUS RECORDED SUSPENSIONS AND REVOCATIONS [24,25]
Actual Value Except:
- 00 — None
- 99 — Unknown

PREVIOUS DWI CONVICTIONS [26,27]
Actual Value Except:
- 00 — None
- 99 — Unknown

PREVIOUS SPEEDING CONVICTIONS [28,29]
Actual Value Except:
- 00 — None
- 99 — Unknown

PREVIOUS OTHER HARMFUL MV CONVICTIONS [30,31]
Actual Value Except:
- 00 — None
- 99 — Unknown

DATE OF LAST ACCIDENT, SUSPENSION, OR CONVICTION [32-35]
Mo. Yr.
- 00 — No Record
- 99 — Unknown

DATE OF FIRST ACCIDENT, SUSPENSION, OR CONVICTION [36-39]
Mo. Yr.
- 00 — No Record
- 99 — Unknown

RELATED FACTORS [40-45]
See Instruction Manual, "Related Factors — DRIVER LEVEL"

HS Form 214A (Rev. 1/83)

Exhibit 3
1983 Fatal Accident-Reporting System (FARS) — Person Level

US Department of Transportation
National Highway Traffic Safety Administration

1983 Fatal Accident Reporting System (FARS) PERSON LEVEL

Form Approved thru 12/31/83
O.M.B. No. 2127-0006
CODED BY: _____
DATE CODED: _____
STATE CASE NO: _____

CASE NUMBER STATE (GSA CODES) [1 2]
CONSECUTIVE NUMBER [3 6]
TRANSACTION CODE [7 8]
31 – Original Submission
32 – Update or Change
CARD NO. [9] 3
VEHICLE NUMBER (Assigned by Analyst) [10 11]
00 – Non-Motorist
PERSON NUMBER [12 13] (Assigned by Analyst)

NON MOTORIST STRIKING VEHICLE NUMBER [14 15]
Assigned Vehicle Number Except:
99 – Unknown

AGE [16 17]
Actual Value
00 – Up to One Year
97 – Ninety-Seven Years or Older
99 – Unknown

SEX [18]
1 – Male
2 – Female
9 – Unknown

PERSON TYPE [19]
1 – Driver of a Motor Vehicle in Transport
2 – Passenger of a Motor Vehicle in Transport
3 – Occupant of a Motor Vehicle Not in Transport
4 – Occupant of a Non-Motor Vehicle Transport Device
5 – Non-Occupant – Pedestrian
6 – Non-Occupant – Bicyclist
7 – Non-Occupant – Other Cyclist
8 – Non-Occupant – Other or Unknown
9 – Unknown Occupant Type in a Motor Vehicle in Transport

SEATING POSITION [20 21]
00 – Non-Motorist
11 – Front Seat – Left Side (Driver's Side)
12 – Middle
13 – Right Side
18 – Other
19 – Unknown
21 – Second Seat – Left Side
22 – Middle
23 – Right Side
28 – Other
29 – Unknown
31 – Third Seat – Left Side
32 – Middle
33 – Right Side
38 – Other
39 – Unknown
41 – Fourth Seat – Left Side
42 – Middle
43 – Right Side
48 – Other
49 – Unknown
50 – Sleeper Section of Cab (Truck)
51 – Other Passenger in Enclosed Passenger or Cargo Area
52 – Other Passenger in Unenclosed Passenger or Cargo Area
53 – Other Passenger in Passenger or Cargo Area, Unknown Whether or Not Enclosed
54 – Trailing Unit
55 – Riding on Vehicle Exterior
99 – Unknown

MANUAL (ACTIVE) RESTRAINT SYSTEM – USE [22]
0 – None Used – Vehicle Occupant / Not Applicable – Non-Motorist
1 – Shoulder Belt
2 – Lap Belt
3 – Lap and Shoulder Belt
4 – Child Safety Seat
5 – Motorcycle Helmet
8 – Restraint Used – Type Unknown or Other including Other Helmet
9 – Unknown

AUTOMATIC (PASSIVE) RESTRAINT SYSTEM – FUNCTION [23]
0 – Not Equipped or Non-Motorist
1 – Automatic Belt in Use
2 – Automatic Belt Not In Use
3 – Deployed Air Bag
4 – Non-deployed Air Bag
9 – Unknown

NON-MOTORIST LOCATION [24 25]
00 – Not Applicable – Vehicle Occupant
01 – Intersection – In Crosswalk
02 – Intersection – On Roadway, Not in Crosswalk
03 – Intersection – On Roadway, Crosswalk Not Available
04 – Intersection – On Roadway, Crosswalk Availability Unknown
05 – Intersection – Not on Roadway
09 – Intersection – Unknown
10 – Non-Intersection – In Crosswalk
11 – Non-Intersection – On Roadway, Not in Crosswalk
12 – Non-Intersection – On Roadway, Crosswalk Not Available
13 – Non-Intersection – On Roadway, Crosswalk Availability Unknown
14 – Non-Intersection – In Parking Lane
15 – Non-Intersection – On Road Shoulder
16 – Non-Intersection – Bike Path
17 – Non-Intersection – Outside Trafficway
18 – Non-Intersection – Other, Not on Roadway
19 – Non-Intersection – Unknown
99 – Unknown

EJECTION [26]
0 – Not Ejected
1 – Totally Ejected
2 – Partially Ejected
9 – Unknown

EXTRICATION [27]
0 – Not Extricated
1 – Extricated
9 – Unknown

POLICE REPORTED ALCOHOL INVOLVEMENT [28]
0 – No (Alcohol Not Involved)
1 – Yes (Alcohol Involved)
8 – Not Reported
9 – Unknown (Police Reported)

ALCOHOL TEST RESULT [29 30]
Actual Value (Decimal Implied before First Digit) (0 xx)
95 – Test Refused
96 – None Given
97 – AC Test Performed, Results Unknown
99 – Unknown

INJURY SEVERITY [31]
0 – No Injury (0)
1 – Possible Injury (C)
2 – Nonincapacitating Evident Injury (B)
3 – Incapacitating Injury (A)
4 – Fatal Injury (K)
5 – Injured, Severity Unknown
6 – Died Prior to Accident
9 – Unknown

TAKEN TO HOSPITAL OR TREATMENT FACILITY [32]
0 – No
1 – Yes
9 – Unknown

DEATH DATE [33 38]
000000 – Not Applicable
999999 – Unknown
MONTH DAY YEAR

DEATH TIME [39 42]
Military Time Except:
0000 – Not Applicable
9999 – Unknown

RELATED FACTORS [43 44] [45 46] [47 48]
See Instruction Manual "Related Factors – PERSON LEVEL"

HS Form 2148 (Rev. 1/83)

NASS sample, in 1981, were alcohol related. This proportion increased dramatically when accidents were categorized according to severity of injuries; 33 percent of serious nonfatal accidents involved alcohol. In 1982, at least 59 percent of fatal accidents involved alcohol, and 48 percent were legally intoxicated according to the laws of most states.[10]

NASS data are likely to underestimate the role alcohol plays in automobile accidents because of the difficulty associated with detecting alcohol as a contributing factor. Alcohol detection often requires sophisticated training and equipment, which is not universally available to law enforcement agencies.[11]

FBI Uniform Crime Report

Uniform Crime Reporting System

The Uniform Crime Report (UCR), a reporting system administered by the Federal Bureau of Investigation (FBI), involves city, county, and state law enforcement programs. UCR provides an analysis of nationwide crime trends based on the submission of data by law enforcement agencies throughout the United States.

In 1930, a voluntary national program to collect crime statistics was initiated by the Committee on Uniform Crime Records of the International Association of Chiefs of Police (IACP). In that same year, Congress authorized the Federal Bureau of Investigation to serve as the national clearinghouse for statistical information on crime in cooperation with the IACP. In order to provide as accurate a picture as possible of nationwide crime trends, the IACP committee determined that a meaningful overview could be obtained through the examination of seven offenses. These offenses, known as the Crime Index Offenses, or Part I offenses, include murder, forcible rape, robbery, aggravated assault, burglary, larceny-theft, and motor vehicle theft. The Part I offenses were selected on the basis of the seriousness of the crime, the frequency of occurrence, and the likelihood of being reported to the police. Currently, arrest information for Part I crime offenses is reported voluntarily on a monthly basis by local and state officials to the UCR.

In addition, local and state arrest data on other significant crimes--termed Part II offenses--also are provided monthly to the UCR. Driving under the influence and public drunkenness are both Part II offenses. The UCR reports information concerning the age, sex, and race of all persons arrested by law enforcement agencies for Part I and II offenses. It does not provide accident information related to Part I and Part II arrests.

Each contributing agency is responsible for compiling its own crime reports and submitting them to the Uniform Crime Reporting Program. The program is an effort to maintain the high quality of data received; it has full-time field representatives who provide reports and procedural training. Also, the FBI publishes annually a handbook concerning uniform crime reports which clearly defines procedures for scoring and classifying offenses. The monthly count of offenses is taken from the records of complaints received by law enforcement agencies from victims, witnesses, and other sources, or discovered by an agency's own investigation. Complaints determined later to be unfounded are eliminated from the aggregate data. Part I crimes are reported without regard as to whether anyone was arrested or stolen property was recorded. Part II crimes are reported only if arrests are made. Verification of monthly reports is performed by national UCR statisticians. "It is standard operating procedure to examine each incoming report not only for arithmetical accuracy, but also and possibly of even more importance, for reasonableness as a possible indication of errors."[12]

National Driver Register

The National Driver Register (NDR) is yet another data system designed to provide nationwide driver information. The NDR was enacted by Congress in 1960 through the National Driver Register--Record of Revocations Act (PL 86-660). The law authorizes the establishment of the NDR to serve as a central index on actions taken by state law enforcement authorities associated with arrests for driving while intoxicated and for fatal accidents, which resulted in suspension or revocation of a driver's license.[13] The National Traffic and Motor Vehicle Safety Act of 1966 (PL 89-563) expanded the NDR to include and transmit state driver's license records concerning all permit denials, terminations, or temporary withdrawals of six months or more.

The NDR, operated by NHTSA, is a cooperative voluntary program between state and federal authorities to assist states in exchanging information about the driving records of certain individuals. The NDR was primarily created to prevent drivers who have had their license suspended or revoked in one state from obtaining a license in another state.

States participate in the NDR by providing reports of license withdrawals and denials for entry onto the NDR file, and by submitting names of license applicants to be checked against the NDR file to determine if a report for license withdrawal or denial is in the file from another licensing jurisdiction. Currently, all states voluntarily participate in the NDR to some degree.[14]

Information on license withdrawal and suspensions contains descriptive data on the individual including name, date of birth, sex, height, and weight. Also, details are noted in the NDR files regarding the action taken against the individual, such as the traffic violation for which the license was suspended or withdrawn, date of the violation, and date of eligibility for license restoration and restoration date if applicable.[15]

A state's request for information is processed against the NDR computer-based file generally within twenty-four hours of receipt. The matching of an inquiry with a record on file produces "a probable identification." An identification is only probable since there is the possibility that the individual noted on the inquiry may not be the same person identified by NDR records. The "probable identification" is mailed to the inquiring states as soon as possible, so that officials may take appropriate actions. The processing time from state inquiry to state receipt of a probable identification notification generally takes about ten days.[16] A response is provided only when a match occurs.

Although the NDR is computer assisted, it relies on the post office to transmit information to and from state licensing agencies. The use of the mail system is a time-consuming activity. By the time a negative response is received on an individual, the individual may have received a new license. This means that there must be a revocation of the new license, which is a lengthy and difficult process. Recently, phone lines have been installed for use with computers to provide overnight service in some places.[17]

The size of the NDR file is continually expanding. This growth is controlled by the use of an automatic purging system, which deletes older records. Currently, records of license withdrawals for serious violations such as drunk driving, hit-and-run accidents, habitual violations, fatal accidents, and driving while license is suspended, revoked, or denied are kept for five years. Alcohol-related driving convictions account for about 52 percent of the records on file, while about 12 percent are for repeated violations.[18]

The most significant problem with the current system is the length of time required to respond to inquiries. The average processing time is ten days. This is a particular problem for twenty-five states which issue a full-term license directly and immediately over the counter.[19] Although these states still send inquiries to the NDR, the results of the NDR file checks are received after a license has been issued.

In 1973, NHTSA conducted a study to identify and determine the extent of NDR program problems. The study's principal recommendation was the development of a computerized "rapid response system" to handle state inquiries. The plans for such a system were laid in April 1978 for the implementation of a "state-of-the-art" federal/state record communication system.[20]

In 1977, Rep. James Oberstar (D-Minn.) introduced a bill to upgrade the NDR through automation. Some states objected, however, to the high costs they would be forced to incur if such an upgrading were to occur. Oberstar's legislation--the Surface Transportation Assistance Act of 1978 (PL 95-599)--was amended to provide for a one-year study of the current system. In 1980, the findings of the study were reported to Congress.

Noted in the study were problems of maintaining recent and accurate data in such a massive data file. The report recommended automation, using a system in which the NDR would serve as a conduit for retrieving information from a state requesting information and then relaying the information found, without interception to the state making an inquiry. This system addressed concerns about privacy, namely that the federal government previously had retained records on the details of adverse driver license actions taken in the states. In addition, since the NDR would no longer be responsible for vast amounts of data, it could rely on the states to provide information as recent and accurate as the data in the state file at the time of inquiry.[21]

However, in June 1981, the Reagan Administration proposed abolition of the NDR. Although there still were questions concerning the NDR's privacy safeguards and accuracy, the primary reason given for the abolition efforts was the high cost of automation.[22] After citizen groups strongly opposed the NDR abolition, the administration reversed its position and supported the 1982 NDR automation legislation.

In 1982, Congress enacted the Alcohol Traffic Safety and National Driver Register Act of 1982 (PL 97-364), part of which upgraded the NDR system. The key feature of the act is section 203(a), which directs the Secretary of Transportation to establish and maintain a NDR system to serve as a link between states seeking and providing information on drivers' records. Only necessary identifying information will be in NDR files; all other pertinent information as to the placement of a person's name in the NDR files will be maintained only at the state level.

The 1982 legislation also expanded the categories of adverse driver licensing actions, which are authorized to be transmitted by the NDR to include convictions for certain traffic offenses that did not involve a license suspension or revocation. This allowed for the reporting of individuals who are convicted of operating a motor vehicle while under the influence of or impaired by alcohol or a controlled substance.[23]

The act also required the Secretary of Transportation to select four states to participate in a one-year pilot program to test and perfect the automated system. The selection process will take place in 1985. Implementation of the four-state system will probably be completed in 1987. Following evaluations of the pilot program, necessary adjustments will be made within the system, and possible amendments to the act may be attempted. Full automation will be completed by October 25, 1989.[24]

RECORDING DWI INFORMATION AT THE STATE LEVEL

Data on DWI arrests, convictions, and DWI-related traffic accidents in Texas are collected by three offices within the Department of Public Safety (DPS). The three offices are the Statistical Services Bureau, the Driver and Vehicle Records Division, and the Uniform Crime Reporting Bureau.

DPS Statistical Services Bureau

DPS receives reports directly from its own officers when a DWI arrest and/or accident occurs. Follow-up reports by DPS officers are forwarded after the disposition of each case. Data from these reports are entered into the DPS computerized information system by the Statistical Services Bureau. Accident data also must be forwarded to DPS by local police agencies. DPS is required to collect accident-related data by Texas Statute Tex. Rev. Civ. Stat. Ann., art. 6701d, sec. 44 (Vernon 1977), and also is required to regularly publish statistical information based on it.[25] DPS is the state custodian of accident records. Each month DPS compiles a year-to-date accident tape, which is derived from the Texas Peace Officer's Accident Report (Form ST-3) and the Driver's Confidential Accident Report (Form ST-2). Accidents that do not meet the state threshold-reporting requirement of at least $250 in property damage and/or involve an injury or fatality are not included in the DPS accident file.

Among the Statistical Services Bureau's reports are monthly and annual alcohol breath testing summaries, DWI-involved motor vehicle traffic accident summaries, and summaries of DWI arrests and dispositions by county. DPS produces an annual publication, Motor Vehicle Traffic Accidents, which is a compilation of information on reported accidents submitted by local police agencies in the state, including data on DWI-related accidents. However, there is no attempt to correlate arrest and accident data.

DPS Driver and Vehicle Records Division

The DPS Driver and Vehicle Records Division maintains information on DWI arrests in individual driver's license records. When a DWI arrest is made by a DPS officer and a citation is issued, a copy is sent to DPS and the information is entered by the Statistical Services staff. Pending arrest information is maintained for up to four years awaiting final disposition. When final disposition occurs, the individual's driving record is updated if there is a conviction or probation.

Although DPS maintains information on DWI arrests made by its personnel, this information is incomplete. It does not include all DWI arrests from local law enforcement agencies because Texas has no law requiring such reporting.

DPS Uniform Crime Reporting Bureau

Data on DWI arrests not related to traffic accidents also are reported on a regular basis to the DPS Uniform Crime Reporting Bureau by local police agencies. A Bureau of Identification and Records was established within DPS by Tex. Rev. Civ. Stat. Ann., art. 4413(14) (Vernon 1976), in 1935. It was charged with collecting information on offenses committed in the state, arrests, and other crime-related data. In January 1976, Texas began to participate in the FBI's Uniform Crime Reporting Program. A Uniform Crime Reporting Bureau was established within the Crime Records Division--formerly the Bureau of Identification and Records--to coordinate the collection, processing, and dissemination of data concerning the extent of crime in Texas. The state also adopted the Uniform Crime Report as the official statewide crime report.[26]

Each month, the bureau mails packets of forms to all 766 county and municipal police jurisdictions located in the state. Each contributing agency is responsible for compiling its own crime reports and submitting them to the bureau. Although participation is voluntary, peer pressure and tradition cause nearly 100 percent of Texas law enforcement agencies to report this information.[27] These reports then are collected, validated, and tabulated by the bureau. The primary objective of the Uniform Crime Reporting Program is to produce a reliable set of criminal statistics for use in law enforcement, administration, operation, and management.[28]

These data are aggregated, computerized, and provided in various formats to the public, the Governor, the Texas Legislature, state criminal justice agencies, and the FBI. Crime in Texas is an annual report compiled by the DPS, which includes information on DWI arrests. The validity of data collected is subject to the vagaries of reporting. Problems exist in attaining uniformity in a voluntary reporting system. Reports are examined for reasonableness, as well as for arithmetical accuracy. They are returned to the contributor if corrections are necessary. Upon resubmission, they are reverified. After all verification is completed, summary statistics are compiled. However, information on the dispositions of cases resulting from DWI arrests is not collected by the Uniform Crime Reporting Bureau.

RECORDING DWI INFORMATION AT THE COUNTY LEVEL

Law Enforcement

Austin Police Department

When investigating a possible DWI offense, the Austin Police Department (APD) completes three forms including the DWI/DUI Traffic Case Report, the Collision Report, and the Field Report. All three are considered incident reports. The Case Report, or the Officer's Arrest Report, contains information pertaining to the possible drinking driver at the time of arrest (see Exhibit 4). The arrest report is given to data entry clerks to file with the APD. A copy also is routed to the traffic

Exhibit 4
Austin Police Department DWI/DUID Traffic Case Report

AUSTIN POLICE DEPARTMENT
City of Austin
DWI/DUID TRAFFIC CASE REPORT

COUNTY TRAVIS

VIOLATOR OR SUSPECT

OFFENSE NO. _____

NAME _____ Last _____ First _____ Middle _____ ADDRESS _____ STATE _____

HEIGHT _____ WEIGHT _____ OCCUPATION _____ DL NO. _____ BIRTH DATE _____ SEX _____ RACE _____

VEHICLE: Color _____ Year Model _____ Make _____ Body Style _____ Registered _____

OFFENSE _____ DATE _____ Day of Week _____ 19 ____ Hour ____ ☐ a.m. ☐ p.m. ☐ Fatal Accident ☐ Non-Fatal Accident ☐ No Accident Number _____

ROAD ON WHICH COLLISION OCCURRED _____ Block Number _____ Street or Road Name _____ Route Number _____ Check and complete one only — AT ITS INTERSECTION WITH _____ — IF NOT AT INTERSECTION ____ feet ☐ N ☐ S ☐ E ☐ W of Street or Road Name _____ Route Number XXXXXXXXX XXXXXXXXX

WITNESSES

Name	Address	Elements of this case witness can testify to
Name	Address	

CHEMICAL TEST

TEST OFFERED (alcohol): ☐ Breath ☐ Urine ☐ Blood ☐ Name ☐ Other, specify

TEST GIVEN (alcohol): ☐ Breath ☐ Urine ☐ Blood ☐ Refused ☐ Other, specify

TEST RESULT _____ %

Subject Driving Motor Vehicle		Person Killed Due to Accident	Accident Occasioned by Intoxicated Condition of Subject
On Public Highway	In Incorp. City XXXXXXXX		

REFUSAL FORM SUBMITTED ☐ Yes ☐ No Intoxicated or Under Influence of Drugs URINE AND OR BLOOD SUBMITTED FOR DRUGS ☐

ARRESTING OFFICER

_____ Ident. No. _____ Dept. _____ Other Officers _____ Officer/Operator _____ Identification No. _____

OBSERVATIONS

CLOTHES—Describe type and color _____ Hat or Cap _____ Shirt or Dress _____
Jacket or Coat _____ Pants or Skirt _____

Condition: ☐ Disorderly ☐ Disarranged ☐ Soiled ☐ Mussed ☐ Orderly Describe _____

BREATH Odor of Alcoholic Beverage: ☐ Strong ☐ Moderate ☐ Faint ☐ None

ATTITUDE: ☐ Excited ☐ Hilarious ☐ Talkative ☐ Carefree ☐ Sleepy ☐ Profanity
☐ Combative ☐ Indifferent ☐ Insulting ☐ Cocky ☐ Cooperative ☐ Polite

UNUSUAL ACTIONS: ☐ Hiccoughing ☐ Belching ☐ Vomiting ☐ Fighting ☐ Crying ☐ Laughing

SPEECH: ☐ Not Understandable ☐ Mumbled ☐ Slurred ☐ Mush Mouthed ☐ Confused ☐ Sure
☐ Thick Tongued ☐ Stuttered ☐ Accent ☐ Fair ☐ Good

BALANCE: ☐ Falling ☐ Needed Support ☐ Wobbling ☐ Swaying ☐ Unsure ☐ Sure

WALKING: ☐ Falling ☐ Staggering ☐ Stumbling ☐ Swaying ☐ Unsure ☐ Sure

TURNING: ☐ Falling ☐ Staggering ☐ Hesitent ☐ Swaying ☐ Unsure ☐ Sure

Fingerprinted By AUSTIN POLICE DEPARTMENT _____ Ident. No. _____ Date of Report _____ Charges Filed _____

Signature of Officer Making Report _____

PD 0014A

Exhibit 4 (cont.)
Austin Police Department DWI/DUID Traffic Case Report

SUMMARY (DESCRIBE WHAT YOU DID AND WHAT YOU FOUND, SHOWING INFORMATION SUCH AS: WHY YOU STARTED CASE; —MANNER OF DRIVING; —CONDITION OF VEHICLE AND DEFENDANT; —POSSESSION OF SPECIFIC DRIVERS LICENSE, BY NUMBER; —PERTINENT REMARKS OF DEFENDANT, WITNESSES, DOCTORS; —PHYSICAL CONDITION OF ROAD, TRAFFIC, WEATHER; —DISPOSITION OF VEHICLE AND DEFENDANT.)

_____
_____
_____
_____
_____
_____
_____
_____

INTERVIEW

Were you operating a vehicle? _____ Where were you going? _____ What street or highway were you on? _____

Direction of travel? _____ Where did you start from? _____ What time did you start? _____

What city (county) are you in now? _____ What is the date? _____ What day of the week is it? _____

INTERVIEWER TO FILL IN ACTUAL Time _____ am/pm Day _____ Date _____ Interviewer's Name _____

When did you last eat? _____ What did you eat? _____ What were you doing the last three hours? _____

_____ Have you been drinking? _____ What? _____ How much? _____

Where? _____ Started? _____ am/pm Stopped? _____ am/pm Are you under the influence of an alcoholic beverage now? _____

What is your occupation? _____ When did you last work? _____ Do you have any physical defects? _____ If so, what? _____

What is the name of your employer? _____

Are you ill? _____ If so, what's wrong? _____ Do you limp? _____ Have you been injured lately? _____ If so, what's wrong? _____

Did you get a bump on the head? _____ Were you involved in an accident today? _____ Have you had any alcoholic beverage since the accident? _____

If so, what? _____ Where? _____ How much? _____ When? _____

Have you seen a doctor or dentist lately? _____ If so, who? _____ (If DUID When? _____ What for? _____

Are you taking tranquilizers, pills or medicines of any kind? _____ If so, what kind? suspected Get Sample) _____ Last dose? _____ am/pm Do you have epilepsy? _____

Diabetes? _____ Do you take insulin? _____ If so, last dose? _____ am/pm Have you had any injections of any other drugs recently? _____

If so, what for? _____ What kind of drug? _____ Last dose? _____ am/pm When did you last sleep? _____

How much sleep did you have? _____ Are you wearing false teeth? _____ Do you have a glass eye? _____ Other information. _____

division to determine whether the defendant had DWI-related offenses in the past ten years. If the offender has been convicted of a DWI violation one one or two previous times, he is charged with a misdemeanor. On his third arrest, a felony is charged, and the case moves to the district court. The district court. The APD forwards copies of the arrest reports involving DWI to the appropriate judicial level: to the county attorney and the county court at law for misdemeanor arrests, and to the district attorney for felony arrests.

In addition, APD records DWI statistics for general information purposes. Included are the number of traffic officers, the number of officers in the Selective Traffic Enforcement Program (STEP), and the number of officers involved in DWI arrests. Records also are kept on the the number of arrests made during STEP patrols, the number of regular DWI arrests, the number of officers per shift, average downtime, the number of stops per hour, and the ratio of STEP citations to total arrests.

Travis County Sheriff's Department

The Travis County Sheriff's Department is involved with DWI arrests in Travis County with jurisdiction outside the city limits of Austin. This office operates on two levels. The trooper arrests suspected DWI offenders and files several forms including the arrest report, Notice of Conviction/Bond Forfeiture/Mentally Incompetent (DL-17), Education Program for DWI (DL-17a), Notice of Final Conviction for Traffic Law Violation (DL-18), and Notice of Suspension DWI or Felony (DL-15).

The hearing officer conducts administrative hearings on driver's license suspensions. He receives the conviction report from the arresting officer and enters it into the defendant's driving record. If the breath test is refused, the sheriff's department presents an affidavit of refusal and the driving record to the county court at law or district court.

The sheriff's department records DWI information on videotaping: the percentage taking and refusing breath tests and the percentage allowing and refusing to be videotaped. This information currently is recorded manually, with plans for automation in the near future.

Texas Department of Public Safety

The Texas Department of Public Safety deals with the justice of the peace daily, with the county court on a weekly basis, and only occasionally with the municipal court. For prosecution, the DPS works closely with the county attorney on a daily basis and with the district attorney occasionally.

Adjudication

The following section describes the activities of three trial courts and an administrative court in Travis County. The trial courts include the the municipal court, the county court, and the district court. The justice of the peace presides over the administrative court, which is concerned with license suspension and the defendant's arraignment.

Municipal Court

The municipal court, as previously noted, gives a magistrate's warning to the defendant, informing him of his rights. The judge reviews the defendant's record and determines which class of offense to charge the defendant. The court handles only Class C misdemeanor cases.

With regard to DWI information, the court is responsible for two forms, the Order of Commitment and the Order of Complaint. Under the Order of Commitment, the defendant is committed to the custody of the sheriff of Travis County to be detained unless he complies with the established conditions of bond or to an amendment or modification of the condition of bond. The Order of Complaint includes some fourteen different forms consisting of charges involving different types of DWI/DUI offenses.

County Court at Law

In Travis County--and all other Texas counties--the county court at law handles Class A misdemeanor offenses. It is here that DWI cases are tried. The county court receives the formal complaint filed by the county attorney's office and the arrest report from the APD. The county clerk also receives a copy of the formal complaint.

District Court

The district court handles all felony cases. The court receives the arrest report from the law enforcement agency. The district clerk oversees the current status of each case, which includes information such as when a petition was filed, its disposition, and the manner of its disposition. Little data collection takes place at this level.

Justice of the Peace

The justice of the peace (JP) is the hearing examiner for DPS license suspensions when a defendant refuses to take a breath test. The JP presides at the arraignment for DPS and sheriff's department's arrestees.

The JP does not have a major role to play in the county DWI system. Data collection is comparable to that of the municipal court.

Prosecution

County Attorney

The county attorney handles misdemeanor cases for the county court in Travis County. The county attorney receives the offense report from the arresting agency. The county attorney creates a file on the defendant consisting of the arrest report from the APD, the complaint against the suspect, and affidavits received from law enforcement agencies. The county attorney then completes a DWI screening sheet.

At this point, the case leaves the county attorney's office to be tried or disposed of in court. After the case is decided, the county attorney completes a postdisposition form recording the penalty received and probation conditions. The lawyer handling the case keeps a hard copy of each form. If the defendant already is on probation due to a previous offense, the attorney's office completes a petition to the court to revoke probation. The court keeps track of case time to ensure speedy completion of cases.

District Attorney

The district attorney serves two functions. The first is to determine if the case against the defendant is complete. If complete, the second function is to present the case to the grand jury. The case already will have been filed and investigated by a law enforcement agency.

The district attorney receives the arrest report from the arresting agency for felony DWI cases. Jail cases--those in which the defendant cannot afford personal bond--are given priority. The district attorney then develops an extraction of the record, which includes all information relating to previous DWI arrests and convictions. In doing so, the attorney must obtain a final conviction packet containing a certified statement that the offender was previously convicted of DWI; this packet must be obtained from the county clerk of the arresting county. Once accomplished, the case may go to the grand jury.

The only DWI data collected are yearly summary data. Disposition data are sent back to the arresting agency. As with the county attorney, the district attorney must operate as swiftly as possible to fulfill the provisions of the Speedy Trial Act.

Case Administration

County Clerk

When a case is said to be filed with the court, it is in effect filed with the county clerk. The clerk manually assigns the case a case number. One copy is kept for internal record-keeping purposes. Other copies are sent to the issuing court, the defendant's attorney, and the prosecuting attorney. Each county clerk's office maintains the record of prior convictions in its own county. However, if the suspect has not been arrested in that county, no record of prior convictions in other counties is available.

The clerk's office receives and files five DWI-related forms. The first is the complaint signed by the arresting officer. The second is the same information as the complaint, but signed by the county attorney. The third form is the Affidavit for Warrant of Arrest and Detention signed by the magistrate of the municipal court. The fourth document is the Order of Commitment placing the suspect in jail, and the final form describes the bond if this option is offered by the court.

District Clerk

The duties of the district clerk are identical to those of the county clerk, except that he or she is responsible for felony cases instead of misdemeanor cases.

TRAVIS COUNTY COMPREHENSIVE ANTI-DWI PROJECT

Project Initiation

In October 1983, the Traffic Safety Section of the Texas Department of Highways and Public Transportation made federal funds available for comprehensive community anti-DWI projects.[29] Supporting a new concept, the funds are aimed in particular at programs which implement better coordination of local efforts to combat DWI. Travis County is one of four counties in Texas which established special projects within the program. The other three are Bell County, Cass County, and El Paso County. The Travis County project is funded for a three-year period to end March 31, 1987. Funding for the first year of the program (fiscal year 1984) totaled $308,439. Federal funding contributes only part of the support for the three-year project. Matching funds must be provided by the county in increasing proportions for fiscal years 1985-87. Funding for continuation of the project by the county beyond 1987 must be sought by the project coordinator and must be authorized by the county commissioners.

Project Description

The program contract describes the project as follows:

The County of Travis will plan and implement a community-wide Comprehensive Anti-DWI Project that will coordinate the cooperative efforts of local agencies and groups toward improving the efficiency of the system for handling DWI offenders from arrest to final case disposition in a more timely manner and with more meaningful sanctions. In addition, two other expected outcomes of this multi-year project are financial self-sufficiency of the project and increased public awareness that DWI is not acceptable conduct in the community. The comprehensive project at a minimum will include the participation of agencies that deal with DWI enforcement, prosecution, adjudication, probation, rehabilitation, and treatment.[30]

Cooperating Agencies

Cooperating agencies in the county include the county attorney's office, the county clerk's office, the county adult probation department, the sheriff's department, the Austin-Travis County Alcohol Counseling Services, the county data processing department, and the Austin Police Department. Staff are provided by the project to assist these agencies in their participation and to ensure implementation of the project.

Project supervision and coordination are provided by a project director and administrative secretary who are located in the county attorney's office. Other staff include:

1. Prosecuting attorney for county attorney's office;

2. Data entry clerk for county attorney's office;

3. Three data entry clerks for the county clerk's office;

4. Alcohol counselor for Austin-Travis County Alcohol Counseling Services;

5. Computer programmer for county data processing department;

6. Two probation officers for county adult probation department; and

7. Two sheriff's officers for sheriff's department.

Project Objectives

The ultimate goal of the Travis County project, according to the contract, is "to improve the efficiency of the local system in controlling the drinking driver." To accomplish this goal, project objectives have been established. These objectives are organized into seven areas including program coordination, enforcement, prosecution, adjudication, probation, rehabilitation and treatment, and public information and education.

Action plans to achieve these objectives were developed by each participating agency in cooperation with the project coordinator. A comprehensive program coordination plan was developed from these action plans by the project coordinator.

The project coordinator also is charged with seeking local financial support for program continuation, working with interested citizens' groups to obtain their vocal and material support, planning and implementing an anti-DWI public information and education program in the community, and developing data collection procedures and a management information system for monitoring DWI offender handling from arrest to disposition. In early 1985, the project coordinator was instrumental in establishing a Travis County Anti-DWI Task Force composed of representatives from various areas of the community.[31]

Management Information System

One of the most significant aspects of the project is the responsibility to develop data collection procedures and a management information system. As a requirement of the project, a number of data elements including statistics on enforcement, prosecution, adjudication, probation, rehabilitation and treatment, and public information and education are being collected and reported by participating agencies to the program coordinator. Most information currently is being maintained and reported manually, but progress is being made on the programming of a management information system in which all data can be stored and manipulated. Automation is essential so that data will be consistent, accurate, and accessible. Data collection requires different agencies to work cooperatively, sometimes for the first time, thereby improving coordination within the project and moving toward the concept of a comprehensive DWI system.

In collecting, coordinating, and automating information on DWI activities, Travis County is serving as a model for the state for a community of its size. The Data Processing Department is providing facilities for the management information system and is training the computer programmer hired for the project. The DWI information system will be added to an existing integrated criminal information system which is being maintained for the county and district courts, the county attorney, and the county clerk. This integrated information system was begun in 1980 with a grant from the Federal Law Enforcement Assistance Act and was subsequently funded from the Governor's Office through the Criminal Justice Division.[32] The DWI information system should be fully programmed by fall 1985.

CONCLUSIONS

The inadequacy of DWI information systems at the federal, state, and local levels frustrates policy changes in the DWI system in Texas. Data systems at the federal level seem to be well organized. But problems of accuracy at the state and local levels challenge the accuracy of federal DWI data. There is no central agency charged with collecting information on all DWI arrests and convictions in Texas. A legislative mandate will be necessary to require local law enforcement agencies to report this information to a designated agency, most probably to the Department of Public Safety.

Data collection activities at the state level are wholly inadequate. Collection at the county level suffers from a lack of adequate computer systems and training to use existing systems, and inadequate numbers of personnel to run the systems. Several counties have recognized this inadequacy. The Travis County Comprehensive Anti-DWI Project is intended to serve as a model to establish a system which involves the city and county in a coordinated effort to combat DWI and to develop and maintain data collection procedures and a management information system to monitor DWI offenders from arrest to case disposition.

NOTES

[1] U.S. Department of Transportation (DOT), National Highway Traffic Safety Administration (NHTSA), Fatal Accident Reporting System (Washington, D.C., 1981), p. v.

[2] Interview by Lisa Norman, Jo Anne Hawkins, and Chris Vein with Mary Lauderdale, Statistician, Statistical Services, Texas Department of Public Safety, Austin, Texas, January 22, 1985.

[3] U.S., DOT, NHTSA, Fatal, p. v.

[4] Ibid.

[5] U.S. Department of Transportation, Federal Highway Administration, Highway Safety Performance - 1982 Fatal and Injury Accident Rates on Public Roads in the United States (Washington D.C., December 1983), p. 13.

[6] U.S. Department of Transportation (DOT), National Highway Traffic Safety Administration (NHTSA), The National Accident Sampling System, Vol. 1 (Washington D.C., December 1978), pp. 2-8; King Mak, The Role of Accident Studies in Problem Identification (San Antonio: Southwest Research Institute, October 3, 1983), pp. 5-6.

[7] Mak, Accident Studies, pp. 5-6.

[8] U.S. Department of Transportation (DOT), National Highway Traffic Safety Administration (NHTSA), The National Accident Sampling System 1981: A Report on Traffic Accidents and Injuries in the U.S. Collected in NASS in the Year 1981 (Washington, D.C.), pp. 7-12 (hereafter cited as NASS 1981).

[9] NASS 1981, p. 7.

[10] U.S. Department of Transportation (DOT), National Highway Traffic Safety Administration (NHTSA), National Center for Statistics and Analysis (NCSA), Fatal Accident Reporting System 1982: An Overview of U.S. Traffic Fatal Accident and Fatality Data Collected in FARS for the Year 1982 (Washington D.C., May 1984), p. i.

[11] Ibid., p. 7.

[12] Ibid., p. 4.

[13]U.S. Department of Transportation (DOT), National Highway Traffic Safety Administration (NHTSA), The National Driver Register Program Users' Guide (Washington, D.C., January 1982), p. 1.

[14]Federal Register 49, no. 191 (October 1, 1984), p. 38648.

[15]Ibid.

[16]Ibid.

[17]Interview by Terri Williams and Chris Vein with Clay Hatch, Director, National Driver Register, Washington, D.C., February 8, 1985.

[18]U.S. DOT, NHTSA, NDR Program Users' Guide, p. 5.

[19]Interview with Clay Hatch.

[20]Federal Register 49, no. 191 (October 1, 1984), p. 38648.

[21]Ibid., p. 38649.

[22]Migdon R. Segal, Auto Safety and Related Issues (Washington, D.C.: Congressional Research Service, April 12, 1983), pp. 58-61.

[23]Interview with Clay Hatch.

[24]Ibid.; Federal Register 49, no. 191 (October 1, 1984), p. 38650.

[25]Interview with Mary Lauderdale.

[26]Texas Department of Public Safety (DPS), Crime Records Division, Uniform Crime Reporting Bureau, Crime in Texas, Calendar Year 1983 (Austin, Texas), pp. 3-4.

[27]Interview by Jo Anne Hawkins with Cal Killingsworth, Manager, Uniform Crime Reporting Bureau, Crime Records Division, Texas Department of Public Safety, Austin, Texas, January 29, 1985.

[28]DPS, Crime in Texas, p. 4.

[29] Interview by Jo Anne Hawkins with John McKay, Traffic Safety Specialist, Traffic Safety Section, State Department of Highways and Public Transportation, Austin, Texas, December 7, 1984.

[30] Texas Traffic Safety Program Contract No. 84-02-03-A1-AC. State Department of Highways and Public Transportation, Traffic Safety Section, Austin, Texas, April 2, 1984. "Comprehensive Anti-Driving While Intoxicated (DWI) Project--County of Travis." Unpaged.

[31] Interview by Jo Anne Hawkins with Lydia McDaniel, Project Coordinator, Travis County Comprehensive Anti-DWI Project, Austin, Texas, November 8, 1984.

[32] Interview by Jo Anne Hawkins with Linda Barta, Coordinator, Criminal and Civil Justice Systems, Travis County Data Processing Department, Austin, Texas, December 7, 1984.

CHAPTER 4

LOCAL PERSPECTIVES ON TEXAS COUNTY DWI SYSTEMS AND SENATE BILL 1

INTRODUCTION

This chapter presents a summary of the DWI systems of eight Texas counties and the views of county officials regarding the effectiveness of reforms in Texas DWI law contained in Senate Bill 1. The results of a survey mailed to all Texas county and district attorneys also are analyzed. One hundred and forty county and district attorneys returned the questionnaire, which posed questions about Senate Bill 1 and solicited recommendations for improvements in existing Texas DWI law. A copy of the survey instrument can be found in Appendix 3.

The eight counties were selected on the basis of geographic dispersion and population size. The larger counties--Dallas, Harris, El Paso, and Webb--all have populations exceeding 100 thousand while the remaining counties--Comal, Gray, Harrison, and Williamson--have smaller populations. Map 1 shows the geographic dispersion of the counties throughout the state and Table 5 contains some comparative county statistics. Recent county DWI data are presented in Tables 6 and 7. These DWI data were obtained from either actual hand counts or computerized lists of county docket books. In some instances, project team members collected the data on their visits to the counties; in other instances, a county public official or resident performed this task upon request.

The information on county DWI systems is intended to supplement Chapter 2 of this report. Project team members collected the information through in-depth interviews of county agencies and departments participating in the DWI process. Whenever possible, interviews were arranged with representatives of the sheriff's department, local police department, district court, district attorney's office, district clerk's office, county court, county attorney's office, county clerk's office, Texas Department of Public Safety (DPS), adult probation department, alcohol council, and the local chapter of Mothers Against Drunk Drivers (MADD). These interviews were conducted in February and March of 1985, following a structured survey instrument format to provide consistency in the type of information received. A copy of the questionnaire can be found in Appendix 2. A more detailed account of these county interviews is presented in Appendix 1.

Map 1
Locations of Visited Texas Counties

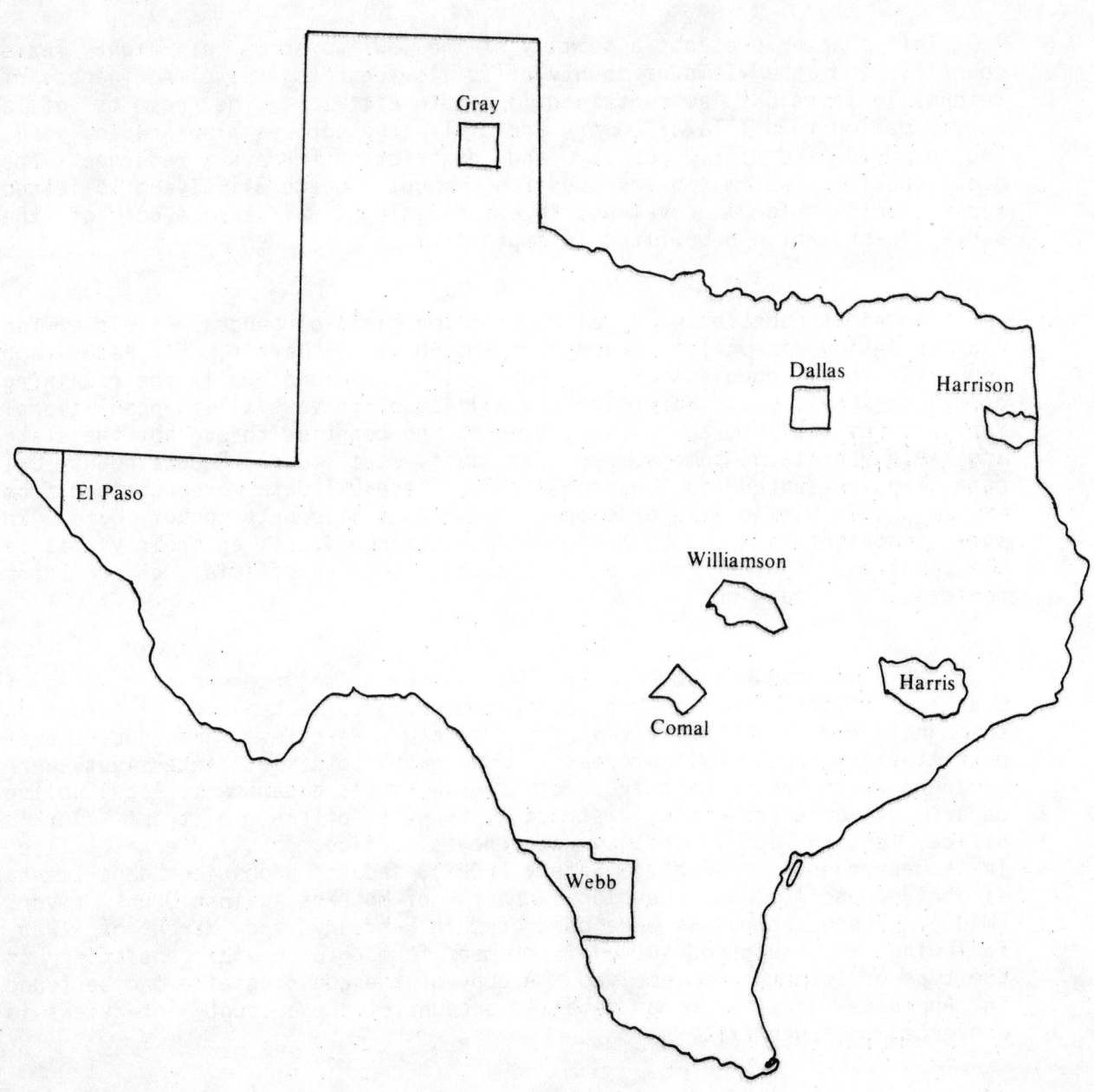

Table 5
Background Information on Visited Texas Counties

	Location	County seat	Size in sq. miles	1982 est. population	1982 number of regular vehicles	Total public road mileage
Comal County	Edwards Plateau region; north of San Antonio on IH 35	New Braunfels	555	39,400	33,135	896
Dallas County	North Central Texas at intersection of IH 35 East, 30 and 40. Blackland Prairie region	Dallas	880	1,641,400	1,475,542	8,594
El Paso County	Far West Texas; borders Mexican city Juarez	El Paso	1,014	513,400	296,161	1,958
Gray County	Rolling Plains region; in Texas Panhandle on IH 40	Pampa	921	27,000	31,695	1,120
Harris County	Coastal Prairie region; Southeast gulf coast on IH 45 and 10	Houston	1,734	2,684,100	2,075,088	11,875
Harrison County	East Texas Timberland region; on IH 20	Marshall	908	55,500	42,288	1,457
Webb County	West of Corpus Christi on IH 35; borders Mexican city of Nuevo Laredo	Laredo	3,363	109,900	64,477	999
Williamson County	North of Austin on IH 35; Blackland Prairie region	Georgetown	1,137	85,700	69,571	1,805

Source: John Clements, *Flying the Colors: Texas* (Dallas: Clements Research), 1984.

Table 6
1983 DWI Statistics on Visited Texas Counties

	Comal	Dallas	El Paso	Gray	Harris	Harrison	Webb	Williamson*
Number of DWI cases filed								
Misdeameanor	1,000	16,486	3,334	272	26,011	571	809	868
Felony	n/a	1,676	1	13	1,873	25	9	64
Total	**1,000**	**18,162**	**3,335**	**285**	**27,884**	**596**	**818**	**932**
Final Dispositions								
Guilty plea	780	12,781	594	238	18,588	504	439	841
Found guilty	16	237	11	0	202	2	2	4
Dismissed	142	5,731	1,252	48	4,026	85	194	82
Other	0	2,572	0	0	0	2	34	0
Punishment								
Probation	649	8,521	213	230	9,502	318	388	609
Fine only	1	602	65	0	123	146	1	151
Jail time	141	4,068	327	8	9,454	40	52	81

Sources: County docket books.

* District clerk's records for felony DWI cases are incomplete; reports for January and September were missing.

Table 7
1984 DWI Statistics on Visited Texas Counties

	Comal	Dallas	El Paso	Gray*	Harris	Harrison	Webb	Williamson
Number of DWI cases filed								
Misdeameanor	506	15,527	4,667	230	22,270	368	406	n/a
Felony	n/a	723	7	15	598	10	0	n/a
Total	**506**	**16,250**	**4,674**	**245**	**22,868**	**378**	**406**	**n/a**
Final Dispositions								
Guilty plea	445	12,677	1,675	205	20,744	322	281	n/a
Found guilty	11	237	18	1	168	3	2	n/a
Dismissed	139	3,992	1,989	68	5,107	74	146	n/a
Other	0	774	0	0	0	0	1	n/a
Punishment								
Probation	319	8,401	1,131	200	11,209	225	219	n/a
Fine only	0	170	8	1	9	48	0	n/a
Jail time	152	4,457	553	5	10,364	38	58	n/a

Sources: County docket books.
* Figures for September 1, 1983 - August 31, 1984 (fiscal year 1984).

TEXAS COUNTY INTERVIEWS

Priority And Focus Of DWI Program Effort

With few exceptions, officials of all eight counties consider DWI as a high priority. Officials in Comal, Dallas, Harris, and Webb counties identified law enforcement and adjudication as the prime focus of their anti-DWI program efforts. Dallas County also concentrates on public information activities. El Paso County stresses prosecution, public information, and education. Harrison County stresses probation, with a secondary interest in rehabilitation and treatment. Gray County did not identify any particular area of the DWI process as being more important than others in focusing its program efforts. The same applies to Williamson County, although county officials take great pride in their treatment and education programs. In spite of these variations, it should be noted that virtually all interviewed county officials acknowledged that public information, education, and treatment ought to be considered integral components of a comprehensive program to combat drunk driving.

Effectiveness Of County Relationships

Working relationships among the county agencies and departments involved in the DWI process appear cohesive and effective in all but two counties. In the smaller counties, officials experience occasional problems in communication with the sheriff's department and the Department of Public Safety (DPS), or friction with the district attorney. Two of these counties perceive the sheriff's department as a minor participant in the county DWI process for varying reasons. Otherwise, the officials consider their small size as an asset in developing friendships and facilitating communication among the agencies.

Gray County officials revealed frustration over differences in philosophy between the agencies in charge of law enforcement and prosecution. County officials noted that strict enforcement efforts are not rewarded with consistent prosecution of these cases. Instead, DWI charges often are reduced to public intoxication or the equivalent. Dallas County officials expressed concern with the perceived lenient attitude exhibited by the county judges, and pointed out a lack of focus in the area of alcohol education and prevention within the system. They indicated a need for greater public awareness. Although Webb County officials cooperate well with one another, they noted the need for a computerized record-keeping system to speed up the information flow within the system.

Individual personalities of county officials can have an enormous impact on the effectiveness of the DWI system and on the working relationships of various agencies and departments. An enthusiastic individual with a strong commitment to the problem of drunk driving can provide focus and energy for the participants in the DWI system.

Special Programs

The largest of the visited counties--Harris, Dallas, and El Paso--have established special DWI task forces to improve the effectiveness of county DWI activities and to increase public awareness. The county commissioner's task force in Dallas initially organized to disseminate information on the legislative intent of Senate Bill 1 to the Hispanic community, and later expanded its audience to the entire city. Harris County has two task forces operating within the community as special law enforcement programs to apprehend drunk drivers. The county attorney in El Paso heads a special task force of attorneys to strengthen the county's commitment to enhanced prosecution of DWI cases and to upgrade community public information and education programs addressing the problem.

Harris, El Paso, and Harrison counties participate in the Selective Traffic Enforcement Program (STEP), directed at increasing DWI enforcement efforts. Police officers patrol areas with high levels of alcohol-related accidents during peak hours. These officers are specially trained to deal with DWI-related cases.

Most counties, large and small, operate some type of alcohol treatment program, whether through private centers and organizations such as Alcoholics Anonymous, or through county alcohol councils or adult probation departments. Some counties support follow-up programs for the problem drinker in an effort to solve the more basic problem of alcohol abuse. Individual counties identified various alcohol/drug awareness programs within their county as an important, but peripheral, part of the county DWI system.

Williamson County's Dial-a-Ride program, El Paso County's Project Graduation, and Dallas County's Holidays Ahead Campaign and Suspect-A-DWI program are useful and worthwhile special programs. These types of special programs--some of which are being used widely in other Texas counties--can be innovative in the way that they disseminate the message to the entire community that drinking often is lethal to the driving public.

Both Harrison and Comal counties maintain successful work release programs which allow the offender, if convicted of a DWI offense, to serve the sentence while earning a living and maintaining self-esteem. Comal County judges, in particular, attempt to take advantage of the offender's talents through community restitution programs that require the offender to make a constructive contribution to society. This action is viewed as the appropriate punishment for the offense. The county's court system successfully uses innovative forms of alternative punishment for DWI offenses that are believed to make a greater impact on the offender than just a simple fine or jail sentence. They benefit the community as well. These alternate sentences also help to alleviate pressure on the overcrowded jail facilities in Comal County.

Alcohol Councils

Only three of the eight counties visited--Dallas, Harris, and Williamson--have functioning alcohol councils. Although an alcohol council exists in Harrison County, its functions are severely limited by an annual budget of $500 per year. The Mental Health and Mental Retardation (MHMR) facility, therefore, has assumed the rehabilitation functions and Mortimer-Filkins Test referrals normally performed by the council. MHMR devotes only one staff member and a secretary to DWI cases, indicating a low priority within the agency. Although MHMR maintains records on all treated individuals, it lacks the funds to record follow-up information.

The alcohol councils in Dallas, Harris, and Williamson counties all work closely with their respective adult probation departments for the evaluation and treatment of DWI offenders. These councils offer alcohol education classes, provide Mortimer-Filkins Test referrals, and offer various public information programs. Each council offers some form of advanced alcohol education program for problem drinkers, and gives high priority to DWI cases. Officials at the Houston Regional Council on Alcoholism, Inc., in Harris County, believe that all convicted DWI offenders should be evaluated, and that treatment should be required by law whenever an individual is identified as a problem drinker.

The Dallas Council on Alcoholism currently is targeting the Hispanic community with bilingual pamphlets on Senate Bill 1 to help educate local residents on the changes in the DWI law. Council officials pointed out the difficulties involved with posttreatment evaluations due to the mobile nature of the Dallas community.

Adult Probation Departments

The role of adult probation departments varies among the visited counties. Although all of the adult probation departments offer DWI evaluation and counseling or sponsor DWI schools, the scope of these programs differs. Adult probation departments in Comal and El Paso counties have taken an especially active role in treatment and evaluation by developing and coordinating unique programs. The Harris County Adult Probation Department conducts research and planning. In Comal County, the adult probation department maintains an eight-week "Discovery Program," and the West Texas Regional Adult Probation Department in El Paso County has developed "Project Home" and Pre-Trial Intervention.

The other visited counties offer standard evaluation and treatment. Two counties, Williamson and Gray, refer probationers for treatment to the area alcohol council or Mental Health and Mental Retardation (MHMR) facility for treatment. Williamson County contracts with the alcohol council for all of its treatment programs, and Harris County works in conjunction with its alcohol council to evaluate and treat DWI offenders.

In each of the eight counties, adult probation officers receive specialized training in alcohol abuse. In Williamson County, officials spend about forty hours a year in this training, and in Harrison County about twenty hours a year. Most counties indicated that additional specialized alcohol training opportunities are taken whenever schedules and caseloads permit. Although specialized training is common, specialized DWI caseloads within adult probation departments appear to exist primarily in the larger counties. Harris and Dallas counties have specialized caseloads for DWI offenders, and El Paso County's "Project Home" is administered by two officers. Since DWI makes up the majority of most county adult probation departments' caseloads, officers spend well over one-half of their time dealing with these offenders. In some counties, this has, in effect, created a "specialized caseload."

Average caseloads for adult probation officers range from one hundred to three hundred cases, with the smallest caseload found in Webb County and the largest in Harris County. Population size does not prove to be especially significant as evidenced by the fact that although both Harris and Webb counties are large, their average caseloads per officer represent opposite ends of the spectrum. All other counties have average caseloads ranging from 120 to 200 per officer. Population size also seems insignificant in terms of the perceived need for additional staff and funding. However, changes resulting from the passage of Senate Bill 1 have increased the workload for most adult probation departments and will likely constrain the effectiveness of this aspect of the system if more funding is not made available.

Record Keeping

The only general statement one can make about the record-keeping systems in the visited counties is that they vary widely. Each of the counties uses the standard D-17 form provided by the U.S. Department of Justice to process DWI offenders, and most indicated that their systems either are computerized or currently are in the process of becoming computerized. Five of the counties report to DPS on a monthly basis. Harris and Dallas counties, both with large populations and a substantial number of persons being processed through their systems, report on a more frequent basis. Harrison County is the exception, as it does not report regularly to DPS; instead, DPS officials come to the county clerk's office about three times a year to collect information.

Information on the number of pending cases and the time from arrest to final disposition leads to no clear conclusion. As expected, the larger counties have a greater number of pending DWI cases, ranging from about 6,711 in El Paso to over 18,000 in Dallas County. The range in the number of pending DWI cases in smaller counties varies from 116 in Gray County to 275 in Williamson County. County officials who consider their records processing to have a backlog do not attribute this situation to a system's problem, but rather to a variety of other reasons--rapid population growth in one case, lack of computerization in another.

Each county's record-keeping system appears to be operated differently. This diversity may be due to individual personalities, long-time habits and procedures, or to a lack of guidelines from the state. The new record-keeping procedures specified in Senate Bill 1 may either exacerbate this situation or improve it. No definitive statement can be made at this time.

Problems with the DWI Process

Problems with the DWI process exist in each of the eight counties. One common problem cited in most counties is a lack of personnel and resources necessary to operate the DWI system effectively or to comply with the changes brought about by Senate Bill 1. Webb and Williamson counties have too few certified officers to administer breath tests, causing substantial delays in the processing of DWI arrests. A general lack of resources for evaluation and treatment of DWI offenders in Harrison, Williamson, and Dallas counties also reduces the effectiveness of their DWI systems.

County officials dislike the legislature's propensity to enact laws without providing adequate funding to assist in their enforcement. The provision for videotape equipment and videotaping of suspects is a noteworthy example. Additional funding was not provided to purchase videotape equipment or to train officers to use the equipment effectively. This lack of funding causes some officers to feel uncomfortable about using the equipment, leading to major processing delays or a reluctance to use videotaping at all. Comal, Harrison, Williamson, Harris, Dallas, and Webb counties all reported these types of negative experiences with videotaping.

Five counties cited the judicial system as an obstacle to an effective DWI system. In one small county, Harrison, some of the interviewed officials indicated that the prosecution of DWI offenders at times can be political, and many borderline cases are not prosecuted. Webb County officials complained of a lack of effort on the part of prosecutors. This is due, in part, to the unique situation which exists in Webb County. The paperwork involved in prosecuting DWI offenders often is a problem for two reasons. First, the large percentage of Hispanics in the population of Webb County makes using names, addresses, and social security numbers inadequate for checking criminal records. Many individuals have the same first and last names, change addresses frequently, and do not have social security numbers. This results in some individuals receiving a misdemeanor charge, when a felony charge is more appropriate. To combat this problem, county officials have begun using date of birth as a primary source of information. Second, a large number of DWI arrests involve Mexican nationals who post bond and return to Mexico, leaving the county with extra paperwork and no ability to follow up.

In Harris County, the difficulty lies in the use of jail time versus probation. Offenders sometimes opt for jail time rather than for probation, because it proves more troublesome to comply with probation requirements and because there is a failure to enforce minimum jail confinement standards. County officials feel that if jail time is viewed only as a minor inconvenience, both the judicial system and the community's understanding of DWI suffer. Problems in El Paso County focus on the requirement that a justice of the peace must be summoned to give the magistrate's warning after arrest before alcohol blood concentration tests can be given. This causes substantial delays in the processing of DWI offenders.

Effectiveness Of Senate Bill 1

One part of the county interviews involved asking county officials about the several reforms in DWI law contained in Senate Bill 1. Officials were asked to respond by rating these "reforms" as very effective, somewhat effective, no change, less effective, or much less effective. Responses varied widely, both within and among counties, indicating that the impact of Senate Bill 1 is an important and diverse issue. The change making .10 percent BAC the per se level of legal intoxication drew the most positive response. Although most counties agreed that this reform is effective in strengthening the DWI system, several problems were noted. One problem arises when the .10 percent BAC rule is combined with the use of videotaping. Officials suggested that if the videotape is not convincing, the application of .10 percent BAC rule as per se level of legal intoxication will be made less effective. Gray County officials indicated that juries are reluctant to convict an offender on a .10 percent BAC and that prosecutors often look for other extenuating evidence. This becomes a problem in the opposite direction, when juries are discouraged from convicting a DWI offender who registered less than a .10 percent BAC level. The only other Senate Bill 1 change that was considered more effective than the .10 percent BAC level was the admission of BAC test refusal as evidence. This important reform has strengthened the DWI system.

The prohibition of deferred adjudication in DWI cases received a variety of responses. El Paso County considers this an effective change and feels that this will result in more offenders being given probation, which (because it is considered a final conviction) will be used effectively for enhancement (upgrading a penalty) and prosecution. Several counties believe this is an important change, but indicated that they had not used deferred adjudication before and, therefore, were not likely to see any change from this reform. In contrast, Gray and Harris counties consider deferred adjudication an effective tool and feel that its removal has made their DWI systems much less effective. Comal County represented a "middle of the road" view. Although officials support an end to the abuse of deferred adjudication by legislative prohibition, they believe a modified system could be effective in certain circumstances.

The provision giving police officers the authority to order alcohol blood and breath tests is given a positive response by most counties, but counties also indicate that this provision would rarely be used. In addition, many counties are not aware this authority exists and do not know how it is to be used. Several counties noted that some hospital and medical personnel are reluctant to take blood samples, when requested or ordered to do so by the police, because they feel the limited immunity to civil suit given to them in the law does not afford sufficient protection. Article 67011, section 3(c) of Vernon's Annotated Texas Civil Statutes, as amended by the Sixty-Eighth Legislature, provides that registered nurses, qualified technicians and vocational nurses under the supervision of a physician may take a blood specimen at the direction of a peace officer using "recognized medical procedures . . . provided further that the foregoing shall not relieve any such person from liability for negligence in the withdrawing of any blood specimen." Quite apart from the issue of who can draw the sample, and under what conditions, the point is that negligence is the basis of medical malpractice law. Both physicians and medical paraprofessionals are sensitive to exposing themselves to possible personal involvement in a separate civil suit arising from their cooperation with a law enforcement agency.

The implementation of new procedures for reporting convictions or probations to DPS is considered to have very little impact in most counties. Several counties were complying properly with reporting procedures before the new law, and they consider these changes to be additional paperwork. In Harrison County, the changes have had no impact because the county clerk's office is not complying with the new procedures. Instead, the DPS comes to them periodically to collect data.

Changes in the implied consent license revocation procedures also drew a mixed response. Comal County believes there has been a substantial reduction in BAC test refusals as a result of this change, but El Paso County believes it is effective because it has shifted the burden of requesting a hearing to the offender. Negative responses focused on the judicial discretion that allows this to be circumvented and the perception that it is being used mostly on low-income offenders. Harrison and Gray counties believe that the poor are at a disadvantage because they are more likely to need a license and are less likely to be in a position to afford counsel to obtain an occupational driver's license.

Responses to the stiffer penalties mandated in Senate Bill 1 vary widely. While Harris and Dallas counties indicated that penalties and fines are not stiff enough, Webb County believes that fines and penalties are too stiff. In Gray County, the majority of low-income offenders could not pay the fines assessed before the Senate Bill 1 changes, making the new fines less effective. Comal and El Paso counties rated the new fines and penalties as an effective change in the system.

The provision concerning the purchase of videotape equipment and the videotaping of suspects received both negative and positive responses. Every county cited the "skilled or experienced drunk" as a major flaw in the use of videotaping. The procedure has become a "double-edged sword" because it aids in prosecution in some cases and destroys the prosecution's case in others. When the videotape is incriminating, it is an extremely useful tool that seems to elicit guilty pleas in most cases. In contrast, the "skilled drunk," even with a BAC level of .10 percent or greater, may be acquitted because of a jury's interpretation of his/her behavior on videotape. Several counties indicated that the lack of funding has made it difficult to acquire high quality equipment and to train officers to use the equipment effectively. If fact, Gray County has not complied with this provision because officials feel that cheap equipment, which is all they can afford, is worse than no equipment at all.

Recommendations for Making Senate Bill 1 More Effective

Recommendations for improvements in Senate Bill 1 are plentiful and diverse. Most county officials expressed the opinion that increased levels of funding would increase the effectiveness of DWI legislation by making compliance with the law's new mandate easier. Another common suggestion is that the DWI program effort, in general, would be boosted by raising the legal drinking age and banning open containers. Others recommend instituting a dramshop law, revoking the license plates of a DWI felon, and giving the Alcohol Beverage Control Commission broader authority.

Specific recommendations covered a variety of areas within the DWI system. In the area of treatment, county officials recommend that more money be spent on treatment; that alcohol evaluation be made mandatory in all DWI arrests; that funding be provided to low-income persons in need of alcohol treatment; and that alcohol education programs be included as a part of the license renewal procedure. As for changes in the occupational driver's license procedure, it is suggested that these licenses should not be given in the case of a second offense, and that for a first offense, there should not be twenty-four-hour licenses. Another county official recommends that for purposes of consistency and effective judicial decisionmaking, the convicting judge should be the same judge to hear the request for an occupational driver's license.

Many officials agree that refusal to take the blood alcohol concentration (BAC) test should carry a stiffer penalty, such as a high fine, which should be immediate and mandatory. Others suggest that the law should specify that a person who actually administers the test should be qualified. If any qualified expert witness could testify, the BAC test could be used more effectively in court. Another recommended provision applying to the BAC test is that the immunity granted to physicians in giving such tests be expanded to include morticians, paramedics, and certain hospital personnel. This change should greatly reduce the reluctance of hospital personnel and others to perform necessary BAC tests. Finally, several county officials recommend that deferred adjudication be restored, but in a modified and limited form.

MAIL-OUT SURVEY OF TEXAS COUNTY AND DISTRICT ATTORNEYS

In addition to the visits to the selected counties, a survey was mailed to every county and district attorney in Texas. The survey is similar to the instrument used for the county visits, and was designed to solicit the views of the attorneys on their DWI-related activities and opinions on Senate Bill 1. Of the 316 surveys mailed, 140 were returned. This return rate of 44.3 percent is quite high for mail-out surveys and probably represents the degree of high interest in this topic. Table 8 contains a list of the 138 respondents who identified themselves. Of these, 134 of the returned surveys arrived in time to perform a statistical analysis of the responses. The responses were encoded and processed using the Statistical Package for the Social Sciences (SPSS). Initial results as well as additional manipulation of the data were possible because of the use of this computer program. All 140 returned surveys were reviewed to summarize individual comments and recommendations. The summary appears at the end of this chapter. A copy of the survey instrument is found in Appendix 3.

Characteristics of Respondents: Questions 1-6

The first six questions of the survey were designed to discover characteristics of the respondents. Of the 134 respondents whose answers were encoded and who identified themselves, 90 or 68.2 percent are county attorneys, and 42 or 31.8 percent are district attorneys. Counties with populations under twenty-five thousand account for 63.6 percent of the respondents; 36.4 percent are from counties with larger populations. The majority, 78.9 percent, reported that one to three persons in their offices deal specifically with DWI, while the remaining 21.1 percent state that four or more persons have these responsibilities. When asked about how DWI activities are financed, most reported that they are not specifically budgeted for, and found it difficult to give a dollar or percentage approximation. Only three attorneys reported receiving special or grant funding for DWI work. And when asked to prioritize their functions, 75.6 percent rated DWI as first, second, or third in priority; 9.9 percent said DWI falls in the middle or low on the priority list; and 14.5 percent reported that DWI is given the same priority as other offenses under the attorneys' jurisdiction.

Interagency Contact: Question 7

The second set of questions asked whether the attorneys have regular contact with other agencies on DWI matters. The following table contains a ranking of agencies by the percentage of respondents who reported regular contact with them. For example, 97.0 percent of responding county and district attorneys reported regular contact with the Texas Department of Public Safety (DPS).

Table 8
List of Responding County and District Attorneys by County

County Attorneys

Anderson	DeWitt	Hale	Jones	Nueces	Stonewall
Austin	Dickens	Hall	Karnes	Oldham	Sutton
Baylor	Donley	Hamilton	Kinney	Palo Pinto	Terry
Bell	El Paso	Hansford	Kleburg	Parker	Throckmorton
Brazos	Ector	Hardin	Lamb	Parmer	Titus
Brewster	Erath	Hartley	Leon	Polk	Travis
Cherokee	Fannin	Hemphill	Liberty	Potter	Upton
Childress	Fayette	Hood	Lipscomb	Reagan	Uvalde
Clay	Fisher	Houston	McCulloch	Red River*	Val Verde
Cochran	Foard	Howard	Matagorda	Reeves	Washington
Coleman	Franklin	Hudspeth	Milam	Refugio	Wharton
Collingsworth	Frio	Irion	Montgomery	Rusk*	Wichita
Cooke	Goliad	Jack	Nacogdoches	San Jacinto	Wilson
Cottle	Gonzales	Jim Wells	Newton	Scurry	Yoakum
Crockett	Gray	Johnson	Nolan	Sterling	Zavala
Crosby	Grimes				

Criminal District Attorneys

Bastrop	Calhoun	Deaf Smith	Harrison	Navarro	Smith
Bexar	Cameron	Denton	Hays	Nolan	Victoria
Bowie	Collin	Gregg	Kaufman	Rockwall	Wood
Caldwell	Dallas	Harris			

District Attorneys

8th Judicial District	Hopkins	109th Judicial District	Winkler
21st Judicial District	Burleson	112th Judicial District	Sutton
25th Judicial District	Guadalupe County	142d Judicial District	Midland
33d Judicial District	Llano	155th Judicial District	Austin, Fayette, and Waller
36th Judicial District	San Patricio	159th Judicial District	Angelina
49th Judicial District	Webb	173d Judicial District	Henderson
52d Judicial District	Coryell	196th Judicial District	Hunt
64th Judicial District	Hale	198th Judicial District	Kimble
69th Judicial District	Dallam and Hartley	229th Judicial District	Jim Hogg
76th Judicial District	Titus	253d Judicial District	Liberty and Chambers
85th Judicial District	Brazos	287th Judicial District	Parmer
90th Judicial District	Young and Stephens	349th Judicial District	Houston
97th Judicial District	Montague County		

* Serves as both county and district attorneys.

Agency Name	Percentage of Attorneys Reporting Regular Contact with Agency
Dept. of Public Safety	97.0%
Dept. of Probation	94.0%
Sheriff	93.3%
Local Police	90.2%
County Clerk	77.8%
District Court	44.3%
District Attorney	40.2%
Alcohol Council	14.2%
MADD	11.9%

Cross-tabulations, which measure the degree of association between responses to selected questions, reveal that both the size of the county and whether the respondent is a county or district attorney affect the likelihood of regular contact with some agencies. Larger counties--those over twenty-five thousand--and district attorneys reported a higher percentage of regular contact with law enforcement agencies than did smaller counties and county attorneys. Of the larger counties, 97.9 percent reported regular contact with local police, as compared to 84.1 percent of the smaller counties. Likewise, 97.6 percent of the district attorneys and 87.5 percent of the county attorneys acknowledged regular contact with local police. All district attorneys and large counties reported regular contact with DPS, while 96.3 percent of the smaller counties and 96.7 percent of the county attorneys responded in kind. Obviously, the larger counties and district attorneys are more likely to acknowledge regular contact with the district court, and the county attorneys work on a regular basis more often with the county clerk than do the district attorneys. Although frequent contact with local chapters of Mothers Against Drunk Drivers (MADD) is not as common, 68.8 percent of those in regular contact are from larger counties. The likely explanation is that only a few of the smaller counties have active chapters of MADD. No association was found between either size of county and/or whether the respondent is a county or district attorney and the remaining agencies--department of probation, sheriff, and alcohol council.

Effectiveness of Senate Bill 1: Question 8

The next section of the questionnaire concerns several changes made by Senate Bill 1 in DWI law. Respondents were asked if these changes made the process of dealing with DWI offenders in their counties more or less effective. Eight changes were listed, and each could be rated as very effective, somewhat effective, no change, less effective, or much less effective. Responses were encoded from one to five, ranging from one as being very effective to five as being much less effective. With this ranking, the perceived effectiveness of the changes can be seen via the calculated mean response for each change. Thus, the lower the mean, the more the change is viewed as being more effective. Similarly, the higher the mean, the more the change in a particular DWI law is adjudged to have produced no change or be less effective. The following table contains a ranking of changes by their calculated means. The provision of DWI law adjudged as most effective is listed first.

Change	Mean Score
Provision allowing admission of BAC test refusal at trial	1.685
.10 BAC per se rule	2.008
Changes in implied consent license revocation procedures	2.118
Stiffened penalties	2.165
Authority for police officers to order BAC tests	2.252
New procedure for reporting convictions or probations to DPS	2.358
Prohibition of deferred adjudication in DWI cases	2.705
Videotaping of all suspects	2.773

In addition to the means, the frequencies with which responses were given help in examining the perceived effectiveness of the changes contained in Senate Bill 1. Regarding the change which allows the admission of BAC test refusal at trial, 85 percent of the attorneys ranked this as very or somewhat effective. The .10 percent BAC rule for per se intoxication is ranked as very or somewhat effective by 70.2 percent of the attorneys. Changes in implied consent license revocation procedures earn a ranking of very or somewhat effective by 65.4 percent of respondents, with the larger counties rating this change more effective more often than the smaller counties (72.4 percent of the larger counties, as opposed to 57.3 percent of the smaller counties, ranked implied consent as very or somewhat effective). Another change, stiffened penalties, is seen as very or somewhat effective by 66.1 percent of respondents. The size of the county is associated with this response by 72.3 percent of the larger counties; only 59.7 percent of the smaller counties view increased penalties as very or somewhat effective. Moreover, 70.9 percent of the county attorneys, who are more likely than district attorneys to be involved with misdemeanor cases, rated stiffened penalties as very or somewhat effective, yet only 58.9 percent of district attorneys responded in kind.

The authority for police officers to order blood and breath tests of BAC levels is rated as no change by 44.9 percent of the attorneys, thus lowering its mean score. New procedures for reporting convictions or probations to DPS also are viewed as having little impact or no change by 46.3 percent of the respondents. District attorneys, though, did rate this change as more effective than did county attorneys. In regard to the prohibition of deferred adjudication, 31.8 percent of the attorneys rate this change as less or much less effective; 36.7 percent of the county attorneys ranked this provision as less or much less effective; and 35.0 of the district attorneys are inclined to view it as producing no change. Finally, the provision calling for the purchase of videotape equipment and the videotaping of suspects is seen by 42.7 percent of the attorneys as no change; 37.3 percent rank it very or somewhat effective; and 20.0 percent regard it as less or much less effective. The size of a county has a high degree of association with this response. This finding is logical since the provision requiring the purchase of videotaping equipment only applies to counties of twenty-five thousand persons or more. Thus, smaller counties are inclined to view this provision as producing no change in their DWI efforts, while 46.8 percent of larger counties rank it as very or somewhat effective; 19.0 percent as no change; and 29.8 percent as less or much less effective. Additionally, more district attorneys rank the provision as very or somewhat effective than do county attorneys.

In summary, the change adjudged to be the most effective in reducing drunk driving is the provision allowing admission of BAC test refusal at trial. The redefining of intoxication as .10 percent BAC also is rated as an effective step. To a lesser degree, changes in license revocation procedures and stiffened penalties also are ranked positively. Ambivalence is revealed toward the changes in authority of police officers to order blood and breath tests of BAC levels and new procedures for reporting convictions. Finally, the prohibition of deferred adjudication and the provision concerning videotaping are rated as the least effective of the changes.

Suggested Improvements and State Involvement: Questions 9-12

The last section of the survey concentrates on improvements in the existing law and statewide involvement in record-keeping, reporting, and videotaping procedures. Improvements were suggested by 65.7 percent of the attorneys; their comments are summarized in the following section. An overwhelming majority, 80.2 percent, of the attorneys feel that their efforts would be more effective if statewide records of DWI arrests and convictions were available. Accordingly, 73.6 percent of the respondents would like to see the enactment of a statute to provide such a record system. Also, 81.7 percent are satisfied that the required county reporting of DWI convictions/dispositions to DPS is carried out in a timely and objective manner. Suggestions were made to improve this reporting;

they are reviewed in the next section. The desire for state involvement in establishing procedures for videotaping DWI suspects is not as strong. In fact, 50 percent responded that the establishment of standard state-approved procedures would improve the usefulness of such evidence in prosecution, while the other 50 percent believed that it would not. The comments received on this question reveal the different sentiments which exist among attorneys on the matter of suggested improvements in existing DWI laws.

Open-Ended Responses: Question 9

As previously noted, three of the questions on the survey are open-ended. The responses were not encoded, but rather were summarized and compiled for review. This summation shows the range of individual comments and the diversity of concerns which they represent. The first of these questions asked the attorneys to suggest needed improvements in Senate Bill 1. This question received the greatest number of responses of the three. In fact, 65.7 percent of all respondents offered one or more suggestions. Although the suggestions addressed a number of areas, several were mentioned repeatedly. Many attorneys called for the return of deferred adjudication in some or all cases for first-time offenders; under extenuating circumstances for first-time unaggravated DWI; and for seventeen-to-twenty-two-year-olds. Although one attorney would eliminate the minimum jail sentence for a first offense, there was a good deal of sentiment to increase minimum and maximum fines and jail sentences, to require mandatory minimum jail time with probation for all levels of offenses, to limit eligibility for probation, to institute a greater range of punishment for felony DWI with many prior offenses, and generally to give prosecutors more discretion.

Attorneys expressed their concerns about the videotaping provision of the law with a number of suggestions. Several called for both videotaping and viewing to be at the discretion of law enforcement officers and prosecutors. Others suggested that suspects should be videotaped only when there is a BAC test refusal, and some emphasized that videotaping should remain optional for all counties. Some attorneys noted that videotaping has caused them to lose cases, and one called for better videotaping facilities.

The BAC test requirement also generated a number of suggestions. These include clarification of driver's license suspension for refusal to take the BAC test; removal of impediments to admissibility of BAC test results and statutory warnings for BAC test refusal; increasing the penalty for BAC test refusal; requiring Intoxilyzers to be tested for electromagnetic interference; and allowing comment at trial as to why a defendant refused the BAC test. A need was seen to increase the number of expert witnesses for Intoxilyzer tests; the available experts are in great demand. Legislative authorization to use other experts or to eliminate the requirement altogether in trial proceedings was viewed as helpful.

One attorney noted that the .10 percent BAC per se level provision for intoxication is under serious attack as a result of the effort to combine two different types of quantitative analyses. Another who sees problems with BAC tests called for a standard field test which, if failed, would prove intoxication. One attorney suggested that it should be illegal for anyone to drive with any alcohol in his blood, and several recommended that the BAC per se level for intoxication should be lowered to a range of .05 to .08 percent.

In addition to the BAC test, several attorneys suggested improvements or changes in the alcohol blood test provision of the law. These include authority for police to order a BAC test without consent, based on probable cause, and mandatory BAC testing for all DWIs. Substantial support was voiced for broadening the limited civil immunity granted to medical personnel who take blood specimens from offenders at the request or order of a peace officer.

Requiring tougher standards for eligibility or prohibiting occupational driver's licenses was suggested by several attorneys. They cited a need for an open container law, and one called for raising the minimum legal drinking age to twenty-one. Another recommended administrative license revocations totally outside the court system.

Several attorneys addressed their concern about the handling of prior convictions at trial. One expressed a need for increased education of county court officials in handling misdemeanor convictions because of their importance in establishing prior convictions in felony DWIs. Others indicated a need to be able to use reports of prior criminal offenses without having to call as a witness the prosecutor or police officer from a distant county to testify as to the identity of repeat offenders in felony DWI cases. Introduction of a defendant's driver's license number as positive identification would be an improvement in the law. Presently, the state must show that the defendant is the same person convicted in previous cases. This can be accomplished only by the testimony of a person present at the prior proceeding or by calling a fingerprint expert; since such experts are scarce in rural counties, the case may be delayed in getting to trial. A further procedural problem is a need for the development of a standard set of forms for guilty pleas in misdemeanor DWIs. Often a prior DWI conviction is unusable for enhancement--upgrading a penalty--on felony DWI because the misdemeanor plea papers are flawed.

Another suggestion is to place sentencing in the hands of the judge, rather than the jury. In some counties, it still is extremely difficult to obtain severe punishment from a jury, largely due to their sympathy for persons who drink. However, one attorney responded that it is easier to obtain a jail sentence for a DWI defendant, but many counties lack jail space and would prefer not to increase their jail populations. His suggested remedy is to consider longer and more easily obtained license suspensions in place of jail sentences.

Some responses reveal the frustrations of the county and district attorneys with the DWI problem, and other responses stem from problems associated with rural and sparsely populated counties. One rather desperate comment was, "Nothing you can do will stop DWI." Another respondent expressed an independent attitude with the remark that his job would be improved if the law would be left alone, and that he was able to be more effective before the passage of Senate Bill 1. One wished for a single place in the statutes where he could find all DWI laws and related information centrally compiled and noted that the statutory cross-references drove him crazy. Another recommended that DWI jurisdiction should be given to both district and county courts. Attorneys from rural areas asked for fine-tuning of the law's provisions in counties where the judge is not a lawyer, and for permission to have six or fewer jurors in smaller counties. One attorney's comment was that trial courts should be allowed to commit persons as alcoholics directly from DWI conviction in court, a one-stop method to deal with the problem drinker and DWI offender.

Assorted other suggestions for improvement in the existing DWI law also were made. One district attorney noted that DPS officers should be fully trained to investigate involuntary manslaughter. To convict, the district attorney must prove that intoxication resulted in a death. Several attorneys commented on the Legislature's proclivity for requiring new duties of public officials and neglecting to provide funding for implementation and administration. And, finally, two attorneys expressed a need to rehabilitate as well as to punish DWI offenders, in view of reports that many have chronic alcohol problems. It may be necessary to decriminalize DWI to deal with problem drinkers effectively.

Suggested Changes to Improve DWI Reporting: Question 11b

The second open-ended question asked what changes could be made at the state level to improve the required county reporting of DWI convictions and dispositions to DPS. Few suggestions for change were made; 81.7 percent of the attorneys are satisfied that their required county reporting is being done in a timely and objective manner.

Of the comments made, though, many focused on problems involved in dealing with the Department of Public Safety (DPS). Several noted that they never receive information from DPS as quickly as it is needed and that prior convictions are not showing up on the DPS computer. This is a particular problem if they are requesting information on convictions in other counties. Others thought that reporting agencies sometimes took weeks to report a DWI arrest or conviction and suggested that there should be a follow-up procedure or enforceable audits of arrests by DPS or police to determine the disposition of a case. Still others requested that additional information such as an indication of whether an injury or death had occurred, a photograph, and fingerprints on conviction papers should be reported to DPS.

Some attorneys suggested that penalties should be set for failure of local authorities to comply with reporting requirements. They indicated that denial of funds could be a means of enforcement if funding of the county clerk is tied to prompt reporting of DWI convictions and dispositions as prescribed by law. One attorney noted that the present disposition of cases is costly and wastes time. Others expressed a need for more uniformity in reporting, step-by-step guidelines for reporting officials, and additional funding from the Legislature. One county attorney said that it is rare for him to go to trial with all information because other counties usually do not report accurately and promptly to DPS. He commented that dealing with Texas counties is much like dealing with 254 different empires.

State-Approved Videotaping Procedures: Question 12

The third and last open-ended question asked for comments concerning whether the establishment of standard state-approved procedures for videotaping of DWI suspects would improve the usefulness of such evidence in prosecution. Responses as to whether standard state-approved procedures should be established were evenly divided, and the comments reflected that split. Many attorneys expressed negative opinions of videotaping on procedural and technical grounds. They said that videotaping often helps persons who have been taped before, because they may know how not to appear intoxicated on the tape; that it hampers prosecution; that a jury cannot determine if a person is intoxicated by viewing a tape; that there are better tests to demonstrate loss of function; and that it gives the defense attorney another area to attack if technical aspects of the procedure are not complied with. A few commented that they are limited in space and equipment for videotaping. Some do not have the equipment, and others do not want it or need it. One attorney asserted that the procedure violates the Fifth Amendment; another said it is a waste of money; and one commented that it probably would aid in obtaining convictions, but that the volume of cases in his jurisdiction would not justify the costs. Other attorneys from small counties said that their population was too small to justify the costs and that juries in some small counties are unwilling to convict their neighbors in any case.

Attorneys who expressed positive opinions about videotaping noted that it should be required in all counties; that it enhances credibility, even if people refuse to cooperate; and that it encourages offenders to plea bargain. One attorney proudly said that his county had a very good videotaping program, and yet another said his county had prepared an instructive procedural tape for videotaping DWI suspects.

In response to the original question about standard state-approved procedures for videotaping DWI suspects, several attorneys indicated that such a requirement should mandate uniform court procedures in the state, and some said that each county presently has its own standards, which are promulgated by prosecutors. One suggested that the state prosecutor could offer seminars in proper procedures, but another said that the recommended procedures designed by the attorney general's office proved to be cumbersome and ineffective. Another noted that such standards would be acceptable if funding were available to maintain them. One thoughtful respondent pointed out that even with state-approval standards, the real answer is in-service training of the officers of arresting agencies. The state-approved standards would be used against the prosecution at trial in any case where the officer did not follow the approved or recommended procedures, even though his procedures might have been proper under the law. One cautious attorney commented that it is too early to alter or examine the procedures until the appellate courts have had a chance to examine them.

CONCLUSIONS

The county DWI systems in Texas are characterized by diversity in the focus of DWI program efforts, and in the perceived problems. In spite of this diversity, county officials identified several common concerns. Each of the counties cited inadequate levels of funding as an obstacle to system effectiveness. While a lack of funding in the areas of probation and treatment has limited effectiveness in several counties, a lack of personnel and resources for videotaping has become a special concern. County officials complained of difficulty in complying with Senate Bill 1 mandates for videotaping without the necessary funding to purchase adequate equipment and to train personnel in its use. The judicial system is perceived as another obstacle to system effectiveness. County officials cited a lack of effort by some prosecutors, an excess of judicial discretion, and political considerations in prosecuting DWI offenders. Finally, many counties expressed the belief that public information and treatment programs are of paramount importance in any effort to deter drinking and driving. Parallel to the diversity in county DWI systems is the diversity shown in the development of more effective DWI programs. Counties have created a variety of unique programs to deal with particular problems; these programs range from county task forces to innovative community service restitution programs.

The survey mailed to every county and district attorney in the state reveals insights into the attorneys' DWI-related activities and opinions about Senate Bill 1. The findings of the survey are similar to those discovered on county visits. Of the agencies listed, attorneys have the most contact with law enforcement agencies. The admission of the BAC test refusal at trial and the provision which defines legal intoxication as .10 BAC percent level are rated as the most effective reforms brought about by Senate Bill 1. The abolition of deferred adjudication in DWI cases and the videotaping requirements are rated the least effective. The majority of respondents suggested improvements in the existing law. The topics of suggestion varied, with videotaping, testing of BAC levels, and establishment of prior convictions receiving the most frequent comments. While an overwhelming majority of the attorneys feel that the required reporting in their county is done in a timely and objective manner, they would like to see a statute enacted to provide for a statewide record of DWI arrests and convictions. Finally, the attorneys expressed mixed views toward the establishment of standard state-approved procedures for videotaping DWI suspects.

CHAPTER 5

PROGRAMS IN OTHER STATES

INTRODUCTION

This chapter presents some of the programs used within a select group of states--Florida, Minnesota, New York, and Pennsylvania--to deter drunk drivers. At the onset of this project, it was determined that one of the objectives would be to look at special programs in other states that addressed different aspects of the DWI system and to ascertain the viability of adopting similar programs in Texas.

Information on the programs was obtained by field visits to the four states. Questionnaires were developed specifically for each state, since the focus of the four state DWI programs differed. Copies of the questionnaires can be found in Appendices 4, 5, 6, and 7. Additionally, while some questions in each state were the same, most varied according to the position of the person interviewed. This format was followed in order to gain a complete understanding of the programs. Within each state, officials involved in the DWI control system were interviewed, as well as those involved in implementing the programs, in order to obtain a balanced perspective for this report. Published material also was collected, and it proved useful in the descriptions of state programs. This material is cited, along with those interviewed, at the end of the chapter.

The surveyed states and their programs were chosen through the recommendations of people affiliated with this research project. A list of possible states was compiled through a literature search and a review of DWI legislation by state. Experts with an overall perspective of DWI activities were contacted by telephone and asked to suggest states that met our criteria. Knowledgeable officials from states most frequently mentioned were interviewed by telephone. On the basis on this information, Florida, Minnesota, New York, and Pennsylvania were selected. Table 9 displays comparative statistics for each state. These states were chosen because of the perceived effectiveness of their programs, the development of their programs into national models, the reputation of the state DWI programs, the specific problems addressed by their programs, and the potential adaptability of their programs to Texas.

While the four states were selected because of special programs, a complete understanding of those programs requires a detailed description of the context in which they function. Therefore, the state program descriptions that follow provide information concerning the overall DWI control system. While some of the programs were solely local initiatives, information about the state system also is included.

Table 9
Background Information on Visited States

	Population[1] (in thousands)	Highway miles[1]	Licensed drivers[1] (in thousands)	Legal drinking age[2]	Per se BAC[2]	DWI arrests[2] 1983 1984	DWI fatalities[2] 1983 1984	Total fatalities[2] 1983 1984
Florida	10,416	93,797	7,979	19	0.10	84,145 NA	1,104 NA	2,729 NA
Minnesota	4,133	131,214	2,397	19	0.10	32,155 40,000+*	318 325*	558 574
New York	17,659	109,825	8,992	19	0.10	67,933† NA	667 NA	1,961 840‡
Pennsylvania	11,865	115,964	7,351	21	0.10	30,100 33,000*	634 610*	1,570 1,583*
Texas	15,280	272,427	10,154	19	0.10	109,621 132,606	1,006 1,049	3,823 3,913

1. U.S. Department of Transportation, Federal Highway Administration, *Highway Safety Performance—1982: Fatal and Injury Accident Rates on Public Roads in the United States* (Washington, D.C., December 1983), pp. 6, 46, and 47.
2. Information obtained from on-site and telephone interviews conducted with officials from the states.

* Estimated.
† DWI/DWAI arrests.
‡ Total fatalities for six months only.

Finally, this chapter does not purport to describe the ideal or the only methods for deterring drinking and driving. Currently, anti-DWI activity is very strong nationally and has many diverse approaches. The programs presented here are selected examples that have proved to be effective.

FLORIDA

Background

The state of Florida has a population of approximately 10.4 million and has 7.9 million licensed drivers. In 1982, there were 8,335,000 registered vehicles in the state. The legal drinking age in Florida was raised from 18 to 19 in October 1980. A person with a blood alcohol concentration (BAC) level of .10 percent or higher is presumed to be legally intoxicated. Florida law enforcement officers made 84,145 DWI arrests in 1983.[1] Alcohol-related accidents in Florida accounted for 40 percent, or 1,104 of the 2,729 traffic fatalities for 1983. In 1984, 1,342 people died in alcohol-related accidents on Florida roadways. Thus, 47 percent of Florida's 2,856 traffic fatalities last year were attributable to drinking and driving.

Relevant Drunk Driving Legislation

Florida is making use of the latest technological innovations to aid in enforcement and record keeping for DWI offenses. In addition to the traditional roadblocks, many counties are using breath alcohol testing mobile units, or "Batmobiles," which are remote units for videotaping and alcohol blood concentration testing. There are twenty-one Batmobiles in Florida, which are informally shared by the law enforcement agencies. Thirteen of the Batmobiles were purchased with section 402 funding from the federal government (these funds support state highway safety programs--see Chapter 1); the remaining eight were purchased with local funds. The cost of each new Batmobile is approximately $50 thousand.

Videotaping of DWI suspects has become quite prevalent in Florida, although it is not legislatively mandated. The Bureau of Public Safety Management currently is conducting a survey to determine exactly where

---

[1]Florida statutes make no distinction as to the proper designation of charges for drinking and driving. The decision is made at the county level. Some counties use DWI while others use DUI. For purposes of consistency in this section, DWI is used to refer to the problem of drinking and driving--whether it be driving while intoxicated or driving under the influence.

videotaping is being used and its effectiveness in obtaining convictions.

In addition, an information management system for tracking DWI offenders is largely in place. Computer terminals are being used in all sixty-seven Florida counties. The system was put in place by the Florida Department of Highway Safety and Motor Vehicles at a cost of $225 thousand.

Florida also has made extensive use of public information and education programs. The Bureau of Public Safety Management, located in Tallahassee, coordinates the public information programs at the state level. It serves as a clearinghouse for disseminating information about local programs to other agencies and the general public.

Following the nationwide trend of heightened awareness about the problem of drinking and driving, Florida also has recently changed its DWI laws. In 1982, it established uniform minimum penalties for all DWI offenses, and increased punishment for first offenders. Each offense results in a fine, automatic license suspension, mandatory completion of a substance abuse course, and a possible jail sentence. The current penalties are detailed below. All penalties are mandatory, unless otherwise stated. DWI offenses which occurred in other states count as previous DWI offenses in Florida for purposes of prosecution as of October 1, 1984. Plea bargaining for DWI is permitted for DWI offenders whose BAC level was .15 percent or lower, and DWI offenses are entered permanently on the offender's driving record. Florida does not grant occupational or "hardship" licenses to any drivers on their second or subsequent DWI offense.

First Offense:
- Fine: $250-$500
- License Suspension: 6 months to 1 year
- Substance Abuse Course: Mandatory completion before license is reinstated
- Community Service: Minimum 50 hours
- Jail: At the judge's discretion; up to 6 months
- Occupational License: Given at the judge's discretion

Second Offense:
- Fine: $500-$1000
- License Suspension: If second DWI offense within 5 years, 5-year suspension; if second DWI offense in over 5 years, 6-month to 1-year suspension
- Substance Abuse Course: Mandatory completion before license is reinstated
- Community Service: At the judge's discretion
- Jail: If second DWI offense within

	3 years, 10 days in jail; if second DWI offense in over 3 years, optional, up to 9 months in jail
Occupational License	No

Third Offense:
Fine	$1000-$2500
License Suspension	If third offense within 10 years, 10-year suspension; if third offense in over 10 years, 6-month to 1-year suspension
Substance Abuse Course	Mandatory completion before license is reinstated
Community Service	At the judge's discretion
Jail	If third DWI offense within 5 years, 30 days in jail; if third DWI offense in over 5 years, optional, up to 1 year in jail
Occupational License	No

Fourth Offense:
Fine	$1000-$2500
License Suspension	Permanent revocation of Florida license, with no possibility of reinstatement
Substance Abuse Course	Mandatory
Community Service	At the judge's discretion
Jail	If fourth offense within 5 years, 30 days in jail; if fourth offense in over 5 years, optional, up to 1 year in jail
Occupational License	No

Notable Features of the Florida Drunk Driving System

When selecting states for comparative study, the project concentrated its efforts on states that were similar to Texas, or had programs that could be applicable to the Texas system. The Florida system is similar to that of Texas in that both systems are relatively new. Also, Florida has adopted programs and policies that are easily adaptable to Texas. Essentially, the visit to Florida focused on three distinguishing features of its system--remote breath alcohol testing mobile units (Batmobiles); the public information and education (PI&E) programs; and the use of videotaping. Interestingly, all three of these factors in the Florida system were initiated by local law enforcement agencies. For purposes of this study, we chose to concentrate our interviews on the Orlando (Orange County) and Clearwater (Pinellas County) metropolitan areas due to their outstanding local public information and education programs and their voluntary use of videotaping. In addition to interviewing officials from the programs in each of these counties, project members spoke with representatives from the Campus Alcohol Information Center at the University of Florida about their alcohol awareness programs for students.

Orange County Sheriff's Department

Program Overview

The DWI program in the Orange County Sheriff's Department, encompassing the Orlando area, is relatively new. The sheriff's department uses a specialized patrol unit for DWI enforcement in the county. These eight men make 60 percent of all DWI arrests. They arrest an average of two hundred DWI offenders per month. The sheriff's office received a three-year federal grant of $440 thousand to pay for eight deputies; equipment such as cars, radios, and uniforms; a computer for tracking DWI offenders; a data technician; and a local project coordinator. Orange County purchased two breath alcohol testing mobile units (Batmobiles) with $100 thousand raised by Mothers Against Drunk Drivers, private citizens, and the local automobile dealers association. The deputies show movies and make presentations to major companies, bar and restaurant employees, and civic groups in the area. One of the most popular programs involves taking the Batmobiles to junior high and high schools for educational demonstrations.

In addition, the deputies make extensive use of videotaping. In Orange County, the sheriff's department videotapes and processes all DWI arrests, including arrests made by the Florida Highway Patrol and local police. The county streamlined the videotaping process with the help of the recently acquired Batmobiles. Prior to its videotaping program, the conviction rate in Orange County was 67 percent; within approximately two years of its implementation, the conviction rate rose to 92 percent.

The Batmobiles in Orange County function effectively as fixed testing centers, rotated among high visibility locations throughout the city. Law enforcement officials bring all DWI offenders to the central processing site, usually the county jail, or the closest mobile site. The Batmobile does not meet the officer at the point of arrest.

Each unit includes the equipment and paperwork necessary for the legal testing and processing of drunk drivers. A trained technician from the sheriff's department performs breath tests inside the vehicle, while a representative from the Florida Highway Patrol conducts the videotaping and sobriety tests outside the unit. As the suspect is tested, the arresting officer completes the necessary paperwork, then returns to duty. The suspect remains at the mobile site until a transport vehicle arrives to take the offender to the county jail.

The Wheeled Coach Corporation in Orlando presently manufactures the Batmobile at an average cost of $50 thousand. The corporation donated the prototype model, developed at an estimated cost of $80 thousand, to the Orange County Sheriff's Department. Although both units were donated, the department remains responsible for any maintenance costs, such as equipment repair or replacement, vehicle upkeep, gasoline, and generator power.

Program Objectives

The DWI system in Orange County evolved concurrently in the legislative and enforcement sectors, prompted by three major factors: the election of a sheriff with a strong desire to strengthen DWI enforcement; the presence and active involvement of the Orlando MADD chapter; and the shift of national and local public opinion against DWI.

The sheriff's department in Orange County traditionally emphasized criminal cases rather than traffic enforcement. When the new sheriff took office in 1981, he initiated a shift in policy toward strengthened enforcement of all the laws within the county's jurisdiction, including traffic enforcement. In the same time period, the Orlando MADD chapter was founded and began the drive for new DWI legislation. In 1982, the passage of significant DWI legislation was achieved. In 1983, state legislators amended the legislation to include driving under the influence of drugs.

Program Implementation

Orange County law enforcement officials praise the success of the videotaping process and agree that, when properly used, videotaping strengthens the prosecution's case and increases the overall conviction rate. They stress that it presents the best and fairest evidence for trial because it "locks, in time and space" the behavior of the individual at the time of arrest. They argue that videotaping provides a cost-effective use of the officer's time and the department's resources, and has increased the Orange County conviction rate from 67 percent to 92 percent.

Some officials do not believe the state of Florida should mandate videotaping. They argue that smaller counties may experience difficulty financing costly video equipment, and fear that if the equipment malfunctions, a case could be thrown out due to a lack of required evidence. They also point out the difficulties involved with the "skilled drunk" who performs well on tape and discredits the scientific evidence, as well as jury misinterpretation of expected behavior at legal intoxication levels. Officials do believe, however, that the trend toward videotaping will continue even if Florida legislators do not require it in the future. They attribute this success to the "snowball effect" within the state.

Orange County officials remain extremely enthusiastic about their recently acquired Batmobiles, which allow timely testing and processing of all county DWI arrests in an effective and efficient manner. The shorter processing time allows for testing immediately following apprehension of the suspect, thereby forestalling any delays which allow the offender to "sober up." This provides more accurate police reports and increases the chances of successful prosecution. It also maximizes the efficient use of the officer's time; as a result, officers are more willing to arrest DWI offenders.

Rotating the Batmobile's location helps to increase its visibility within the community, an important aspect of the public information and education effort. As an unexpected benefit, these units provide a deterrent to crime in the area where the Batmobile is deployed. Businesses have begun to request the units and offer the use of their facilities in return. Surprisingly, the Batmobiles also provide evening "entertainment" for local citizens who come to watch the DWI enforcement process, thus providing another aspect of public information.

Before Orange County purchased the Batmobiles, the processing time for each DWI arrest averaged five hours. At present, arrests and processing average thirty to forty-five minutes, allowing the officer to return to active duty in a short period of time. The Batmobiles also play an important role in the county public information and education program. Officials take the units to area schools and organizations to teach citizens and students about the threat of drinking and driving on the lives of friends and loved ones. The Batmobile, therefore, is appropriately described as a "showpiece by day and a workhorse by night."

Different actors within the county DWI system work together to advance public information and education in the area. MADD works actively toward this end, as does the sheriff's department. Public speaking strategies differ for different groups, but the general message concerns awareness of the consequences of drinking and driving.

Working with the private sector, the county implemented several successful campaigns against drinking and driving. One such program targeted the designated driver as a nondrinker in a group patronizing a bar or restaurant. Distinguished as such by a "Designated Driver" button or sticker, the individual is eligible to receive free soft drinks, half-price meals, and other discounts from participating establishments. The stickers and posters publicizing this program have become increasingly popular in the Orlando area. Another interesting program involves a "two for one" offer providing a drink and an hors d'oeuvre for the price of one. This promotes the idea of combining food and alcohol consumption.

With increased enforcement and resulting arrests, DWI cases now overload the court system. Although an increased caseload speaks well of the DWI process, county officials feel it may increase the need for plea bargaining. At present, Orange County allows plea bargaining in cases with a BAC level of .15 percent or below. Involvement by family members and friends of the drunk driver's victim can increase the chance that the case will come to trial. MADD's role is to help educate the victim's family about this process. MADD will become actively involved if the family requests such assistance.

County officials feel the practice of mandatory license suspension is relatively ineffective in Florida because the suspension process becomes bogged down in paperwork and notification procedures. The immediate suspension provision requires the arresting officer to notify the state license bureau of the pending suspension. The bureau must notify the offender within thirty days and allow ten days for his response. Even if the license is suspended, the offender can request an occupational driver's license on the first offense or risk driving without a license. The process would be more effective if the burden fell on the offender to set up the hearing or face automatic license suspension.

Although the DWI system as a whole needs further fine-tuning, the Orange County Sheriff's Department deserves credit for instituting an innovative and effective enforcement process. An important factor in the success of the Orange County DWI system involves the successful combination of law enforcement and public information and education. Neither element in the system must be relied upon to fight the battle alone.

Pinellas County "Arrest Drunk Driving" Program

Program Overview

The "Arrest Drunk Driving" program, initiated by the Clearwater Police Department, has received favorable notice from the U.S. Department of Transportation's National Highway Traffic Safety Administration and is generally recognized as one of the nation's most successful programs in combatting drunk driving. The "Arrest Drunk Driving" program, implemented in 1983, is a deliberate attempt to create an innovative approach to a local DWI system. Originally a cooperative effort between the cities of Clearwater and Largo, the program now includes the neighboring cities of Dunedin and Tarpon Springs. The combined area the program encompasses is about seventy-five square miles, and includes a population of approximately 800 thousand people. Pinellas County is the smallest, yet most densely populated, county in Florida. Its cities use a three-tiered approach to combat DWI, concentrating on public information, enforcement, and specialized training for police officers.

Program Objectives

The "Arrest Drunk Driving" program involves the cities of Clearwater, Largo, Dunedin, and Tarpon Springs in Pinellas County, near the Tampa Bay metropolitan area. Before the program was implemented, research indicated that, in the years 1979-82, there was a 55 percent increase in automobile accidents. This increase was coupled with an alcohol involvement rate of over 65 percent in all accidents producing fatalities and serious injuries.[2] Before the "Arrest Drunk Driving" program, there were no interagency traffic enforcement programs directed toward the drunk driver problem in the Pinellas County area.

The cities of Clearwater and Largo combined resources and philosophies to combat the DWI problem beginning in July 1983. Their coordinated and cooperative approach is a multiphase enforcement and public information and education campaign. It involves extensive police officer training, increased selective and directed enforcement, and the establishment of five fixed-site testing centers for the processing of DWI suspects.

Within six months, the success of the project led to the expansion of the "Arrest Drunk Driving" program to include the neighboring cities of Dunedin and Tarpon Springs. The program objectives aim to achieve a 20 percent reduction in the number of alcohol-related fatal and nonfatal serious injury accidents; a lessening of the time spent on each case by one hour for the arresting officer; and an increase in the number of DWI arrests by 25 percent.

There are three major components to the "Arrest Drunk Driving" program. They are police officer training, enforcement strategies, and public information and education. In the area of training, the "Arrest Drunk Driving" program operates on the premise that each individual police officer on patrol is responsible for addressing the particular problem of drunk driving in his particular patrol zone or sector. Therefore, each police officer associated with the "Arrest Drunk Driving" program in the four participating agencies receives extensive DWI enforcement training. The sixteen hours of training for officers include legal review, report-writing skills, standardization of field sobriety testing, and instruction in detection cues, breath testing, and videotaping. Moreover, the agencies now have seventy Intoxilyzer operators, each of whom has received forty hours of specialized training.

The second tier of this DWI program is enforcement. Enforcement

---

[2]The latter figure is substantially higher than the national average. This is partially due to the fact that the Clearwater Police Department makes use of the coroner's reports to calculate the number of fatal alcohol-related accidents. Most other agencies use the accident report prepared by the police officer at the scene for calculating this figure. Since in most instances the accident report indicates only the officer's perception that alcohol may have been a factor, the coroner's report is a more accurate measurement.

strategies used in the "Arrest Drunk Driving" program include directed patrol, deployment of personnel in high DWI accident locations, and DWI sobriety checkpoints. Rather than selecting certain law enforcement officers to conduct DWI enforcement in the jurisdictions--as with the Selective Traffic Enforcement Program (STEP)--Pinellas County officials decided every patrol officer should be an important part of the enforcement strategy. Therefore, every officer patrolling the streets performs DWI enforcement. The four cities have increased their use of roadblocks, taking advantage of the situation by turning roadblocks into a "media show." Although the county has used only twelve checkpoints altogether, the media has publicized the roadblocks so extensively that it appears to the public that there are many more than twelve checkpoints.

Law enforcement officers videotape all DWI offenders and refer to the videotapes as "witness for the prosecution" in their public service announcements. The four-city cooperative program has no Batmobiles; instead, they have established five fixed testing sites in addition to the facilities at the police departments, so that at any given time officers are only ten minutes away from a fixed-site testing facility. Each testing facility contains videotaping equipment, Intoxilyzers, and a holding cell.

Since the education of the public is critical to the longevity of any enforcement program, public information and education is a major component of the "Arrest Drunk Driving" program. It commenced with a press conference announcing the program and includes the following: a speaker's bureau, television public service announcements, radio public service announcements, television and radio talk shows, newspaper advertisements, magazine articles, news releases, billboards, brochures, bumper stickers, posters, press folders, street signs, police cruiser decals, window stickers, key chains, and much more. A particularly effective feature of the PI&E projects is that they all address the drinking and driving problem by using the "we will catch you" theme. The underlying philosophy is twofold: that an enforcement program cannot survive without a proper public information and education campaign to support it, and that public information and education is the most effective tool in changing societal attitudes about drinking and driving.

Program Implementation

All activities associated with the "Arrest Drunk Driving" program occur at the municipal law enforcement level of government. The Clearwater Police Department (CPD) is responsible for the administration of the federal grant and the evaluation of the project. Each participating agency designated a coordinator responsible for that jurisdiction's participation in the project. The coordinators of the project usually are the traffic enforcement supervisor or a member of the planning and research staff of the given law enforcement agency.

The "Arrest Drunk Driving" program has benefited from many funding sources. The original equipment for the project was funded by section 402 highway safety grants from the Department of Transportation to the Florida Bureau of Public Safety Management. Concurrent with these funds the project received aid from a section 403 highway safety grant awarded to the University of North Carolina's Highway Safety Research Center. The section 403 grants are specified federal funds distributed to organizations or agencies conducting research, projects, or studies the Department of Transportation is particularly interested in (see Chapter 1). The Florida program became a test site for the university in a study on the effectiveness of public information and education in a continuing DWI enforcement project.

The section 402 grants provided by the Florida Bureau of Public Safety Management paid for the acquisition of the original equipment. In addition to videotaping equipment and Intoxilyzer machines, these funds also covered the cost of public information and education materials and resources for the establishment of three fixed-site breath-testing laboratories in Clearwater and Largo. Subsequently, the section 402 grants funded the acquisition of additional equipment for fixed-site testing locations in Dunedin and Tarpon Springs. The University of North Carolina's Highway Safety Research Center section 403 grant assisted the "Arrest Drunk Driving" program by channeling funds into public information and education material, preprogram and postprogram surveys, training, equipment acquisition, and consultant services.

The "Arrest Drunk Driving" program has been responsible for the reduction of costs associated with court time, specifically in the area of officer overtime for appearance in traffic court. Payroll savings also have been realized in streamlining the processing of DWI suspects and the reduction of overtime associated with late calls. Additional savings have been achieved in printing the public information and educational materials. Printing now is being performed by inmates of the state prison system as part of a prison rehabilitation program and has reduced printing costs by as much as 50 percent.

The "Arrest Drunk Driving" program has resulted in many benefits. Since the program's inception, two additional cities, Dunedin and Tarpon Springs, have come under the project umbrella. Additional cities in Pinellas County also have contacted the Clearwater Police Department for inclusion in the project. In counties surrounding Pinellas County, individual agency efforts have increased the awareness and enforcement of DWI activities. In some instances, former STEP programs have been revitalized and enhanced. The training associated with the project is available upon request to other agencies in the Pinellas County area. Numerous agencies have taken advantage of this opportunity, resulting in standardization of some policies, procedures, and individual field sobriety testing. Publicity surrounding the program has resulted in contact between the "Arrest Drunk Driving" staff and jurisdictions both around the state and across the nation. The public information and education material has been of particular interest. Over three hundred individual packets of information have been distributed nationwide.

Particularly important is the television public service time donated to the project by four television stations. The estimated value of the air time donated to the "Arrest Drunk Driving" program is in excess of $40 thousand. Coupled with this is an estimated $24 thousand in donated billboard space.

Citizen involvement occurred early in the "Arrest Drunk Driving" program. Specifically, it began with the development of a citizen advisory board. The advisory board included actors from all aspects of the local DWI system: the judiciary, the state attorney general's office, teachers from local high schools, the Pinellas County chapter of the National Safety Council, MADD, SADD, and members of certain peer groups associated with the public school system. The purpose of the advisory board is to provide community input into the inner workings of the project itself, to assist with the dissemination of public information and education material, and to develop and identify future funding resources. Moreover, the Clearwater Police Department also has requested the advisory board's participation in periodic evaluations to identify key areas overlooked by the project staff. By involving so many groups in the planning phase of the program, many potential problems were successfully averted.

Evaluation of the "Arrest Drunk Driving" program currently is being performed by several different groups. The "Arrest Drunk Driving" project staff measures the productivity of arrests, the officer time of involvement, the fatality rate in the different jurisdictions, and the number and severity of injuries associated with the drinking driver. The University of North Carolina Highway Safety Research Center will be evaluating the public information and educational aspects of the "Arrest Drunk Driving" program.

Northwestern University's Traffic Institute also is participating in the evaluation stages of the program. It is studying the impact of officer training on enforcement and apprehension of DWI offenders. Preliminary evaluations indicate the program has been highly successful. The total number of DWI arrests has doubled since the program's implementation; Dunedin's DWI arrests alone have increased 400 percent since joining the program. The conviction rate for arrests jumped from 65 percent to 96 percent in the first two years of the program. The time an officer spends per DWI arrest has decreased by more than one hour. Thus, in a short two years, "Arrest Drunk Driving" has been successful beyond the program's original expectations. Enthusiasm for the program remains high, and there is no indication of any potential problems to prevent further success.

The Campus Alcohol Information Center at University of Florida

The Campus Alcohol Information Center at the University of Florida conducts two programs concerned with DWI-related offenses. One of the programs, Boost Alcohol Consciousness Concerning the Health of University Students (BACCHUS), is a nationwide college program, which originated at the university. BACCHUS deals with all aspects of college students' drinking habits, including drinking and driving. The second program is part of the Florida Department of Health and Rehabilitative Services (HRS). It is a prevention program designed for university students convicted of DWI.

BACCHUS

In the past, many officials have not reviewed the education of young adults about alcohol and its safe and appropriate use as a tool for decreasing widespread alcohol abuse. Analyses of drinking problems often conclude that youth itself is a major contributor to alcohol abuse. Laws, punishments, and warnings directed at young people's drinking habits appear to have done little more than challenge the independence of youth and dared young people to experiment with alcohol.

Collegiate drinking and socializing often are inseparable. Students away from home for the first time experience acceleration of the rites of passage, and are under considerable pressure to "fit in" with the crowd. This group interaction may include drinking frequently. Decisions to drink often are made without an understanding of responsible drinking choices.

In response to this lack of education for young people, BACCHUS was formed in 1976 by Dr. Geraldo Gonzales, Assistant Dean of Student Services at the University of Florida, and a group of university undergraduates. The goals of BACCHUS are to provide a strategical framework and peer network for ongoing education, and to provide peer support for making responsible personal decisions about alcohol. BACCHUS members believe that college students will be more successful in modifying the attitudes and behavior of their peers than would traditional authority figures. The founders chose the name BACCHUS in order to convey that the group is not an antialcohol or antidrinking group; Bacchus was the Roman god of gaiety and wine.

BACCHUS has grown from about fifteen chapters in 1980 to almost two hundred chapters in 1985. Located on university and college campuses throughout the United States, BACCHUS also serves as a national clearinghouse for information and idea exchange involving student-oriented campus alcohol education. The BACCHUS Board of Trustees and National Advisory Council are responsible for the organization's overall policy direction. Delegates and staff advisers from each chapter meet in an annual general assembly to hear reports and pass rules and regulations. The national organization also runs regional training workshops on alcohol education programs for students, professionals, and groups interested in starting BACCHUS chapters. Campus visits are made to provide technical assistance and consultation in the formation and implementation of educational programs. BACCHUS also has a network of speakers knowledgeable and interested in addressing alcohol-related subjects. Recently, BACCHUS created a regional network of six consultants to improve communication among chapters and to increase accessibility to the national office.

Recent BACCHUS publications include the "BACCHUS Drinking-Driving Packet," produced in cooperation with the Metropolitan Life Foundation. This publication gives interested administrators and student organizations step-by-step instructions for implementing a campaign against drinking and driving. BACCHUS also edited a manual called Model Programs of Alcohol Education in Institutes of Higher Education. It covers the full range of alcohol programs and issues on college campuses. The organization also offers a ten-minute slide presentation and a ten-minute film, CHOICES, showing appropriate drinking behavior and effective peer dynamics. In the near future, CHOICES may be shown to all incoming freshmen in public universities in Florida.

Articles about BACCHUS have appeared in Newsweek, The Chronicle of Higher Education, The New York Times, and U.S. News and World Report. The dramatic increase in BACCHUS chapters across the United States suggests heightened student awareness and concern about alcohol abuse. College students around the country are taking the initiative in educating peers about alcohol and encouraging them to make an informed choice about drinking.

Health and Rehabilitative Services Community Service Program

The second program of the University of Florida's Campus Alcohol Information Center involves students attending state universities who have been convicted of DWI. This secondary prevention program, funded by the Florida Department of Health and Rehabilitative Services (HRS), is coordinated by the BACCHUS chapters on state university campuses throughout Florida. The statewide program coordinator is located at the Campus Alcohol Information Center in Gainesville.

The HRS funds provide money to hire a part-time graduate assistant doing work in a counseling field at each state university. Currently, seven of the nine state universities are actively participating in the HRS program. The graduate assistant helps the offender to find opportunities to perform his mandatory community service and provides group and individual counseling sessions. Offenders participate in support groups and alcohol information classes. The amount and type of counseling an individual receives depends on the evaluation done as a result of his arrest. Substance abuse counseling also may be recommended or required as part of the offender's sentence. The Health and Rehabilitative Services program is a very new one and is not yet completely operational. No evaluations of the project have yet been attempted.

State Recommendations

Florida officials pointed out several loopholes in the 1982 DWI legislation. The law allows punishment for DWI crimes to be measured from conviction to conviction rather than from offense to offense. This allows greater possibility for manipulation by defense attorneys to keep conviction penalties as low as possible. The law also permits implied consent license suspensions for refusal to submit to breath or blood tests to be served concurrently with license suspensions due to convictions. These sentences should be consecutive, not concurrent, in order to provide a greater deterrent.

The Orange County Sheriff's Department recently purchased the Intoxilyzer 5000, which measures alcohol levels by infrared rather than chemical analysis. Florida law, however, permits only "chemical" testing to be submitted as evidence for the prosecution. Although the infrared analysis is more accurate than chemical tests, defense attorneys challenge the submission of infrared tests. Lawmakers simply need to update the wording to avoid this loophole.

Florida officials recommend shifting the burden of license suspension to the offender rather than the county in order to strengthen the enforcement and punishment phase of the process. They also stress the need for education of the public, who are all potential jurors, on the legal definition of blood alcohol concentration level and what behavior to expect at Florida's statutory BAC level of .10 percent or above.

Law enforcement officials also must emphasize the importance of the strongest case possible against a given DWI offender in order to reduce the probability of going to trial. The court system is too overloaded to try marginal cases. The clearer the case against the offender, the less likely it is to be tried before a jury. Officers may want to videotape the suspects for a longer period of time to effectively show the behavior of the DWI offender.

Officials from the Orange County Sheriff's Department and Pinellas County pride themselves on the efficiency of their programs, which were effectively put into place in only two years. They suggest an emphasis on fund-raising efforts and donations from the private sector to finance potentially costly components of a program, such as the Batmobiles and videotaping equipment. They also suggest federal grants to supplement initial equipment and implementation costs for an infant program. Pinellas County has shown that limited resources can be maximized by sharing facilities and manpower with neighboring communities. Florida officials emphasize the importance of innovation and enthusiasm in the success of any DWI program that is undertaken.

Conclusions

The DWI system in Texas could implement many of the successful elements of the Orange County program. The Batmobiles seem to work much better in combatting drunk driving than does the standard videotaping already in use in Texas cities. Other than the momentum provided by specific personalities in Orange County, the state of Texas could achieve similar success by implementing Florida's techniques to streamline DWI processing, strengthen DWI cases, and generate outside funding sources.

Similarly, the Texas DWI system could be enhanced by implementing programs such as "Arrest Drunk Driving" at the local level. The law enforcement agencies in Pinellas County have enjoyed strong public support for their DWI program, which is a major factor in its success. Local police officers have experienced a renewed enthusiasm in enforcing DWI laws since their time of involvement has decreased and the use of videotaping has significantly increased the possibility of conviction. Pinellas County officials are confident that their program would be suitable for use in many localities, particularly the more metropolitan areas in Texas.

BACCHUS currently has eight chapters in Texas. They are located on the campuses of North Texas State University, Sam Houston State University, St. Mary's University, Stephen F. Austin State University, Southern Methodist University, Texas A & I University, Texas A & M University, and Texas Tech University. Information on the effects of alcohol use on college campuses could be greatly improved in Texas if the number of BACCHUS chapters were increased. Also, the secondary prevention efforts funded by the Florida HRS and coordinated by BACCHUS could be replicated on Texas campuses. Although no evaluations have been formally done on the project, preliminary indications suggest its usefulness in preventing DWI recidivism. The program provides counseling, education, and peer support for young people who have been caught drinking and driving.

In summary, the DWI system in Texas could be strengthened considerably by adopting some features of the Florida system. Since Texas is so geographically and demographically diverse, it would be most useful for Texas to implement both the Batmobiles and videotaping at fixed testing sites. Officials in Florida felt that the Batmobiles functioned best in the rural areas, and that fixed testing sites are best in urban areas. Sharing of these testing resources has been another important factor in the success of the Florida DWI system. The four cities involved in the "Arrest Drunk Driving" program have demonstrated that much more can be accomplished through a cooperative effort than by municipalities acting autonomously. Orange County officials have shown that private groups often are willing to contribute additional resources to aid in purchasing new equipment. Texas administrators should explore the possibilities of implementing cooperative efforts among cities and between the public and private sectors.

MINNESOTA

Background

The state of Minnesota has a population of 4.1 million, and has 2.4 million licensed drivers. In 1982, there were 3,278,000 registered vehicles in the state. The legal drinking age in Minnesota, as of January 1985, is nineteen. A person is presumed to be legally intoxicated if an alcohol concentration test records a BAC level of .10 percent or more. In 1983, Minnesota peace officers made 32,155 DWI arrests. In 1984, that number rose to over 40,000 DWI arrests. During 1983, alcohol-related accidents in Minnesota accounted for 57 percent, or 318 of the 558 traffic fatalities. It is estimated that in 1984, 325 people died in alcohol-related traffic accidents.

Relevant Drunk Driving Legislation

The Minnesota state legislature first addressed the DWI problem in 1911 when it passed a bill making it a misdemeanor to operate a motor vehicle "while in an intoxicated condition." Since that first bill, a more complete set of laws evolved for addressing the problem of drinking and driving. Today, when a person is stopped and suspected of driving while intoxicated, the driver must submit to an alcohol concentration test or the individual's driver's license is revoked for one year. Minnesota began using the term "alcohol concentration" in 1978 instead of "blood alcohol concentration" in order to include breath and urine tests under the statute.

A preliminary breath test (PBT) may be used by the peace officer, though the results are not admissible in court. Refusal to take a PBT or an alcohol concentration test is, however, admissible as evidence. All drivers whose blood, breath or urine tests show an alcohol concentration level of .07 percent or more have this recorded on their driving record. If a second test of .07 percent or more occurs within two years, the Commissioner of Public Safety can require an alcohol assessment of the driver. If a driver has an alcohol concentration test of .10 percent or more, the state automatically revokes the person's license for ninety days. The peace officer acts for the Commissioner of Public Safety by giving the driver the notice of revocation, which takes effect after seven days.

A driver who is convicted of DWI is required by state law to undergo an alcohol problem assessment. Minnesota was the first state to require that all convicted DWI offenders be assessed. The assessment report includes information on the driver's traffic record, prior alcohol problems, and amenability to rehabilitation. The court considers the assessment report when determining punishment.

A first conviction of DWI is a misdemeanor, punishable by a maximum $700 fine and ninety days in jail. Typically, a first offender receives a $200 to $300 fine and at least two days in jail, which are not served at the offender's convenience. Additionally, the driver's license of a first offender is revoked for not less than thirty days. A driver convicted of DWI within five years of a prior offense or within ten years of two or more convictions is guilty of a gross misdemeanor, and is subject to a maximum $1,000 fine and one year in jail. Also, persons convicted of their second DWI offense within five years have their license revoked for at least ninety days and until the court has certified that treatment was completed. A third offense within five years results in a license suspension of at least one year, and the suspension remains in effect until rehabilitation is completed. A fourth or subsequent offense leads to a license revocation of at least two years and also requires completion of a rehabilitation program.

The legislature wanted to make it more difficult to escape conviction on felony charges, so in 1983 the state legislature made it a felony to seriously injure or kill a person through gross negligence or a DWI violation. Hit-and-run offenses which result in injury or death, whether alcohol related or not, also became felonies.

Minnesota does not attempt to enact the strictest possible laws for punishing convicted DWI offenders. It prefers instead to enact legislation which affects the largest number of DWI offenders. The state legislature believes strongly in fairness and has tried to develop laws whereby many DWI offenders lose their driving privileges as opposed to a situation where a few DWI offenders are punished severely and used as examples.

Notable Features of the Minnesota Drunk Driving System

Minnesota's concern for the problem of drunk driving is evident from the innovative methods it has used to address the problem. The preliminary breath test (PBT), selective enforcement, and the administrative per se law were all pioneered in Minnesota. Of these three innovations, state officials view the administrative per se law as the most effective in dealing with the drinking and driving problem. The original law, which authorized administrative license revocations, was passed in 1976. Twenty-two other states, including Texas, now include some form of license revocation in their DWI laws. As the first state to pass this type of legislation, Minnesota has had the longest time to work out any deficiencies, resulting in a model administrative license revocation system.

The administrative per se law in Minnesota provides for a maximum ninety-day license suspension for any driver with an alcohol concentration test result at or above .10 percent, or a one-year suspension for any driver refusing to be tested. Both of these suspensions are automatic, regardless of whether or not the person is ultimately convicted of driving while intoxicated. The license revocation can be served directly by the peace officer, who takes the driver's license and issues a seven-day driving permit. During the seven days, the driver must either make other driving arrangements for the period of revocation, such as public transportation or car pooling, or apply for an occupational driver's license. The Commissioner of Public Safety, who issues occupational licenses, may require proof that use of public transportation or car pooling would be a hardship.

Arrests for DWI increased dramatically with the implementation of the administrative per se law, rising from 16,976 DWI arrests in 1977 to 22,788 arrests in 1980 and 32,155 arrests in 1983. Initially, the license suspension was stayed pending the outcome of a judicial review, but this caused a backlog of cases awaiting review. In 1982, the state legislature amended the law to improve the revocation process. Under the present system, drivers may request an administrative and/or a judicial review; however, the suspension is not stayed pending the outcome of either review. By not delaying the suspension, the number of requests for hearings has decreased by 82 percent; thus, delay tactics are eliminated. A written petition for an administrative hearing can be filed anytime during the revocation period. The Commissioner of Public Safety must respond within fifteen days of receipt. A petition for a court hearing must be filed within thirty days of the suspension, and the driver pays the filing fees. The judicial hearing must occur within sixty days of the filing date.

Adopting a system similar to Minnesota's administrative driver license revocation process is not costly. Since the peace officer is generally the person issuing the revocation, postage costs are low. The peace officer must complete a few more forms, but this process puts the officer in charge. Minnesota does not allow a prerevocation hearing or a hearing which stays the revocation. When available, such hearings often were requested simply to delay the license revocation.

The administrative per se law has resulted in some unexpected, but positive, side effects. Peace officers have a renewed interest in stopping drivers suspected of DWI because of their ability to take the driver's license and issue a revocation for those drivers who refuse the test or who have an alcohol concentration test result at or above .10 percent. The officers know that the driver is unlikely to avoid punishment. The judicial process was streamlined in order to meet the sixty-day time limit for hearing petitions concerning license revocations. And, by eliminating delay tactics, judges hear fewer cases and generally only those cases where there is a legitimate argument against the license revocation.

A driver charged with DWI in Minnesota faces possible criminal penalties in addition to the automatic license suspension for refusing to take the test or for an alcohol concentration test result of .10 percent or more. This two-track system for dealing with DWI offenders eliminates some of the effects of plea bargaining. In the past, prosecutors often bargained down charges to an offense which did not require a license revocation and which eliminated any mention of an alcohol-related offense on the driver's record. Today, Minnesota automatically notes the reason for the license revocation on the driver's record. Actors in the Minnesota DWI system do not consider plea bargaining to be a major problem in Minnesota.

Forst Lowery, Safety Program Coordinator for the Minnesota Department of Public Safety, believes that the loss of driving privileges is feared by drivers and ought to be considered a severe penalty. Minnesota's efforts to increase the certainty and swiftness of the loss of driving privileges for violating the DWI laws takes advantage of this fear, and as a result the state feels it has created a stronger deterrent to drinking and driving. The two-track system of dealing with DWI offenders, especially the administrative license revocation process, has increased the certainty and swiftness of punishment.

Program Objectives

Minnesota first passed the administrative per se law in 1976, providing for license revocation for having an alcohol concentration test result at a level at or above .10 percent. Since 1961, drivers who refused to take the test had their driver's licenses revoked for six months under the implied consent law. It seemed only reasonable that if drivers who refused the test had their licenses revoked, then drivers who failed the test also should have their driving privileges automatically suspended. The legislature set the period of revocation for failing the test at three months, half the time of the revocation period for refusing to take the test, in order to provide an incentive to take the test. In 1984, the state increased the revocation period for test refusal to one year to further reduce the number of refusals.

The 1976 administrative per se law was passed through the efforts of a state senator concerned about the prevalence of plea bargaining in DWI cases. Often, judges reduced DWI charges to careless driving, with no record of the original charge. This practice meant that repeat offenders were not identified and avoided losing their licenses. The automatic license revocation for failing the alcohol concentration test now is placed on the driver's record, and repeat offenders can be identified regardless of the outcome of the criminal charges.

Beginning in 1978, peace officers were allowed to act as agents for the Commissioner of Public Safety, serving notice of revocation and seizing the licenses of drivers refusing the test or who tested at or above .10 percent. The proposed revocation notice issued by the officers became self-executing if the driver did not file a request for a hearing within thirty days; the notice also served as a thirty-day temporary license. This change reduced the number of drivers who were avoiding conviction for driving after revocation by denying that they had received their notice of revocation. The ability to seize licenses also encouraged officers to make more DWI stops, which increased the workload of the attorney general's office.

If the defendant requested a judicial hearing, the license revocation was stayed pending the outcome of the hearing. Because requests for judicial hearings created a backlog in the courts, legislators decided to reduce the number of hearing requests by not delaying the revocation until completion of the hearing. Several things occurred prior to the 1982 session which led to the elimination of prerevocation hearings. Both the attorney general and the governor wanted to attack the drunk driving problem. MADD organized in Minnesota. Also, a man awaiting trial on two DWI cases killed two ladies, ages 89 and 85, just before Christmas as they were returning from church. The man's alcohol concentration exceeded .10 percent. In the 1982 session, legislators changed the implied consent law, which covers both refusal to take the test and testing at or above .10 percent, to provide for the revocation to take effect in seven days, and to prohibit the revocation from being stayed pending the outcome of a hearing. To meet due process requirements, time limits for judicial review of the revocation were made shorter, and the administrative review was added. The elimination of prerevocation hearings was immediately challenged as violating due process, but it was upheld by the Minnesota Supreme Court.

Another tragic incident resulted in the legislature changing the laws that relate to violations resulting in death or serious injury. The accident involved a high school swimming coach who killed two young girls in a hit-and-run offense. One of the girls was on his swim team. The coach was arrested days later, and it was found that he had several DWI charges on his record. It now is a felony to kill or seriously injure a person as a result of gross negligence, a DWI violation, or a hit-and-run offense. In 1984, Minnesota eliminated the "right" to refuse to take an alcohol concentration test under the implied consent warning, and the revocation period for refusing to take the test was increased from six months to one year.

Minnesota's administrative per se law and other DWI laws are continually evolving as problems arise. The catalysts behind the legal changes are numerous--examples of drunk drivers who were "beating the system" when they killed someone, heavy media involvement, the governor's and attorney general's close cooperation, the efforts of MADD, experts testifying before the legislature, and favorable decisions by the state's courts.

The overall goal of DWI program efforts in Minnesota is to reduce the number of alcohol-related traffic accidents. Through the use of the administrative per se law, the state hopes to use the deterrence mechanisms of certainty, severity, and swiftness of punishment. Automatic revocation for refusing to take an alcohol concentration test, or testing at or above .10 percent, leads to certainty of punishment. A study by the Minnesota House Research Department (cited at the end of this chapter) found that the loss of driving privileges is considered a severe punishment by Minnesota drivers, and that not staying the revocation prior to a hearing leads to swifter punishment. Of course, the drunk driver must first be apprehended; experts estimate that the probability of a drunk driver being arrested range from 1 in 300 to 1 in 2,000. The ability to seize immediately the plastic licenses of drivers refusing or testing at or above .10 percent is a proven incentive for officers to make more DWI stops. Also, the number of DWI arrests increased in Minnesota with the introduction of new preliminary breath test (PBT) units. For example, when the state patrol began using the new PBT units, the result was an increase of 171 DWI arrests per month coupled with an additional 6.8 DWI arrests each month thereafter. By arresting as many drunk drivers as possible, instead of arresting a few and punishing them severely as examples, the state hopes to increase the perception and probability of being caught.

The study by the Research Department of the Minnesota House of Representatives also suggests two areas for future concentration. First, Laurence H. Ross found that changes in DWI laws often have only temporary effects. Therefore, the state must continually review and amend the DWI laws. Second, societal disapproval of drunk driving and moral commitment to upholding the laws must be encouraged for any long-term reduction in the drinking and driving problem. Encouragement can be in the form of increased public education and awareness of the seriousness of the problem. In the past, the state has revised the DWI laws and has shown that it is not afraid to implement innovative programs. Additional improvements to the existing legislation are being discussed in order to further reduce the number of alcohol-related traffic accidents.

Program Implementation

Enforcement

The overall effect of Minnesota's administrative per se law on the enforcement of DWI offenses has been overwhelmingly positive. Although the license revocation process requires that an additional form be filled out, peace officers are making more DWI arrests, apparently due in part to the assurance that the drunk drivers will receive some form of punishment. DWI enforcement training, both in the Minnesota State Patrol (MSP) and in the localities, is done in-house and as a portion of their normal training programs. The MSP requires five days of training in Breathilyzer operation and mandates that part of an officer's in-service training be DWI related as well.

Currently, while many communities use videotaping in their DWI arrest procedure, it is not required by the state and depends on the policy of the individual booking agency. Almost all parties interviewed expressed a similar attitude toward videotaping--it can be a useful tool in prosecution, but it also can damage a case when the person being taped does not appear "drunk." The use of roadblocks and DWI checkpoints similarly is left to the discretion of each community. The state patrol has decided not to use roadblocks for the time being so as not to compromise the public support already attained for DWI enforcement.

Prosecution and Adjudication

Minnesota's two-track system for handling DWI cases also has generated mostly positive reactions from state and local officials, although a few problems were mentioned. Workloads for almost all members of the DWI system have increased, and with the added workloads have come increasing financial burdens. Plea bargaining still is a prominent method of handling the tremendous volume of DWI cases, but it is not considered a major problem since some punishment is levied (namely, automatic license revocation) and since an alcohol-related offense remains on an individual's driving record. There is naturally some negative feeling about plea bargaining on the part of police officers; however, they see it as a necessary evil until additional funding becomes available.

Prosecutors in the state do believe, however, that the current implied consent law generally strengthens their case against alleged drunk drivers. The statute allows for prehearing license revocations without delays for hearings, and it permits the officer to decide which test will be offered. Also, while the new implied consent law initially meant that police had to spend more time in court (since it was continually being challenged), there probably has been a net decrease in the total amount of time police officers spend in court.

Other problems that plague the administrative per se law and the two-track system are the disparity of sentencing from judge to judge and the remaining overlap between the administrative and judicial processes. Although sentencing for the criminal charge is somewhat standardized through communication among judges, there still is a great deal of variance in the penalties that are being assessed, particularly in the jurisdictions outside of the Minneapolis-St. Paul metropolitan area. The courts still use license revocation as part of the plea bargaining process. A guilty plea generally results in a reduction in the length of the revocation from ninety days to thirty days.

The thirty-day jail sentence given in most cases is generally reduced to two days in the workhouse, and other requirements are imposed (for example, required attendance at a DWI course and further alcohol assessment) in lieu of the remaining jail time. These requirements may vary from case to case, depending largely on the alcohol assessment provided by the probation department. Judges in Minnesota are not specifically required to receive training in DWI or alcohol-related crimes; however, they must attend continuing education courses, and DWI courses are offered.

Administration

Minnesota presently uses the administrative hearings for spotting major mistakes (such as mistaken identity or switched licenses); the hearings rarely result in a reversal of the revocation. Only four reversals occurred in 1984 as a result of an administrative hearing. If there is no reversal, the driver may apply for an occupational driver's license, and if sufficient need can be proven, the person almost always receives one if it is his first offense. Repeat offenders either do not receive occupational licenses or must go at least one-half of the revocation period without one. The incident is immediately recorded on the driver's record when the person applies for the occupational license. The Driver's License Division must wait for the police report to come in, usually between four to ten days, for confirmation of the offense.

Minnesota law also allows the ordering of an alcohol assessment for a driver who is caught twice within two years with an alcohol concentration of .07 to .10. As a practical matter, this rarely happens. A BAC test result in this range tends to highlight an officer's mistake in judgment when pulling over possible drunk drivers.

The biggest problem facing the licensing system in Minnesota, at least administratively, has been dealing with the higher number of repeat offenders. The overall DWI system has become very adept at identifying these individuals, but questions of proper license restrictions and penalties still remain. Adherence to the penalties given to repeat offenders is also more complex and difficult, placing an additional strain on the Driver's License Division of the Minnesota Department of Public Safety.

Probation and Treatment

Along with the administrative revocation procedure, the alcohol problem assessment is considered by treatment officials to be one of the strongest features of Minnesota's drunk driving system. The assessment is mandatory for each first-time conviction. The assessment takes into account family situations and financial status as well as strictly alcohol-related concerns.

Approximately 5 percent of those convicted of DWI--whether first or higher offense--are placed on probation. Hennepin County--greater Minneapolis--has twenty-two probation officers and numerous volunteers who are used for monitoring programs and support. Following the alcohol problem assessment, a level of alcohol problem is assigned--no identifiable problem, identifiable problem, severe problem, or other. A level of probation also is assigned to the offender--monitoring, minimum, medium, or maximum. The frequency of interaction between the offender and the probation officer is dependent on the level of probation assigned.

Probation level is also a factor in determining what treatment will be recommended (for example, a residential treatment facility or participation in Alcoholics Anonymous).

Minnesota places a heavy emphasis on treatment. It is one of the leading states for treatment, with the most total treatment beds for chemical dependency in the country. Those on probation must complete a DWI education course offered by the Minnesota Safety Council or a similar program, such as Operation Foresight, Be Aware, or CREATE. Repeat offenders usually attend some sort of alcohol abuse program such as Alcoholics Anonymous. These programs generally involve a great deal of self-evaluation and personal assessment of the individual's drinking problem.

The screening or referral system used for determining the type of treatment varies a great deal. It often is a function of the particular judge or assessor. Probation and treatment officials expressed some interest in standardizing the process, and to that end a computer system has been developed for the screening. The computer program is called MACH (Minnesota Assessment of Chemical Health). Initial results in Hennepin County have been very favorable.

Treatment generally is believed to be effective. Less recidivism occurs with offenders who have good family lives, financial situations, jobs, and the like. Employee assistance programs also have lessened the occurrence of recidivism. Now the problem for the state is what to do with the repeat offender who will not learn from the education classes or treatment.

Minnesota also is beginning to see the need for an emphasis on prevention as well as treatment. The Minnesota Institute, a consulting firm active in the area of public health, has initiated an advertising campaign focused on certainty of punishment and license revocation, in order to advance the cause of prevention. It also is involved in a program called Control Factor that is aimed at junior and senior high school students. The purpose of the program is to initiate peer pressure against drinking to excess and more specifically against drinking and driving.

Legislation

The Minnesota legislature has been a key element in the state's fight against drinking and driving. In response to lobbying by the public, MADD, the media, and others, it has enacted what some safety experts consider to be some of the most unique and effective legislation in the country. Legislators perceive Minnesota's administrative per se law as being effective because penalties are severe enough that drivers fear the consequences, yet at the same time are reasonable enough not to dissuade judges from sentencing. Also, the administrative revocation process is smoother and offers reassurance to the arresting officer that he or she is being effective.

There are no changes in the current DWI laws proposed for the 1985 legislative session. There is some interest, however, in raising the drinking age to twenty-one and enacting a dramshop law, penalties for those who test between .05 and .10 percent, and a nickel-a-drink tax to promote a self-financing DWI system. The issue of drinking and driving is very important to the legislators' constituents. Public awareness of the problem and the laws is great. MADD was the initial driving force behind improving the DWI laws in the state, and since that time, its concerns have become the concerns of many citizens.

Public Advocacy and Information

The contributions of citizen lobbying groups and interested public organizations to the problem of drinking and driving are very visible in Minnesota. Mothers Against Drunk Drivers (MADD) is active in the state with twelve chapters. Other public interest groups include the Criminal Justice DWI Task Force and the Minnesota Institute.

Comprised of representatives from enforcement, prosecution, adjudication, probation, treatment, and administration, and funded by National Highway Traffic Safety Administration monies distributed to the Minnesota Department of Public Safety, the Criminal Justice DWI Task Force meets approximately once a month to address both long- and short-term aspects of the DWI problem. In the short term, the task force's primary objective is to react to existing and proposed legislation as it affects drinking and driving in Minnesota. Over the longer run, it examines the entire DWI problem and considers a variety of solutions for Minnesota policy. These remedies primarily are directed at legislation, education, and enforcement.

The Minnesota Institute is a nonprofit consulting firm that handles work in the field of public health. Advertising campaigns, research studies, public education, and informational programs directed at the problems of alcohol and drugs are the main thrust of the institute's efforts.

The public advocacy groups in Minnesota are in basic agreement that the issue of drinking and driving must continue to be publicized and highlighted before the general public. Prevention and deterrence will be at their strongest when it becomes socially unacceptable to drink and drive. The Minnesota license revocation procedures are seen as very strong tools in this effort, for some sort of punishment is guaranteed to any driver caught driving while intoxicated. Some of the advertising campaigns of the Minnesota Institute come right to the point. For example, "In Minnesota, anyone who can't walk a straight line will get a month to practice."

Two suggested areas of improvement highlighted by public advocacy interests are the need for better handling of repeat DWI offenders and the need for some sort of financing alternative to supplement the DWI system. The breadth of Minnesota's administrative revocation procedures is reflected in their outcome. Increased efforts to punish first offenders have resulted in more first offenders being noted on the record books. For example, in 1984 the Department of Public Safety took approximately forty-three thousand license actions, and about forty thousand DWI prosecutions occurred statewide. While most states are worried about catching that first offender, Minnesota now is concerned about the rising number of second or higher offenders.

Part of the problem is that repeat offenders often receive slower treatment in the courts. In some cases, the referrals by probation officers are not being completely followed in that inappropriate treatment assignments are made and some problem drinkers go unassisted. Advocacy groups suggested more mandatory minimum sentences and consistency of punishment for the repeat offenders.

Without question, one of the more forceful proposals from the public advocacy sector concerned the nickel-a-drink designated tax on alcohol. Designed to tax the entire pool of potential DWI offenders, it is estimated that a surcharge of five cents on every drink sold in Minnesota would generate approximately $120 million in revenues annually. By not using general revenues to fund the DWI system and by taxing liquor consumers, this tax would directly target the population who commits the offenses. The funds would be used for treatment, incarceration, restitution, and education. The aims of such a tax are sixfold:

1. Remove the financial burden of enforcing existing statutes. (Each DWI offense is estimated to cost $1,000 <u>without</u> going to trial.)

2. Increase apprehension and prosecution levels.

3. Apply funds to other problem areas associated with alcohol abuse (e.g., battered women, child abuse).

4. Reimburse the victims of those who abuse alcohol through a state Victims Compensation Fund.

5. Increase treatment programs.

6. Fund massive educational programs both in and out of the schools, beginning as early as kindergarten.

In all, the public advocacy and information factors in Minnesota's DWI system remain active in the ongoing efforts to reduce drinking and driving in the state. They devote themselves to propelling new ideas and supporting innovative alternatives while also promoting every effort to improve upon existing capacities, whether they be enforcement, prosecution, or treatment. For most programs, the essential problem is one of money. If Minnesota is to continue at the forefront of DWI control systems across the country, it must not fail to address the financial aspects of drinking and driving.

State Recommendations

Recommendations were made by those people interviewed to improve Minnesota's DWI system. Their suggestions include:

--Uniformity and absolute certainty of punishment, possibly facilitated through statewide meetings among judges;

--Increased funding for DWI arrests or at least a streamlining of the access to funds currently available;

--Totally divorce the courts from license revocation;

--Make efforts to educate those convicted of DWI during their period of incarceration;

--Chemical dependency treatment and rehabilitation dispositions for DWI offenders must be emphasized as part of any long-term resolution of the DWI problem;

--Allow the courts to sentence sixteen- and seventeen-year-olds to jail terms for drunk driving;

--Impose tougher penalties for individuals who refuse alcohol concentration tests;

--Impose mandatory jail terms and higher fines for all DWI offenders;

--Impose a license tag tax on repeat offenders;

--Videotape arrests for future courtroom proceedings;

--Hire physicians to examine individuals arrested for drunk driving and to provide expert testimony concerning the defendants' state of intoxication as well as their potential need for chemical dependency treatment;

--Develop a "scared straight" program for young people
which would include sessions at local hospitals on
weekend nights and holidays to observe emergency
room activities in connection with drunk driving
accidents;

--Impose an alcohol consumption tax to pay for
education and treatment programs, and to compensate
victims;

--As a warning to motorists, statistically identify
and mark road areas which involve a high risk of
encountering drunk drivers;

--Conduct new roadside surveys to measure the incidence
of drunk driving in Minnesota.

Conclusions

In reviewing the current status of the DWI control system in Minnesota and seeking to apply it to Texas, one basic difference must be understood. General acceptance of the government's role in regulating and overseeing its citizens' daily actions seems to be much greater in Minnesota. What might be interpreted as an intrusion in Texas would likely be seen as a necessary protection in Minnesota. This should not, however, impede consideration of Minnesota's DWI program efforts for adoption by Texas. Instead, it should be viewed as part of the framework governing program implementation.

The primary Minnesota program that Texas should examine is the administrative per se law with its license revocation procedures. Since passage of the initial legislation in 1976, Minnesota officials have had sufficient time to discover and correct any serious problems. The license revocation period, extended for those refusing to take the alcohol test, resulted in a decrease in refusals. Also, the backlogs confronting the administrative appeals process were eliminated. The revocation is no longer stayed pending the result of an individual's appeal. Likewise, by changing from a solely administrative revocation process to one in which arresting officers issue forms making the revocation effective after seven days, Minnesota accomplished two improvements. It eliminated many of the delays blamed on the process itself--such as paperwork and postal delays-- and it also gave officers a greater awareness of their impact in removing drunk drivers from the roads.

In all, the concerted efforts of all parties involved in the Minnesota DWI programs should be closely examined by their Texas counterparts. Alcohol-related driver's license revocations increased from 14,251 in 1976 (53 per 100 million vehicle miles traveled) to 30,481 in 1980 (107 per 100 million vehicle mile traveled). By 1984, revocations were up to nearly 40,000, reflecting the most recent legislative changes. To the extent that a similar removal of drunk drivers from the roads remains as a primary objective of the Texas system, the Minnesota policies should not be overlooked.

NEW YORK

Background

New York state has a population of 17.7 million. There are 9 million licensed drivers, and 8 million registered vehicles in the state. In 1982, the legal drinking age was raised from eighteen to nineteen. A person is presumed to be legally intoxicated if an alcohol concentration tests record a BAC level of .10 percent or higher. Also, a person with a BAC level of .06 percent or higher is presumed to be alcohol impaired. In 1983, New York law enforcement officers made 67,933 DWI arrests. In 1983, alcohol-related accidents accounted for 34 percent, or 667, of New York's 1,961 traffic fatalities--a decrease from 884 alcohol-related traffic fatalities in 1981 and 761 in 1982.

Relevant Drunk Driving Legislation

In New York, an important distinction is made in the offenses of drinking and driving. As opposed to relying upon the traditional criminal charge of driving while intoxicated (DWI), New York also utilizes driving while ability impaired (DWAI), which is defined as a BAC level of greater than .06 percent. This lesser charge is used as the minimum charge for a drinking and driving offense. It is impossible to plea bargain below the DWAI charge to a nonalcohol-related offense, such as a traffic violation, due to legislative changes made in 1980. This legislation, coupled with increased penalties for the DWAI offense, has aided the state in reducing the DWI problem.

Since 1980, legislation has been the primary focus in confronting the problem of drinking and driving. In 1981, the legislature established the Special Traffic Options Program for Driving While Intoxicated (STOP-DWI). This is a comprehensive, financially self-sustaining alcohol and highway safety program. It enables the counties to receive the fines collected for future use in alcohol and highway safety countermeasures. Upon approval of its program and budget, a STOP-DWI program allows the different localities to act autonomously to combat the drinking driver problem in their jurisdictions while benefiting from state coordination and guidance.

A second area of legislative change involves penalties for the convicted. In order to make the laws more efficient and a stronger deterrent, a mandatory $250 fine and a ninety-day license revocation were levied on a first-offense DWAI. A second offense carries a $350 minimum and $500 maximum fine, as well as a minimum six-month license suspension. A third offense entails a $500 minimum and $1,500 maximum fine, and a minimum six-month revocation if the driver had no convictions within the past five years. Jail is rarely used, although maximums of fifteen, thirty, and ninety days for the first, second, and third DWAI offenses, respectively, are established.

The penalties for DWI are stiffer. A first offense is subject to a minimum fine of $350, but shall not exceed $500. In addition, a first time DWI offender is subject to a maximum one-year jail sentence and a six-month license revocation. A second offense incurs a $500 minimum to a $5,000 maximum fine, as well as a maximum four-year jail sentence and a minimum one-year license revocation.

Other legislative highlights include mandatory license suspension for a chemical test refusal and a six-month revocation after a hearing on the refusal coupled with a $100 civil fine. A second offense for a DWI or DWAI conviction within the past five years entails a one-year revocation and a $250 fine for a chemical test refusal. The chemical test is mandated upon an accident resulting in serious injury, death, lawful arrest, and chemical test refusal. These are all contingent upon a court order. Presently, there is a mandatory seven-day jail statute for driving with a suspended or revoked license. Furthermore, if an accused drunk driver has a DWI or DWAI conviction within the previous three years, license suspension is immediate.

One final law related to DWI legislation was enacted in 1984--the first mandatory seat-belt restraint regulation. All front passengers, regardless of age, and rear passengers under age ten, are required to wear a seat belt at all times. Though not a deterrent to the drinking and driving problem, this safety feature perhaps will aid the state in reducing the number of fatalities and serious injuries resulting from alcohol-related traffic accidents.

Notable Features of the New York Drunk Driving System

A major feature of New York's drunk driving system is the Special Traffic Options Program for Driving While Intoxicated (STOP-DWI). The STOP-DWI program was the result of two task forces. The Governor of New York set up a task force in 1980 for the purpose of empowering all agencies to study and examine the drinking driver problem for future direction. Sixteen state agencies were involved including six working committees with a special coordinating group in the Department of Motor Vehicles' Office of Alcohol and Highway Safety. The recommendations from this group were to implement a systems approach and to create a perception in the public's mind about the likelihood of apprehension while drinking and driving and the possible penalties. Simultaneously, Senator William Smith led a state senate task force seeking to uncover revenue sources for program development and implementation while retaining a community focus. Senator Smith was the catalyst for change; he had a personal interest in addressing the DWI problem and he personally lobbied strongly for more rigorous legislation. The resulting senate bill forced the alcohol abuser to pay for solving the problem and encouraged community involvement through local options and plans.

STOP-DWI's new approach to the drinking and driving problem leaves the county free to develop a program and budget best suited to its location. The program allows decisionmaking activities to focus on the level of government which is responsible for enforcement, adjudication, education, and rehabilitation. Currently, there are fifty-eight programs serving sixty-two counties. The Commissioner of Motor Vehicles reviews and approves all programs. State requirements placed on the counties are minimal. Participating counties must appoint a coordinator and file a letter of intent with the Department of Motor Vehicles. To be eligible, a county program had to be a new initiative and could not be a simple duplication of a state program.

Another important aspect to the STOP-DWI program is the structuring of fines. Normally, any fine collected in the courts would be posted with the Office of the State Comptroller. Through the STOP-DWI program, all fines collected are posted with the state comptroller and then are given back to the finance officer of the participating county to apply to STOP-DWI programs. Fiscal officers must certify that the monies are spent according to plan. Rollover (unspent) money which results from program delays remains with the county for future STOP-DWI program efforts. The program monies for the county plans come solely from collected fines--no state monies are added to the program. In 1983, the program generated $10.7 million in fines and roughly $14 million in 1984.

The role of the county coordinator is to develop a budget and program to which the fine monies will apply. The coordinator is appointed by the county executive, or county legislative body. There are no legal requirements defining the qualifications of the coordinator, although political knowledge of the county is essential for satisfying all factions in the county. Coordinators must report regularly to the Department of Motor Vehicles on their programs and expenditures and other important data concerning arrests and dispositions of cases. The coordinator's office functions as an accountability mechanism which requires police, prosecutors, and judges to report their activities. State oversight is minimal, focusing on the appropriation of funds in accordance with each county's original program design.

The STOP-DWI Coordinators Association is divided into six regions, and its committees meet four to five times per year. The purpose of the association is to represent the coordinators across the state. The association often acts as a liaison between the Department of Motor Vehicles and the individual coordinators. One of its main objectives is to effect administrative changes within the entire policymaking process. It also serves as a self-help organization. In the STOP-DWI program, both the state and the counties have obligations to perform their respective tasks effectively and not abuse the system. The association is a forum for coordinators to discuss such issues and provide inner support systems among coordinators. Each fall, the coordinators set the agenda for a meeting conducted by the Department of Motor Vehicles. Communication among counties is provided through regional county coordinators' meetings. Regionalism is important since the state is too big and diverse for them to meet at one time. Both the Department of Motor Vehicles and the coordinators conduct conferences which serve as an exchange of ideas about programs and technology.

One basic benefit of the STOP-DWI program, aside from its autonomous structure, is that the agencies and localities have no fear of a change in administrative priorities which may cancel funding. Since the program is self-sufficient, a new administration or agency head cannot eliminate the programs.

Another feature of the STOP-DWI program is that it works within the existing criminal justice system. This eliminates any redundancy from a dual system and reduces the communication problems associated with a dual justice system.

Currently, the Institute for Traffic Safety Management and Research, an independent state agency, is evaluating the STOP-DWI program in New York. Though the success of the program still is under investigation, data regarding STOP-DWI do exist. In 1979-81, the annual average for fatal accidents was 2,294. In 1982, this was reduced to 1,947, and in 1983, to 1,981 for 15 percent and 16 percent reductions respectively. There was also a large decrease in fatal accidents occurring between 10 p.m. and 5 a.m., the most likely time for alcohol involvement. The 1979-81 average was 984. In 1982, there were 691 fatalities between 10 p.m. and 5 a.m., a 23 percent decrease, and in 1983 there were 614 such fatalities, a 37 percent decrease. Obviously the efforts of New York State have had some effect; the impact of the program needs to be investigated further.

Program Objectives

The objectives for the STOP-DWI program center on autonomous, county-based, self-sustaining programs. Specifically, STOP-DWI programs were conceived and enacted to place the creation of solutions where the problems occur--at the local level. This allowed each county to be unique and create the programs it citizens felt were most needed and appropriate. STOP-DWI programs were designed to establish real deterrence for drunk driving and to provide the necessary resources to achieve this goal.

In creating these county-based programs, the legislature hoped to increase communication among the counties concerning drunk driving. County coordinators serve this role, encouraging the sharing of program ideas and plans and creating an arena for interchange concerning problems and difficulties. It also was hoped that the coordinators at the county level would have the freedom to act within the political environment to ease conflict, thus creating effective programs to meet the needs of their respective counties.

The objectives for the county programs were broadly defined. Much flexibility was given to each coordinator, since specific program requirements were not a part of the 1980 legislation. By placing the monies at the local level, it was hoped that the problem of drinking and driving would not be dismissed but would instead be attacked effectively and creatively by concerned members of the community.

Program Implementation

As mentioned earlier, each county in New York was encouraged to design its own STOP-DWI program. Hence, the implementation of the overall program objectives came in many different forms. At present, all counties have a STOP-DWI program which has been custom designed by and for its citizens. Each program places different weights on various ways of approaching the drinking driver problem. The major program areas include enforcement, prosecution and adjudication, rehabilitation, public education, and public information. Fine monies are spent to fit the particular problems of the county. In the aggregate, 45.1 percent of all money was spent on enforcement and 15 percent on prosecution in 1983. The remainder was spread evenly across adjudication, probation, rehabilitation, public information, and education. Another large percentage, 12.7, was allocated for administration. Obviously, enforcement and prosecution receive the greatest attention. This disturbs those who espouse the public-health approach, where emphasis is placed on rehabilitation and treatment for the alcoholic as a balance to the punitive approach.

The implementation of the county programs was, of course, made possible because of the funding mechanism created by the state. Ample, if not overly plentiful, amounts of money were generated by fines from DWI offenders. Revenues in 1984 approached $14 million. Coordinators are responsible for the allocation of these monies. Although their job was made more difficult because specific guidelines for STOP-DWI programs were not provided by the state, coordinators have created unique programs and shared information and ideas.

The original implementation of the county programs was a simple process. Each county that wanted to participate in the program had to file a letter of intent with the Department of Motor Vehicles. This earmarked all fines collected by the county from that point on for its future DWI plans. After the appointment of a coordinator, a county STOP-DWI plan was submitted to the Office of Alcohol and Highway Safety in the Department of Motor Vehicles. This was reviewed, and if it met minimal requirements, approval was automatic. The main requirement was that the programs be unique and not mere duplications of previous county or state efforts. This implementation process took up to twelve months from letter of intent to final approval.

Upon approval, fine monies are channeled to the county to be spent according to the local STOP-DWI plan. Although line item allocations are not detailed, any major expense change not in accordance with the plan is submitted for future approval. During the year, coordinators are obligated to report on activities and monies spent, without being required to justify the logic or reasonableness of a program. Aside from some administrative changes, the approval process remains the same in the following year.

New York City's STOP-DWI Program

A representative STOP-DWI program is that of New York City, which covers the five boroughs which include Manhattan, Brooklyn, Bronx, Staten Island, and Queens. The total budget for fiscal year 1985 is $1,517,306 and is divided among enforcement, public information, administration, public education, rehabilitation, and prosecution. The overall objectives of the plan are reduction of traffic fatalities, injuries, and amount of drunk driving; increased enforcement, conviction, and education; and continuation of the existing advisory committees.

One unique aspect of the New York City program involves the STOP-DWI program advisory committees. These committees are composed of citizens, professionals, academics, and politicians. The committees address areas of concern such as legislation, public education, insurance, rehabilitation, criminal justice, and citizen issues. The committees exist to recommend programming and determine the needs of the five boroughs in confronting the drunk driver problem.

In enforcement, there is a FY 1985 budget of $555,520. One component to be increased is the "Roving Patrol Program" or STOP-DWI Task Force. During FY 1984, it included eighteen officers and one supervisor engaged in specialized traffic patrol on both limited access highways and streets. Each group is equipped with "alco-sensors" to conduct breath tests prior to arrest. These are prescreening devices used to make an initial determination of alcohol involvement. Other programming includes sobriety checkpoints. During the past year, there were 1,678 checkpoints which stopped 743,000 motorists and led to 3,242 arrests.

Public information is budgeted at $285,000 for FY 1985. One component is the "Dry Driver Program," which began in Staten Island in cooperation with bar and restaurant owners. Under this program, the group member identified as the "dry driver" for the evening receives complimentary nonalcoholic beverages. Other components include increased television, radio, and printed advertisements as well as increased use of bumper stickers and general literature. FY 1985 will expand the "Dry Driver Program" and coordinate activities with the various civic groups.

In administration, the FY 1985 budget is $240,000, which will be used to identify problem areas, increase staff training, and create a liaison with the state Department of Motor Vehicles and other citizen groups. There also will be an emphasis on evaluating the STOP-DWI programs and a concentrated effort to coordinate activities in the five boroughs.

Public education has a budget of $160,000 for FY 1985. This includes expansion of the "Starting Early Program." This education program addresses groups from kindergarten to the sixth grade. In FY 1985, this should expand to junior high schools as well as presentations being formulated for the high schools. There will be increased coordination with the Board of Education, the Archdiocese of New York, and the Automobile Club of America. A Students Against Driving Drunk conference is scheduled for fall 1985 as well as participation in campus "Alcohol Awareness Days."

Rehabilitation has a FY 1985 budget of $150,000, which will concentrate on efforts to expand treatment centers and on reviewing proposals to determine the necessary components for a strong rehabilitation program.

The remainder of the budget, $126,784, is for prosecution and adjudication. Other programs include appointing an assistant district attorney in each borough to deal exclusively with prosecuting DWI cases. There will be experimental use of Batmobiles and a study to determine if all fine monies are recycled back to the STOP-DWI programs.

The New York City budget breakdown is 37 percent for enforcement, 18 percent for public information, 16 percent for administration, 11 percent for public education, 10 percent for rehabilitation, and 8 percent for prosecution and adjudication. Revenues from fines are estimated at $1,205,500. When added to $1,080,414 of 1984 rollover, this leaves New York City with a potential of nearly $2.3 million to combat the DWI problem. In FY 1984, fatalities decreased 27.2 percent from FY 1982 to 491; arrests increased 138 percent, from 3,260 in FY 1982 to 7,752 in FY 1984. Obviously, the approach New York City has undertaken has been successful, and 1985 promises to see an even stronger effort.

Nassau County's STOP-DWI Program

Another representative county STOP-DWI program is that of Nassau County, a large county located outside of New York City. The 1984 plan is broken down into individual budgets for enforcement, prosecution, adjudication, probation, rehabilitation, public information, education, program evaluation, and program administration. These are followed by a summary budget and narrative. Included in these individual budgets is a statement, which outlines the problem and the objectives to be achieved.

For example, the total enforcement budget was $525,000 for 1984. The stated problem was a decline in the number of arrests due to staff reductions. The main objectives were to include all enforcement agencies in programs and increase the number of enforcers to reduce the alcohol-related fatalities. Other objectives were to train officers in the implementation of tests and arrests at the lower BAC levels.

Highlights of the 1984 budget include the allocation of $120,000 for prosecution with the goal of preventing backlogs in the courts as county arrests increase, especially at the lower BAC levels. Another goal was to dedicate prosecutors to only DWI. No monies were allocated for adjudication. Probation was allocated $195,000 with the goal of maintaining liaisons with courts, prosecution, and treatment services as well as decreasing the number of recidivists from probation. Rehabilitation was allocated $260,000 to provide increased treatment services.

The Nassau County 1984 budget was $1,200,000, of which $1,115,864 was for personal service. The budget narrative emphasized the need to concentrate on enforcement due to the drop in arrests from previous years. It further advocated better relations between police officers and the coordinator, as well as a continuation of working relationships with business, civic, and educational organizations such as MADD and SADD. The final note of the summary was to encourage continuous vigorous public information programs especially the distribution of pamphlets and posters.

State Recommendations

The people in New York are extremely pleased with their STOP-DWI program in its present form. Most officials would not change anything. However, some administrative problems have been identified for which there are no definite, viable solutions. These unsolvable problems will be addressed here. Although many of the problems cannot be presently dealt with in New York, some of them could be addressed if the program were implemented in Texas.

The biggest problem is that not enough groundwork was done before the program was started. One especially unfortunate mistake was the failure to collect data on the status of the DWI problem in New York; these data could have been used as a baseline for evaluating the STOP-DWI program after it was implemented. As a result, there is not an adequate "before" picture to accurately assess the impact of the program. Along the same lines, every county in New York was included in the new program, so no control group exists to isolate the STOP-DWI program effects from other factors contributing to a decrease in drunk driving accidents. For example, nighttime crashes, which are used as a proxy for driving while intoxicated, have recently decreased throughout the United States. The largest decrease in accidents in New York came immediately after the STOP-DWI program was implemented and may not be solely attributable to the STOP-DWI program. Rather, it may be part of a larger nationwide trend.

Another problem developed because the New York Department of Motor Vehicles failed to determine precisely what data needed to be collected from the counties before implementing the program. The state originally asked for all collected information, intending to discard the useless data. The result was that many counties were overwhelmed. Perhaps the state should have consulted with a research institution before implementing the program to determine the essential data necessary for a comprehensive evaluation of the program. Then New York could have stressed quality over quantity and been more insistent in demanding that the data be sent to the state as a requisite for participation in the program.

Another problem which surfaced before the program began was an insufficient staff at the state level to handle the processing of the county plans. Many counties needed guidance in designing their programs in the first few years to ensure that they used a sufficiently detailed line-item budget and spent the money properly. The counties also needed to communicate with other counties to discover what their plans were like; the counties possibly could have benefitted from a prototype program designed by the state as a base from which to work.

Certain budgeting techniques led to the current problem of a lack of accountability. Many New York officials agree that a professional audit is necessary and that the state needs to substantially tighten its oversight function. The state does not seek to threaten county autonomy, because autonomy is the backbone of the program, but access to the large quantities of money generated by the program must be closely monitored to avoid problems of corruption.

The fact that so much money has been generated so quickly has led to another unexpected potential problem. According to the law, the interest generated from STOP-DWI does not have to be spent on DWI-related activities. In addition, the STOP-DWI fund does not have to be spent in its entirety every year; the money can remain in the account indefinitely. This provision was designed to encourage counties to spend the money wisely rather than rushing to use the money up every year for fear of losing it. The problem is that some accounts have become so large that a substantial amount of interest is being earned and channeled into the counties' general revenue funds. The earning of interest could encourage counties to use the accounts for this purpose rather than to spend the money on STOP-DWI functions. Although rollover has not yet become a serious problem, a possible solution is to earmark the interest for STOP-DWI activities. The accounting of such a program is so complex that close scrutiny by Texas officials is essential.

One obvious problem is that the design of STOP-DWI places emphasis on enforcement and adjudication. Each county can only spend as much money as is generated by fines resulting from arrests and prosecutions. Hence, the more prosecutions, the more fine monies there are to be spent within the county. A county with little previous enforcement must thereby generate these fines through increased arrests before any money is made available for other areas of programming such as treatment and rehabilitation. This might result in questionable arrests conducted solely for the purpose of generating more funds. One solution for this would be a statewide distribution of those STOP-DWI funds that counties fail to spend. Or, the legislature might allocate money to those areas which are in greatest need.

In sum, New York officials have no recommendations at this time for changing the program as it now exists, but they do offer some valuable insights into what should be done differently if the program were to be implemented in Texas. Texas should not rush into the program before the necessary groundwork has been accomplished. Also, Texas should expect the program to change and mature over the years as the counties become more confident in both themselves and the state's role, learning to trust that the funding will continue.

Conclusions

The STOP-DWI program offers much to states interested in innovative programs to combat the problem of drinking and driving. The program is attractive because it makes the DWI offender, not the taxpayer, assume the costs associated with the program. It has been successful in encouraging long-range planning because the money is guaranteed and continues to increase. Furthermore, STOP-DWI allows the counties to develop a program suited to their particular needs and interests. The state is only minimally involved. This approach puts the incentive and money at the local level, where the problem occurs. The STOP-DWI program is politically popular with the residents of New York and undoubtedly will continue to be used.

On the negative side, the program has the potential to create conflict in the counties. There always will be disagreement about how the money should be spent, so in-county squabbling can be expected. Most important, there is no concrete evidence that the program works to stop or significantly reduce driving while intoxicated. Throwing money at a problem, even money that is readily available, may not do anything to solve the problem.

The STOP-DWI program has excellent potential for implementation in Texas. Texas could benefit from New York's experience by hiring a research organization to thoroughly study the New York STOP-DWI program, conduct the necessary baseline research, establish a control group, and design a similar program suited to Texas's needs. The group could determine in advance the data needed from the counties for evaluation purposes and design a prototype program for the counties.

Before implementing the program here, several issues should be examined. Texas might consider including the Department of Public Safety's Highway Patrol in the program. This was not seen as necessary in New York, but in Texas the Highway Patrol arrests a significantly higher proportion of the DWI drivers than in New York. This has the potential problem, however, of blurring the separation between the state and county. On the other hand, excluding the Highway Patrol might cause animosity between local and state law enforcement officials.

The New York legislation contains a built-in emphasis on spending money for enforcement and prosecution. This places a strain on other elements in the DWI system, namely treatment and rehabilitation. These functions get overloaded with handling the DWI offender, but do not receive their share of dollars to deal with the problem. Texas may wish to alter the wording of the legislation to address this imbalance. It has not yet been proven that emphasis on any one component is more effective in stopping the DWI problem, so it seems unwise to spend a majority of resources in one area. Other areas which need attention, according to the New York Division of Alcoholism and Alcohol Abuse, include the stricter enforcement of the minimum age to legally purchase alcohol and more education programs on the hazards of drinking and driving.

Overall, this is a program with great potential for Texas. It could be very beneficial in reducing the DWI problem, with no costs imposed on the non-DWI taxpayer. The problems thus far identified are all minor and could be avoided when developing a similar program for Texas.

PENNSYLVANIA

Background

The Commonwealth of Pennsylvania has a population of approximately 11.9 million, with nearly 7.4 million licensed drivers. In 1983, there were 7.6 million registered vehicles. The legal drinking age in Pennsylvania is twenty-one. The state defines a BAC level of .10 percent as being "illegal per se." In 1983, Pennsylvania law enforcement officers made 30,100 DUI arrests.[3] In 1984, officials arrested almost 33,000 people for DUI. During 1983, alcohol-related accidents accounted for 40 percent, or 634, of Pennsylvania's 1,570 traffic fatalities. It is estimated that in 1984, 610 people died in alcohol-related traffic fatalities on Pennsylvania roads and highways.

Relevant Drunk Driving Legislation

Pennsylvania's major legislation dealing with the problem of drinking drivers is Act 1982-289, Title 75 (Vehicle Code), which became effective January 1, 1983. The law authorizes the use of a nonevidentiary preliminary breath test (PBT) in order to determine the need for full testing, and establishes the right for a law enforcement official to request full chemical testing of DUI offenders. Properly trained civilians may administer the official breath tests. Test refusal, admissible as evidence, results in a mandatory twelve-month license suspension. Pennsylvania does not grant "hardship" allowances or exceptions for license suspensions. No reduction or modification of the DUI charges is allowed at the preliminary arraignment, and a BAC level of .10 percent is considered an offense per se.

All persons charged with DUI must be evaluated by a state-certified analyst and the evaluations entered into the Court Reporting Network (CRN) before sentencing. The CRN uses a presentence investigation questionnaire to gather information on an offender. This information is then combined with the person's driving record, and the Pennsylvania Department of Transportation (PennDOT) generates a report. Output from the CRN evaluation can be used to adjudicate the case. In addition, the Secretary of Transportation may enter into reciprocal agreements with other states on DUI matters, such as sharing driver information kept on the CRN system or requesting records on out-of-state drivers.

---

[3]The charge of drinking and driving is referred to in Pennsylvania statutes as driving while under the influence, so as to encompass both alcohol and drug abuse. Since this section of the report deals specifically with Pennsylvania and its programs, the term DUI, as opposed to DWI, will be used.

Pennsylvania has a process whereby first offenders who meet certain criteria may receive Accelerated Rehabilitative Disposition, or ARD. Pennsylvania law does not consider acceptance of ARD as a conviction, but ARD is noted on the offender's driving record. A person is not eligible for ARD if he has had a prior ARD or was convicted of DUI in the past seven years. Also, a person is not eligible for ARD if guilty of committing a serious traffic violation in connection with the present offense, or if a DUI-related accident resulted in death or serious injury. If the offender accepts ARD, he must agree to pay restitution, go through probation, and have his license suspended for one to twelve months. The judge can revoke ARD for failure to meet program conditions or commission of another serious traffic offense. After seven years, PennDOT drops the ARD from the offender's driving record. Acceptance of ARD is viewed as a first conviction--for enhancement purposes--if another DUI-related conviction occurs within seven years. Persons convicted of DUI or sentenced to ARD must attend and pay the required costs for the state-sponsored alcohol highway safety school and treatment deemed necessary by the court or probation office.

Pennsylvania law classifies DUI as a misdemeanor offense, with a fine of not less than $300 or more than $5,000, and up to two years in prison. Minimum terms of imprisonment for DUI are forty-eight consecutive hours for a first conviction, thirty days for a second conviction, and ninety days for a third conviction; subsequent convictions result in terms of not less than one year. The commonwealth can appeal any sentences not meeting these minimum guidelines. DUI-related homicide by vehicle is a felony offense with a minimum prison sentence of three years. Any DUI conviction results in a flat twelve-month license suspension, which cannot be appealed. Driving while under a DUI-related license suspension is a summary offense with a fine of $1,000 and a minimum imprisonment of ninety days.

Notable Features of the Pennsylvania Drunk Driving System

The strongest aspect of Pennsylvania's drunk driving program is the emphasis on management information systems. The Pennsylvania Department of Transportation (PennDOT) maintains a computer-assisted information system known as the Court Reporting Network, or CRN. The CRN links county DUI programs into a statewide network which evaluates persons charged with DUI and catalogs standardized summary information about offenders. The Pennsylvania Department of Health (DOH) maintains another system of computerized records known as the Uniform Data Collection System (UDCS). The UDCS reporting system records the number and types of admissions to alcohol and other treatment programs. The system does not actually track individuals as they progress through the treatment because of client confidentiality considerations. Finally, the City and County of Philadelphia operate an independent system known as NEXUS. Once a person is assigned a trial date or enters treatment specified by ARD probation requirements, the offender's progress is tracked through information provided to NEXUS. NEXUS information is available only for Philadelphia.

The CRN's role begins with a legally mandated evaluation by a certified evaluator. Everyone charged with DUI must go through a CRN evaluation. The questions on the survey are designed to solicit information on types of beverages consumed, age and educational background, emotional condition, BAC at the time of arrest, and other variables. Evaluations are done by county personnel who take an average forty-five minutes to one hour to complete an assessment. The information then is sent to PennDOT headquarters and keyed into the agency's computer. The resulting printout incorporates survey information with a person's driving record, puts the accused into a "drinker classification," and recommends a sentence. CRN data analysis takes four to five days, and the printout is sent to the presiding judge for the case. Many judges take the CRN assessment into account during the sentencing phase of the trial; in other cases, the CRN is used to help decide on probation conditions.

The CRN also lets county officials know if a person is eligible for pretrial diversion or Accelerated Rehabilitative Disposition (ARD). A first offender may be sentenced to ARD if he or she meets certain criteria. Persons on ARD must attend the alcohol safety school, have their licenses suspended, and go through probation, which involves alcohol treatment in some cases. The CRN notes the ARD on the person's driving record, but PennDOT erases the citation after seven years if the individual does not commit another DUI offense. Almost 70 percent of Pennsylvania's offenders participate in the ARD program, which in turn relieves the courts and jails.

Persons not eligible for ARD go to trial. Upon conviction, an offender must enroll in an alcohol highway safety school, serve whatever prison term is assigned, and often undergo alcohol treatment or counseling. Should the person be sentenced to treatment as well as to the alcohol highway safety school, the Pennsylvania Department of Health takes responsibility for monitoring the individual's progress. UDCS records each admission and notes the reason for admission. Because the UDCS intake form (see Exhibit 5) allows the admissions clerk to chose only one of several different options--including probation, a court sentence, or DUI--it is difficult to gather statistics on the number of DUIs a facility has admitted. There is no evaluation to test the effectiveness of the program regarding the client's progress or possible change in attitude toward drinking. Each facility defines successful completion of a program as a person's attendance at every meeting. Pennsylvania currently does not track offenders as DUIs within the UDCS. Although the Department of Health compiles summary statistics for all counties, the department does not have definitive information on total DUI-related admissions.

Philadelphia's NEXUS system records information about convicted DUI offenders from the time the municipal court system assigns them a number until they complete the terms of their sentence, including any alcohol treatment. ARD candidates are added to the system if and when they enter a treatment program. The Philadelphia NEXUS system works in conjunction with the municipal court's management information system.

Exhibit 5
Pennsylvania Uniform Data Collection System — Client Admission Form

UDCS

UNIFORM DATA COLLECTION SYSTEM
CLIENT MANAGEMENT
OFFICE OF DRUG AND ALCOHOL PROGRAMS
DEPARTMENT OF HEALTH

CA

IF ANOTHER SCA REFERRED THIS CLIENT, ENTER THE CODE OF THE REFERRING SCA (SEE SCA CODES ON BACK) — REFERRING SCA

CLIENT ADMISSION (CHANGE °☐)

A.
- FACILITY NUMBER
- CLIENT NUMBER
- ADMISSION DATE (MO DAY YR)
- SEX (1-M 2-F)
- DATE OF BIRTH (MO YR)

CLIENT REFERRED BY:
- 01 SELF
- 02 HOSPITAL
- 03 COMM. MENTAL HEALTH CENTER
- 04 COMM. SERVICES AGENCIES/INDVS
- 05 FAMILY/FRIEND
- 06 EMPLOYER
- 07 SCHOOL
- 08 DWI
- 09 OTHER VOLUNTARY
- 10 TASC
- 11 DIVERSION PROGS
- 12 CO. PROBATION
- 13 STATE PROBATION
- 14 FED. PROBATION
- 15 CO. PAROLE
- 16 STATE PAROLE
- 17 FED. PAROLE
- 18 OTHER NON-VOLUNTARY

ADMIT TYPE:
- 1 FIRST ADMISSION ANY FACILITY WITHIN PROJECT
- 2 READMISSION ANY FACILITY WITHIN PROJECT
- 3 TRANSFER FROM ANY FACILITY WITHIN PROJECT

IF TRANSFERRED, ENTER LAST FACILITY NUMBER — 9

B. WHY IS CLIENT IN TREATMENT?
- 10 | 1 OWN D/A PROBLEM
- 2 OTHER'S D/A PROBLEM

IF ENTRY IS NOT OWN D/A PROBLEM SKIP TO E.

PREVIOUS TREATMENT
- 1 NONE
- 2 DRUG
- 3 ALCOHOL
- 4 BOTH

IF ENTRY IS NONE SKIP TO C.

- NUMBER OF PRIOR TREATMENT EXPERIENCES
- MONTHS SINCE LAST TREATMENT EXPERIENCE

REASON FOR DISCHARGE FROM LAST TREATMENT EXPERIENCE:
1. COMPLETED TREATMENT AND NOT TRANSFERRED OR REFERRED
2. LEFT WITH FACILITY ADVICE
3. LEFT AGAINST FACILITY ADVICE
4. NON-COMPLIANCE WITH FACILITY RULES
5. TRANSFERRED OR REFERRED
6. JAILED

WHAT KIND OF FACILITY:
1. D&A FACILITY
2. NON D&A FACILITY
3. CORRECTIONAL FACILITY

C. PATTERN OF DRUG USE
Columns: DRUG | SEVERITY | FREQ. | HOW TAKEN | AGE OF FIRST USE
- 17 | 1 | | 19 |
- | | | 24 |
- | | | 29 |

DRUG CODES:
- 02 HEROIN
- 03 ILLEGALLY OBTAINED METHADONE
- 04 OTHER OPIATES AND SYNTHETICS
- 05 ALCOHOL
- 06 BARBITURATES
- 07 TRANQUILIZERS
- 08 OTHER SEDATIVES, HYPNOTICS (METHAQUALONE)
- 09 AMPHETAMINES
- 10 COCAINE
- 11 MARIJUANA/HASHISH
- 12 HALLUCINOGENS
- 13 INHALANTS (GLUE)
- 14 NON-PRESCRIPTION OVER-THE-COUNTER
- 15 PCP
- 99 OTHER

SEVERITY: 1 MAJOR 2 SECOND 3 THIRD 9 USED IT DURING MONTH BEFORE ADMISSION BUT DO NOT CONSIDER IT A PROBLEM

FREQUENCY:
- 0 NO USE DURING MONTH PRIOR TO ADMISSION
- 1 MORE THAN 3 TIMES A DAY
- 2 2 OR 3 TIMES A DAY
- 3 ONCE A DAY
- 4 SEVERAL TIMES A WEEK
- 5 ONCE A WEEK
- 6 LESS THAN ONCE A WEEK

HOW TAKEN: 1 SWALLOWED 2 SMOKED 3 SNORTED 4 SNIFFED 5 SKIN POPPED 6 MAINLINED

D. NUMBER OF ARRESTS IN 24 MONTHS BEFORE ADMISSION
- 31 DWI
- 32 FELONY
- 33 MISDEMEANOR

E. RACE ETHNIC
- 1 WHITE
- 2 BLACK
- 3 HISPANIC-PUERTO RICAN
- 4 HISPANIC-MEXICAN
- 5 HISPANIC-CUBAN
- 6 HISPANIC-OTHER
- 7 AMERICAN INDIAN
- 8 ASIAN OR PACIFIC ISLANDER
- 9 ALASKAN NATIVE

CURRENT COUNTY OF RESIDENCE (SEE CODES ON BACK)

CURRENT MARITAL STATUS:
- 1 NEVER MARRIED
- 2 MARRIED
- 3 SEPARATED
- 4 DIVORCED
- 5 WIDOWED

LIVING ARRANGEMENT: 37
- 1 ALONE
- 2 WITH PARENTS
- 3 WITH SPOUSE AND/OR CHILDREN
- 4 WITH OTHERS

DOES CLIENT PROVIDE PHYSICAL CARE FOR ONE OR MORE DEPENDENTS? 38 — 1 YES 2 NO

HIGHEST GRADE COMPLETED — ENTER 00-20

STUDENT IN EDUCATION OR TRAINING PROGRAM — 1 YES 2 NO

CURRENT EMPLOYMENT STATUS:
1. FULL TIME (35 OR MORE HOURS PER WK)
2. PART TIME (LESS THAN 35 HOURS PER WK)
3. RETIRED
4. UNEMPLOYED-HAS SOUGHT EMPLOYMENT IN LAST 30 DAYS
5. UNEMPLOYED-HAS NOT SOUGHT EMPLOYMENT IN LAST 30 DAYS
6. LEAVE OF ABSENCE

NO. OF MOS. EMPLOYED IN LAST TWO YEARS — ENTER 00-24

F. IF MEDICATION IS A PRIMARY PART OF TREATMENT, ENTER CODE
49
1. METHADONE
2. LAAM
3. NALOXONE
4. CYCLAZOCINE
5. DISULFIRAM (ANTABUSE)
6. OTHER ANTAGONIST
7. NALTREXONE
8. OTHER

USUAL OCCUPATION:
- 01 PROFESSIONAL, TECHNICAL, MANAGERIAL
- 02 OFFICE, CLERICAL, SALES
- 03 CRAFTSMAN
- 04 ENTERTAINER, MUSICIAN
- 05 OPERATIVE
- 06 SERVICE WORKER
- 07 LABORER
- 08 OTHER
- 09 NO WORK EXPERIENCE
- 10 STUDENT
- 11 HOUSEWIFE

ACTIVITY/APPROACH

CURRENT GROSS WEEKLY LEGAL INCOME: PERSONAL | PUBLIC ASSISTANCE
- 1 NONE
- 2 GENERAL
- 3 MEDICAL
- 4 ADC
- 5 SSI
- 6 SRS

DOES CLIENT HAVE HEALTH INSURANCE: 48
- 1 NONE
- 2 BLUE CROSS/BLUE SHIELD
- 3 OTHER PRIVATE INSURANCE
- 4 MEDICAID/MEDICARE
- 5 CHAMPUS
- 6 OTHER PUBLIC INSURANCE

ACTIVITY/APPROACH MATRIX

ACTIVITY ↓ / APPROACH →	DETOX	MAINTENANCE	DRUG FREE	OTHER CHEMOTHERAPY	EXPERIMENTAL
INPATIENT NON-HOSPITAL	821		823	824	825
INPATIENT HOSPITAL	831		833	834	835
CORRECTIONAL INSTITUTION	841		843		845
PARTIAL HOSPITALIZATION	851		853	854	855
OUTPATIENT	861	862	863	864	865
SHELTER	871		873		875

G. FOR SHORT TERM DETOX CLIENTS ONLY
- DATE OF DISCHARGE (MO DAY YR)
- REASON FOR DISCHARGE

1. COMPLETED TREATMENT AND NOT TRANSFERRED OR REFERRED
2. LEFT WITH FACILITY ADVICE
3. JAILED
4. LEFT AGAINST FACILITY ADVICE
5. NON-COMPLIANCE WITH FACILITY RULES
6. TRANSFER WITHIN PROJECT
7. REFERRED OUTSIDE PROJECT
8. JAILED
9. DEATH

H. STAFF I.D.

GCDAA 207 1/79   **COUNCIL COPY**

Program Objectives

Of the approximately eight million licensed drivers in Pennsylvania, about 10 percent, or 800 thousand, are estimated to be problem drinkers. The Commonwealth of Pennsylvania recently began an integrated health and legal systems approach to DUI, incorporating the law enforcement, judicial, education, and rehabilitation sectors. A key element in this system is the information gathered through the Court Reporting Network (CRN).

Until recently, Pennsylvania dealt with its drinking drivers in a punitive fashion, paying little attention to the need to change the behavior patterns of the DUI offender. Law enforcement officials arrested individuals driving under the influence of alcohol or other drugs, while the courts adjudicated, sentenced, and imposed various sanctions on the offender. Often, judges found drinking drivers not guilty or else allowed a person to plead guilty to a lesser charge. In rare instances, judges required convicted offenders to seek treatment as part of their sentences. No agency collected information on DUI charges or convictions, and one could not be sure if it was a person's first offense or if they were a repeat offender.

Compounding the problem of inconsistencies in the court system, the commonwealth did not have a standardized educational process. Pennsylvania has since developed a comprehensive alcohol highway safety school program, with attendance required of persons charged with DUI or diverted through the ARD program. Moreover, the state moved to educate judges and county officials concerning the scope of the drinking driver problem. In addition, Pennsylvania now requires more alcohol counseling and/or intensive treatment of all persons convicted of DUI or diverted through ARD.

Because Pennsylvania's policymakers did not feel they were addressing the drinking driver problem adequately, they decided to try a new method. The health and legal approach is based on the premise that a successful DUI program requires a close working relationship between the judicial system and the community health network in each county. The Commonwealth provides oversight and direction, but the counties are responsible for carrying out the program. This cooperative systems approach partially originated in the Pennsylvania Motor Vehicle Code, Title 75, Act 1982-289. Title 75 mandates CRN evaluation and the designation of a DUI coordinator for each county. The coordinator facilitates interactions between the criminal justice system and the alcohol education and treatment agencies. The DUI coordinators are responsible for planning, implementing, and monitoring the county alcohol highway safety program.

Court Reporting Network (CRN)

The CRN gives county DUI coordinators vital statistical information, which enables them to do their jobs. By gathering and meshing information of past driving history, alcohol use, prior alcohol-related treatment, license and insurance status, source of income, and an alcohol highway safety evaluation, the CRN generates a Client Profile Form (CPF), which not only details this information but also recommends appropriate treatment strategies. Because Title 75 mandates the CRN evaluation by a state-certified evaluator, Pennsylvania is able to gather statewide, standardized information on drinking drivers.

The CRN process begins with the evaluation interview. The Client Intake Form (CIF)--see Appendix 8--is a screening tool designed to aid the county evaluation unit in the analysis of DUI offenders. Evaluators must complete three days of training before the state issues certification. Training includes learning how to identify drug and alcohol abusers, how to elicit answers from an evasive person, and the significance of each section of the CIF. The CIF includes approximately seventy-five questions taken from the Mortimer-Filkins Test to identify problem drinkers, a quantity-frequency index, and an alcohol impairment index. The form profiles the alcohol-related history and current status of the offender while analyzing his behavior.

The answers to the CIF are sent to PennDOT, whose staff enter the information into the PennDOT computer; they then send the resulting Client Profile Form (CPF) to the originating county. If the CIF is not completed properly, PennDOT staff return it to the county and request a corrected form. The CPF is an individualized summary of a person's driving record, alcohol use, the results of the Mortimer-Filkins test, and recommendations for sentencing and treatment. In addition to generating individual reports, PennDOT computers generate both a statewide statistical report and reports on each county.

The state expended $300 thousand of section 402 funds over a four-year period on the Court Reporting Network (CRN) to cover development and implementation costs and to train personnel. An outside consultant was hired to develop the CRN. This expenditure does not include the hidden cost of two computer programmers who worked for a year to put the CRN on line-- that is, to make the CRN an operating system. Furthermore, every fiscal year, $40 thousand of section 402 funds are provided for updating manuals, continued training of personnel, and program evaluation. The state incurs another $40 thousand to $50 thousand in personnel costs for keypunching, processing, and verifying the information appearing on CRN forms. The counties are not supposed to incur any out-of-pocket costs. Counties receive the fees paid by DUI offenders.

Uniform Data Collection System

A judge may sentence a person charged with DUI or require an individual who has been diverted through the ARD to take treatment as part of the terms of probation. Publicly funded alcohol treatment programs in

Pennsylvania, with the exception of Veterans Administration (VA) hospitals and federal prisons, treated over 43,110 clients in 1983. The Office of Drug and Alcohol Programs (ODAP), a subunit of the Pennsylvania Department of Health, administers the state's drug and alcohol treatment programs. ODAP's Division of Program Monitoring ensures accountability for drug and alcohol services by regularly reviewing each county's programs. The DOH computers help in the process by analyzing data collected through the UDCS and the automated fiscal system. The Technical Support Section of ODAP has primary responsibility for UDCS. Section staff interact with the State Health Data Center and the Division of Data Processing. Additionally, the section staff train treatment facility and county health department staff members, and develop reporting compliance standards.

Pennsylvania designed the UDCS several years ago as the result of a grant from the federal government. State health department staff enter data from forms completed by individual treatment facilities. ODAP provides forms for client admission, client discharge, and facility summary information. The state also instructs facility personnel on form completion and provides a reference manual. The DOH aggregates admission and discharge information following treatment. The DOH uses facility summary forms to compile data on monthly activities.

The UDCS gathers information on the aggregate number of persons treated for drug and alcohol programs and compiles individual facility statistics. This allows Pennsylvania officials to calculate treatment costs per client and to predict trends and funding needs. The system also allows the commonwealth to monitor publicly funded treatment programs. There is no centralized clearinghouse for information from all treatment facilities in Pennsylvania. All publicly funded facilities, except VA hospitals and federal prisons, send in reports. Private facilities do not have to file reports. Several private programs receive some public funds and report on clients supported by those monies.

The UDCS reporting system records only the number of admissions to treatment in the facilities monitored by the DOH. The system is not set up to track an individual's progress through treatment because of difficulties with legislated confidentiality requirements. Consequently, an individual may move from one program to another and be counted as a new admission. Moreover, the initial intake form lists DUI as only one of several options for the reason for referral. Other options include court-ordered probation and referral by another program. A person may be sent to the treatment program as part of his DUI-related probation, but the intake staff may choose probation instead of DUI on the intake form because the questionnaire only allows for one choice.

The City and County of Philadelphia use the NEXUS system to track persons convicted of DUI or diverted into the ARD program and assigned to alcohol treatment. Philadelphia uses the CRN system to evaluate the DUI offender; the NEXUS program monitors the offender's progress through the use of court records, the CRN results and recommendations, and treatment records. The NEXUS program communicates with the municipal court system, tracking the offender by the municipal court case number.

Unlike the UDCS, NEXUS does allow specific monitoring of DUI cases throughout the treatment phase of the sentence. The Coordinating Office for Drug and Alcohol Abuse Programs (CODAAP) administers NEXUS. CODAAP is an agency of the City and County of Philadelphia, so information compiled for NEXUS is only for Philadelphia and does not cover the entire state.

Program Implementation

Implementation of Pennsylvania's DUI program occurs at the county level. Each county has a DUI coordinator appointed by the President Judge. The coordinator may be in the county's probation office, health department, or specialized drug and alcohol office. As an alternative, the county may contract with a private consultant or agency to do the work. In most cases, however, control remains in a public agency. Currently, probation officials administer 45 percent of county DUI programs. County health departments run an additional 45 percent of the programs, and private providers administer the remaining 10 percent of the programs. The county coordinator usually is a person who has the desire to push the DUI agenda and who also has good rapport with all of the various actors in the process. In some instances, sparsely-populated counties have joined together to form single-county authorities (SCAs), using a shared coordinator in order to save money.

Although Title 75 requires the CRN evaluation, and most counties have either an alcohol highway safety school or have established a school in conjunction with another county, each county has some discretion as to the comprehensiveness of its DUI program and when to administer the CRN evaluation. The law states that persons must be evaluated prior to being sentenced or diverted through ARD; however, this does not always happen. Most county officials view the CRN as an excellent tool for assessing treatment needs and use the CRN results, although some judges resist using the CRN results shown in the Client Profile Form (CPF) as a basis for sentencing because they do not wish to be told how to do their job. There also is some division as to how necessary it is for a judge to see the CRN results before deciding a case disposition. In general, ARD judges tend to rely more heavily on the CPF results than do judges who hear cases for repeat offenders. Title 75 does not require judges to read the CRN report or consider its recommendations for sentencing.

In Dauphin County, Pennsylvania, there is a three-week backlog for CRN evaluations. Harrisburg, the state capital, is the largest city in Dauphin County. Instead of requiring the person charged with DUI to undergo the CRN evaluation before coming to court, judges sometimes ask the county detectives to check for prior convictions or an ARD. The judge then either assigns the person to ARD or sentences the offender to jail and/or probation, stipulating that the CRN evaluation must be conducted before probation terms are set. The probation department then uses the CRN results to determine what type of probation the person should be required to follow. Dauphin County generally has about 85 percent of its DUI charges evaluated by the court date. The percentage for persons eligible for ARD is closer to 100 percent.

The City and County of Philadelphia require all persons charged with DUI to take the CRN evaluation prior to court appearance. Staff from the National Council on Alcoholism (NCA) evaluate the ARD candidates. The NCA is a private provider designated by the court to do CRN evaluations, oversee the alcohol highway safety school, and evaluate ARD candidates. Persons not eligible for ARD go to the Coordinating Office for Drug and Alcohol Abuse Programs (CODAAP) for assignment to a private agency for assessment. In Philadelphia, once a person has been to the CODAAP offices and been assigned to a CRN evaluator, that person also is logged into the NEXUS system. ARD candidates are put into the NEXUS system when and if they are assigned to a treatment program. NEXUS tracks all persons being treated on an alcohol-related charge, whether they are treated by a public or private facility.

According to county officials, over one-half of DUI offenders need treatment, but probably only one-third participate in an alcohol treatment program either as an outpatient or inpatient. Judges often are reluctant to assign indigents to treatment because they are expected to pay for the programs as specified by state law. Moreover, unless treatment is made a mandatory part of probation, participation in such programs is voluntary and patients cannot be forced to complete their stay. Probation is, however, revoked if the person does not complete the treatment. There is no provision for posttreatment evaluation of DUI offenders at this time, and treatment facilities do not usually give tests to determine if the client's attitudes toward alcohol use have changed as a result of treatment.

Although county probation officers know if a person is going through court-ordered treatment, the Commonwealth does not gather data on alcohol offenders as they complete treatment nor does it calculate recidivism rates for DUIs. There also is no easy way for one county official to tell what kind of treatment, if any, a judge or probation officer in another county may have required of an offender. The Office of Drug and Alcohol Programs currently is designing a new admission reporting form, which will help Pennsylvania gather information on DUIs admitted for treatment.

A significant problem in the modification of the Uniform Data Collection System, designed to "track" the DUI offender, is that of client confidentiality. Social security numbers and driver's license numbers cannot be used; instead, a facility assigns a client number to each individual as treatment begins. Should a client return to the same facility, the same number would likely be used again, while a different treatment center would issue a new number. The Pennsylvania Department of Health does not issue a unique client number per individual for the entire state. There are 490 service providers in Pennsylvania, including both outpatient and residential facilities.

PennDOT uses federal section 402 highway safety funds for the state program, and also provides "seed money" for the county programs. The county coordinators then may use these grants to develop subsystems or improvements to their programs. Day-to-day local program expenses, however, must be funded by the county. Funding for the local DUI programs comes from a combination of fines and fees. Title 75 mandates the distribution of fines for convicted offenders: 50 percent goes to the arresting municipality, 25 percent to the county in which the municipality is located, and 25 percent to either the county department of drug and alcohol services or the county health department. In some counties, such as Dauphin County, the DUI coordinator retains control of all of the funds collected from DUI fines, disbursing special grants to municipalities and health programs for DUI-related expenses. Persons attending the alcohol highway safety school must pay approximately $150 to cover its costs. The CRN assessment charge generally is $25. Individuals undergoing alcohol treatment must pay for those sessions as well. A sliding scale determines fees for indigent offenders.

Besides providing both the commonwealth and the counties with reliable statistics, the CRN saves Pennsylvania money by helping local program coordinators to work together as a statewide network. County officials have access to a comprehensive driving record and have a quick assessment tool at their fingertips. Moreover, the CRN's Client Profile Form rapidly identifies first offenders and recommends diversion into the ARD program, if appropriate. The ARD program saves about $10 thousand per offender in arrest, prosecution, and trial costs. With emphasis on education and prevention activities such as the self-supporting alcohol highway safety school, the state can intervene in the costly "repeat offender" syndrome so prevalent in DUI cases.

State Recommendations

Although Department of Health staff members expressed some concern over maintaining client confidentiality, in general Pennsylvania officials felt the state's information management process should be expanded to track offenders from the CRN evaluation to final treatment and/or end of the sentence. Some officials in Philadelphia felt a statewide system like NEXUS would fulfill this goal. The DOH would act as a centralized data collection system for the state--one which would assign a unique treatment number per individual and could look at statistics such as recidivism rates, types of treatment received, place of treatment, emergency room activities, and probationary terms. All parties in the DUI process should have direct access to the information. The system should be simple and require only data relevant to state policy decisions; some data currently collected is irrelevant and should be dropped from the forms. Pennsylvania officials also would like to have more information on persons treated in private facilities, prisons, and VA hospitals.

Dauphin County Health Department officials would like to see a formal referral, intervention, and treatment system for DUI clients. This system should emphasize rapid treatment referral, thorough and accurate client evaluations, and the development of short-term or intervention programs. The client monitoring system needs to document client evaluations and client progress, provide feedback to the courts or probation officers, and identify the need for court appearances or urinalysis monitoring, if appropriate. Pennsylvania should place special emphasis on repeat offenders by developing methods to ensure continued treatment after the mandatory jail sentence.

Another area of concern is young drinkers, specifically persons from eighteen to twenty-five years of age. While twenty-one is the minimum drinking age, eighteen is the age of legal maturity, and insurance rate breakpoints come at age twenty-five. Pennsylvania officials feel that persons in this age group tend to have different drinking habits than older individuals. Currently, PennDOT is developing a specialized CRN for this age group, which should address some of these concerns. Moreover, some county health officials feel there should be specialized alcohol treatment programs offered to young offenders.

In the future, PennDOT officials would like to see a "fast track" process for adjudication. Offenders could waive their right to a preliminary hearing and go to court within sixty days. PennDOT also plans to develop standardized kits, endorsed by the courts, which would set down procedures for processing offenders and would expedite offender processing. Further improvements would include legislation requiring counties to meet state program guidelines, and the establishment of standardized treatment guidelines for repeat offenders. Finally, PennDOT would like an amendment to Title 75, which would require judges to follow the CRN sentencing recommendations or explain why they chose another option.

State officials also see the need for standardized BAC testing. PennDOT staff suggested requiring a parallel system of blood tests to back up the breath test. Using a urine test may be another option. The state should also require hospitals to gather information on drinking drivers involved in accidents.

Finally, PennDOT officials hope to expand their public information program, both for public schools and the officers making the arrests. Because of recent trends involving the liability of beverage servers, Pennsylvania officials also will begin educational programs for bartenders, bar owners, and party hosts. Prevention activities are very important at the county level as well; Dauphin County officials recently chose "DUI Duck" (pronounced Dewey Duck) as the mascot for their campaign to stop drinking and driving.

Conclusions

Texas needs a management information system for its DWI program. The system should be capable of tracking offenders from arrest through the completion of their punishment and/or treatment. In order for this system to be sufficiently comprehensive, all actors must be required by law to submit standardized information on every person arrested for DWI. There are a great number of political complexities inherent in requiring local officials to comply with legislated standards; however, it is imperative that the DWI program be coordinated at the state level.

Texas officials should consider mandating a CRN-like evaluation, administered by certified, non-law-enforcement county staff. Evaluator training should emphasize dialogue and accuracy. In order to relieve the court backlog, Texas officials also should consider a statewide pretrial diversion program, which, like Pennsylvania's ARD, would stay on an offender's driving record. After the evaluation, the state should track the progress of the accused via the unique court number. Treatment should be part of the sentence, and tracking should be done as part of court requirements; however, records should continue to maintain client confidentiality. The initial start-up costs for a computerized tracking system would be high, but by using an ARD-type diversion program and a centralized conviction file, counties could save thousands of dollars in court costs. Presentence investigations would be easier and more efficient because every county would report all convictions to a central source. Counties also could access information on a DWI offender rapidly and inexpensively.

The comprehensive health and legal approach has merit. Instead of viewing the drinking problem as a health problem and the drinking driver problem as a legal problem, both must be addressed before the problem of drinking drivers will subside. Health officials should develop methods to determine whether various treatment strategies are working. Treatment should be tied to methods acknowledging the interactions between the health and legal aspects of the situation.

Finally, without some state agency to coordinate the information, this proposed system would not achieve its fullest potential. One agency should have responsibility for the system, and all counties must have access to information on treatment and prior convictions. A comprehensive approach to the problem of identifying the drinking driver can be achieved; without such an approach, Texas lawmakers will have difficulty enforcing even the current legislation.

SUMMARY

The preceding state program descriptions were comprehensive and detailed. It may prove helpful to briefly highlight the aspects of each program relevant to Texas. The following summary descriptions emphasize the areas of applicability to Texas.

Two Florida counties, Orange and Pinellas, provide excellent examples of effective DWI activities at the local level. While operating under Florida laws, the counties took the initiative in developing their programs. Both counties created programs that emphasize enforcement, public information, and education.

In Orange County, the sheriff's department's breath alcohol testing mobile units (Batmobiles) are the primary feature, used for both enforcement and public information and education. In terms of enforcement, the Batmobiles function most effectively as fixed testing sites while being rotated among high-visibility locations. Each Batmobile includes the equipment and paperwork necessary for testing and prosecuting DWI offenders. With closer access to a testing site, offenders are tested soon after being apprehended. With trained personnel in the Batmobile to perform the tests and videotape the offender, the officers' average arrest processing times decreased from five hours to thirty to forty-five minutes.

The Batmobiles also are used to inform and educate the public. The units are taken to junior and senior high school demonstrations. The deputies also are active in showing movies and making presentations as a part of their public education and information activities.

In Pinellas County, the "Arrest Drunk Driving" campaign focuses on officer training, enforcement, and public information and education. Police officers associated with the campaign received extensive enforcement training. As a part of the enforcement efforts, the use of roadblocks was increased. Altogether, only twelve checkpoints have been set up. The media publicized them to such an extent, however, that the public perceives them as a regular occurrence. Public information and education activities have centered on the "we will catch you" theme. The philosophy behind such publicity is that an enforcement campaign cannot survive without proper public information and education, and that public information and education is the most effective tool for changing societal attitudes regarding drinking and driving.

In both Orange and Pinellas counties, the use of videotaping was highly touted. Officials in both counties considered it as the main reason behind their increased conviction rates (which went from 67 to 92 percent in Orange County, and from 65 to 96 percent in Pinellas County). In regard to the increases in the conviction rates, several things must be considered. Other factors, such as the national awareness of DWI, occurred at the same time these two counties began using videotaping. This could account for some of the increase. Both counties emphasize close proximity to a test site; with the offender videotaped soon after arrest, there is less time for the driver to sober up. Videotaping currently is not mandated by Florida law, and some local officials strongly support the discretion left to the individual counties. They believe that law enforcement officers are generally more enthusiastic over voluntary practices initiated to satisfy local needs.

One other public education program in Florida that deserves to be mentioned are the efforts directed at college students. Through the BACCHUS program, an attempt is being made to provide peer support and education for making responsible decisions about drinking and driving. Also, the Florida Department of Health and Rehabilitative Services is providing help to students at Florida state universities who have been convicted of DWI.

The programs in Orange and Pinellas counties are specific examples of what can be accomplished through local initiative in a short period of time. The examples also lend support to the idea that local levels of government should be allowed the freedom to design programs that will most efficiently and effectively meet their needs. Finally, without the latitude given them by the state, and the generous support from the private sector, the programs in the two counties would not have achieved the same measure of success.

The most prominent feature of Minnesota's DWI system is its two-track method for handling DWI offenders. In the administrative track, a driver automatically loses his license for one year for refusing to take an alcohol concentration test, or for six months for testing at or above a level of .10 percent. The officer is authorized to take the license from the driver and issue a seven-day permit. The revocation is not stayed pending the outcome of a hearing, if one is requested by the driver. The administrative revocation is automatic, regardless of the outcome of any criminal charges. Because they have the ability to take the plastic license and know that the offender will receive some form of punishment, officers have dramatically increased the number of DWI arrests made in the state.

In the criminal track, the offender faces additional penalties if convicted. In the Twin Cities metropolitan area, first-time DWI offenders are generally sentenced to two days in jail and fined $200 to $300. Even if the sentence is plea bargained down, the driver's history contains a record of an alcohol-related offense due to the administrative revocation.

Minnesota was the first state to require that all convicted DWI offenders undergo an alcohol problem assessment. The assessment includes alcohol-related questions as well as questions about family situation and financial status. The assessment report includes information on the driver's traffic record, prior alcohol problems, and amenability to rehabilitation. The assessment is used to assign a level of alcohol problem and level of probation. It is used as an aid by the judge when sentencing.

A recent report by the Minnesota House Research Department recommended that to maintain a long-term reduction in alcohol-related accidents, DWI laws must be reviewed continually and amended. Also, societal disapproval of drinking and driving and moral commitment to upholding the laws must be encouraged. Encouragement can be in the form of public information and education. Several catalysts have helped in the continuous development of the DWI laws, including tragic examples of the damage drunk drivers can incur, heavy media attention, the joint effort by a governor and an attorney general, the efforts of citizen groups, expert testimony before the legislature, and favorable rulings by the state's courts.

Minnesota's strongest DWI efforts are at the state level, in areas that are the state's traditional functions, such as driver licensing and legislation. Changes to help the state's DWI control system also have facilitated local level DWI efforts. Also, along with increasing local enforcement efforts, the administrative license revocation automatically and immediately gets DWI offenders off the road.

New York, interested in retaining a community focus on the DWI problem, developed the Special Traffic Options Program for Driving While Intoxicated, or STOP-DWI. Counties that develop STOP-DWI programs and budgets receive all the fine money from DWI offenders in that county. While the state did not mandate participation, most counties have developed their own STOP-DWI program. Participating counties are required to appoint a coordinator, who has the responsibility of developing the DWI program and budget. Otherwise, state requirements are minimal.

There are several benefits to the STOP-DWI program. The county governments are granted the autonomy to develop DWI programs that are appropriate for that locale, while the state government still remains the overall coordinator and overseer. The county programs are funded by those who abuse the DWI laws; as more offenders are convicted, county funding increases. The counties do not have to fear that their funding will be cut off or that their priorities will be changed unexpectedly. Also, the STOP-DWI program is compatible with the existing criminal justice system.

All the counties have STOP-DWI programs designed by and for their citizens and facilitated by their county coordinators. Soon after STOP-DWI was initiated, the county coordinators formed an association. This has resulted in an additional benefit--the STOP-DWI Coordinators Association provides a forum for the exchange of ideas and information among the counties. In sum, STOP-DWI has provided New York with a state-coordinated, locally implemented, self-financing approach to the DWI problem.

Within the context of its health and legal approach, the Commonwealth of Pennsylvania has developed several programs for addressing the drinking driver problem. The three programs that would be most applicable to Texas are the Court Reporting Network (CRN), the Accelerated Rehabilitative Disposition (ARD), and the use of county coordinators to facilitate interaction between the criminal justice system and the alcohol education and treatment agencies.

The CRN gives the Commonwealth the capability to combine information on an offender's driving history, alcohol use, prior alcohol-related treatment, license and insurance status, income source, and an alcohol-highway safety evaluation. This information is generated into a Client Profile Form (CPF), which also recommends appropriate treatment, including diversion into the ARD program. The CRN also provides vital information to the county coordinators through aggregated county data and access to statewide information. Because of the CRN, the Commonwealth has centralized and standardized statewide information on drinking drivers.

The ARD program is a pretrial diversion mechanism used throughout the Commonwealth. In order to qualify for the ARD, certain basic criteria must be met. Participants in ARD must agree to pay restitution, attend an alcohol safety school, go through probation, have their licenses suspended for one to twelve months, and, in some cases, undergo alcohol treatment. ARD is not considered a first conviction for enhancement purposes unless another alcohol-related conviction occurs within seven years. The program saves time and money in the adjudication process and relieves overcrowding in jails.

While the Commonwealth provides oversight and direction for drunk driving activities, the counties are responsible for carrying out the programs. Pennsylvania law requires each county to have a DUI coordinator. Therefore, similar to Florida and New York, local government activities for attacking the drinking and driving problem are emphasized. The coordinator may be located in the county's probation office or health department or the county may contract with a private consultant.

The county coordinators are responsible for planning, implementing, and monitoring the county alcohol highway safety program. While the county coordinators must implement state programs, they also may develop additional programs of their own. Funding for county activities comes from federal section 402 highway safety funds dispersed by the Commonwealth and from a combination of fines and fees. Through the county coordinators, the Commonwealth ensures that counties adopt a minimum level of DWI activity, while at the same time allowing the counties the autonomy to develop additional programs.

CONCLUSIONS

In addressing the DWI problem, the programs surveyed take alternative means to deter drinking and driving. In two Florida counties, enforcement and public information and education are stressed. The State of Minnesota chooses to emphasize administrative procedures to ensure that their DWI system provides certainty of punishment. New York believes in a community-based approach to the problem. Pennsylvania, within its health and legal context, provides for a statewide management information system.

While the approaches taken within each state are varied, a few common themes are obvious. All of the programs were either locally initiated or facilitated local activity. DWI is a problem within each locality; the evidence appears to show that local programs, supported or encouraged by the state, are the most effective. Encouragement can be in the form of financial incentives, access to statewide information, or even the ability to take the offender's plastic license. This focus on local programs suggests that programs should not be mandated for each local government, rather localities should be granted the latitude to develop their own programs to meet their individual needs. The state does have a role to play, however. Local government programs need to meet minimum requirements and some state supervision is desirable. Some of the DWI control functions belong at the state level, such as legislation and driver licensing. Other functions require close state supervision, such as adjudication, probation, and treatment. Any action taken by the state should be sure not to hinder local efforts.

The programs surveyed appear to be functioning effectively. It is helpful to review the modifications that were made in each program as it developed. A review of these changes is a necessity for any attempt to reproduce the programs. It must also be remembered that these programs developed in response to the needs and situations found in each state. For any attempt to be successful in deterring drinking and driving, programs must be implemented that are compatible with the needs and situation of the given jurisdiction.

INTERVIEWS

FLORIDA

<u>Orange</u> <u>County</u> (Orlando)

Mark Van Arnam, President, Wheeled Coach Industries, February 6, 1985.

Capt. Walt Gallagher, Commander, Specialized Patrol Division, Orange County Sheriff's Department, February 6, 1985.

Jim Humphries, DUI Liaison/Consultant, Orange County Sheriff's Department, February 5 and 6, 1985.

Judge Tony Johnson, Orange County Judge, February 5, 1985.

Sgt. Cleveland Lee, DUI Enforcement Supervisor, Orange County Sheriff's Department, February 6, 1985.

Mary Wylie, Chapter President, Mothers Against Drunk Drivers, Orlando Chapter, February 4, 1985.

<u>Pinellas</u> <u>County</u> (Clearwater)

Diane Fradin, Chapter President, Mothers Against Drunk Drivers, Pinellas County Chapter, February 18, 1985.

Capt. Robert E. Kennedy, Division Commander, Technical Services Specialist, Support Services Division, Clearwater Police Department, February 15, 1985.

Sgt. Michael Stuart, Computer Programming Coordinator, Research and Development Unit, Clearwater Police Department, February 15, 1985.

<u>Alachua</u> <u>County</u> (Gainesville)

Elizabeth Browten, Graduate Assistant, Campus Alcohol Information Center, University of Florida, February 18, 1985.

Beverly H. Saunders, University of Florida Chapter Consultant, BACCHUS of the United States, February 18, 1985.

MINNESOTA

Anoka

Richard Neuner, Executive Director, Minnesota Institute, February 14, 1985.

Bloomington

Jim Abercrombie, Cofounder, Minnesota State Chapter of Mothers Against Drunk Drivers, February 14, 1985.

Fridley

Tim Turnbull, Special Projects Coordinator, Fridley Police Department, February 14, 1985.

Minneapolis

Judge Debra Hedlund, Hennepin County Municipal Court, February 15, 1985.

Stephen M. Simon, Clinical Attorney, University of Minnesota, and Member, Criminal Justice DWI Task Force, February 14, 1985.

Ed Vennewitz, Director, Municipal Probation Division, Department of Court Services, Hennepin County, February 13, 1985.

St. Paul

Michael F. Driscoll, Assistant City Attorney, City Attorney's Office, February 14, 1985.

Major Glenn E. Gramse, Director, Legal and legislative Affairs, Minnesota State Patrol, Minnesota Department of Public Safety, February 14, 1985.

Forst Lowery, Safety Program Coordinator, Minnesota Department of Public

Safety, February 13, 1985.

Harold Peterson, Assistant Director, Drivers License Division, Minnesota Department of Public Safety, February 13, 1985.

Rep. Kathleen Vellenga, Minnesota House of Representatives, February 15, 1985.

Joel Watne, Special Assistant to the Attorney General, Attorney General's Office, State of Minnesota, February 13, 1985.

NEW YORK

Albany

Jean Bave-Kerwin, Director, Division of Traffic Safety, Program Planning and Development, New York Department of Motor Vehicles, February 5, 1985.

Sgt. Ray Ducher, New York State Police, February 4, 1985.

Dennis Foley, Coordinator, Albany County STOP-DWI Program, and Member, New York State's STOP-DWI Coordinator's Administrative Committee, February 6, 1985.

Jerry Friedman, Intergovernmental Relations Specialist, Office of the Assistant Commissioner for Motor Vehicle Affairs, New York Department of Motor Vehicles, February 4, 1985.

Rob Lillis, Research Assistant, New York State Division of Alcoholism and Alcohol Abuse, February 4, 1985.

Clarence W. Mosher, Director, Division of Traffic Safety Records, New York Department of Motor Vehicles, February 4, 1985.

Marcus Salm, Assistant Director, Division of Traffic Safety, Program Planning and Development, New York Department of Motor Vehicles, February 5, 1985.

Donald F. Savage, Executive Director, Senate Special Task Force on Drunk Driving, New York State Senate, February 5, 1985.

Richard D. Smith, Assistant Director, Division of Traffic Safety, Program Planning and Development, New York Department of Motor Vehicles, February 4, 1985.

Tim Williams, Research Assistant, New York State Division of Alcoholism and Alcohol Abuse, February 4, 1985.

Bill Williford, Assistant Director for Highway Safety and Criminal Justice, New York State Division of Alcoholism and Alcohol Abuse, February 4, 1985.

New York City

Kathie Keegan, Assistant Coordinator, STOP-DWI Program, New York City Department of Transportation, February 6, 1985.

Joel W. Stahl, Assistant Commissioner, New York City Department of Transportation, February 6, 1985.

PENNSYLVANIA

Harrisburg

Gregory Curtis, Program Analyst, Office of Drug and Alcohol Programs, Division of Program Monitoring, Pennsylvania Department of Health, February 13, 1985.

Terry Davis, DUI Coordinator, Dauphin County Adult Probation Department, February, 13, 1985.

Ike Golden, Program Analyst III, Supervisor, DWI Section, Office of Drug and Alcohol Programs, Division of Program Monitoring, Pennsylvania Department of Health, February 13, 1985.

Lou Rader, Manager, Pennsylvania Alcohol Safety Program, Bureau of Safety, Programming and Analysis, Pennsylvania Department of Transportation, February 13, 1985.

David Stockton, Executive Director, Department of Drug and Alcohol Services, Dauphin County, February 14, 1985.

Philadelphia

Dorris Cohen, Executive Director, Pennsylvania Chapter, National Council on Alcoholism, February 15, 1985.

Frank F. Colanfuno, Director, Alcohol Highway Safety Program, Coordinating Office for Drug and Alcohol Abuse Programs, City and County of Philadelphia, February 15, 1985.

Eugene P. DeVine, Director, Pennsylvania Chapter, Alcohol Highway Safety Program, National Council on Alcoholism, February 15, 1985.

Nicolas L. Piccone, Ed.D., Executive Director, Coordinating Office for Drug and Alcohol Abuse Programs, City and County of Philadelphia, February 15, 1985.

CITATIONS

FLORIDA

BACCHUS of the United States. "Alcohol and the American Campus." Gainesville: University of Florida Campus Alcohol Information Center, February 1981.

_____. "BACCHUS Handbook: A Guide for Community Action to Promote Responsible Decisions about Drinking." Gainesville: University of Florida Campus Alcohol Information Center, Fall 1981.

_____. "1984 Annual Report." Gainesville: University of Florida Campus Alcohol Information Center, n.d.

City of Clearwater. Arrest Drunk Driving Project. "Arrest Drunk Driving Conceptual Summary." n.d.

_____. Clearwater/Largo Cooperative D.U.I. Enforcement Program. "Grant Proposal to the Florida Bureau of Highway Safety." Project period, July 1, 1983, to September 30, 1983.

_____. "Noteworthy Project-Arrest Drunk Driving." N.d.

Orange County Sheriff's Office. "Orange County Comprehensive D.U.I. Program." Project period October 1, 1984, to September 30, 1985.

State of Florida, Department of Highway Safety and Motor Vehicles. Division of Driver Licenses. "Report on DWI Convictions by Age Group." Tallahassee, 1984.

_____. Division of Administrative Services. "Alcohol/Nonalcohol-Related Accidents." Tallahassee, 1984.

Vaugh, Jerald R., and Sid Klein. "Arrest Drunk Driving: A Comprehensive Cooperative Approach." Police Chief (July 1984): 32-34.

MINNESOTA

Gerval, Jean, and Cynthia Long. D.W.I. Prosecutors' Update. St. Paul: Minnesota County Attorneys Association, September 1984.

Lowery, Forst. Some Notes on Minnesota's 1982 and 1983 Traffic Death Record, as Related to Drunk Driving. St. Paul: Minnesota Department of Public Safety, May 1984.

Minnesota Department of Public Safety. "Drunken Driving and Problem Drinkers: Punishing the Offense and Treating the Affliction." St. Paul: Minnesota Department of Public Safety, January 1985.

_____. "Drunken Driving in Minnesota: 1976-1983." St. Paul: Minnesota Department of Public Safety, June 1984.

_____. Young Drinking Driver." St. Paul: Minnesota Department of Public Safety, March 1984.

Minnesota House of Representatives Research Department. Analysis of the Effect of Recent Changes in Minnesota's DWI Laws. Part 1, The Perceptions of Minnesota's Drivers, August 1983. Part 2, Perceptions of Members of the DWI Control System, January 1985. St. Paul.

National Commission Against Drunk Driving. Success in Minnesota: Among State's Achievements an Administrative Per Se Law. Washington, D.C., 1984.

National Safety Council. Assessment of Drunk Driving Countermeasure Activities: State of Minnesota. Chicago, June 1984.

U.S. Department of Transportation. National Highway Traffic Safety Administration. Study of Minnesota DWI Law Shows That Prompt License Suspension Is Effective. Washington, D.C., July 6, 1984.

NEW YORK

Ameruso, Anthone R. '83-'84 Action Plan: New York City STOP Program. New York: Commissioner of Motor Vehicles, 1983.

Brodie, Kathie. "Action Plan 1985: New York City STOP-DWI Program." New York: Office of Commissioner of Transportation, January 1985.

Governor's Alcohol and Highway Safety Task Force. "DWI--Driving While Intoxicated." Albany, 1983.

Institute For Traffic Safety Management and Research. Survey of New York

State Licensed Drivers: Attitudes, Knowledge, Perceptions, and Behaviors Related to Drinking and Driving: Summary Report. Albany, December 1983.

_____. Two Years of Accident Experience Under STOP-DWI, December 1981-November 1983: Interim Report. Albany, April 1984.

Lillis, Robert P., Timothy P. Williams, and William R. Williford. Estimating the Number of Drinking Drivers: Examination of Blood Alcohol and Highway Safety. Albany: New York State Division of Alcoholism and Alcohol Abuse, Fall 1982.

McGuirk, James F. New York State's STOP-DWI Program: A Model for the Nation. Albany: New York State Department of Motor Vehicles, n.d.

New York State Department of Motor Vehicles. Office of Alcohol and Highway Safety. "Administrative/Impact Evaluation Quarterly Report: STOP-DWI." Albany, 1984.

_____. "Analysis/Discussion: Accident Trends Since Implementation of STOP-DWI." Albany, April 1983.

_____. "STOP-DWI Media Campaign." Albany, n.d.

_____. "STOP-DWI Plan, 1984: Monroe and Nasau Counties." Albany, 1984.

Smith, Senator William T. "Driving Reform in New York State: 1980-1984 Strategy, Results, Recommendations." Albany, n.d.

_____. STOP-DWI: New York's Response to Drunk Driving. Albany, February 1982.

_____. "Testimony of Donald F. Savage, Executive Director New York State Senate Special Task Force on Drunk Driving." Oklahoma City: Legislative Committee, Presidential Commission on Drunk Driving, 1982.

PENNSYLVANIA

Commonwealth of Pennsylvania. "Act 1982-289, Laws of Pennsylvania, Amending Titles 75 (Vehicles) and 42 (Judiciary and Judicial

Procedures) of the Pennsylvania Consolidated Statutes." Harrisburg, n.d.

_____. "Governor's DUI Task Force Report." Harrisburg, October 14, 1984.

_____. "The Governor's Traffic Safety Council Reporting Network (CRN): Program Management and Evaluation Procedures Manual." Harrisburg, September 1, 1980.

County of Dauphin. "Annual Report, Department of Probation and Parole." Harrisburg, n.d.

_____. "Interim Report to the Dauphin County Board of Commissioners by the Dauphin County Driving Under the Influence Task Force." Harrisburg, November 1984.

Pennsylvania Commission on Crime and Delinquency. Statistical Analysis Center. "Deterring Drunk Driving in Pennsylvania." Harrisburg, n.d.

Pennsylvania Department of Health. "Drug and Alcohol Treatment Trend Report." Harrisburg, January 1985.

_____. "FY 1984-85 Management Plan." Harrisburg, n.d.

Pennsylvania Department of Transportation. Bureau of Safety Programming and Analysis. "Annual Work Plan, 1984-1985." Harrisburg, n.d.

_____. "Commonwealth of Pennsylvania Highway Safety Plan, Fiscal Year 1984." Harrisburg, n.d.

Pennsylvania National Safety Council. "Assessment of Drunk Driving Countermeasure Activities." Harrisburg, June 1984.

APPENDIX 1

REPORTS ON TEXAS COUNTIES

INTRODUCTION

This appendix contains the detailed findings of visits to Comal, Dallas, El Paso, Gray, Harris, Harrison, Webb, and Williamson counties to investigate the nature of county DWI systems and to solicit opinions regarding the effectiveness of the reforms to the DWI law contained in Senate Bill 1. Whenever interviews could be arranged, project team members visited representatives of the sheriff's department, Texas Department of Public Safety (DPS), district attorney, district clerk, district court, county attorney, county clerk, county court, adult probation department, alcohol council, local police department, and the local chapter of Mothers Against Drunk Drivers (MADD). The field trips took place in February and March of 1985. All county interviews are cited at the end of this appendix. Summarized DWI statistics were obtained by hand counts or from automated lists of county docket books.

COMAL COUNTY

Background Information

Comal County is located in South Central Texas. The county seat is New Braunfels, situated on the southeastern edge of the county. The city of New Braunfels extends into Guadalupe County on this southeastern boundary and is the major city in Comal County. Comal County covers 555 square miles and is located north of San Antonio on Interstate 35 in the Edwards Plateau region. The 1982 estimated population of 39,400 indicates a continued growth. Comal's population growth rate between 1970 and 1980 was one of the highest in the state, with rural areas increasing 121 percent and urban areas increasing 26 percent. Residents with German ancestry make up 36 percent of the population, followed by 24 percent Hispanic and 21 percent of English descent. Much of the county courts tourists with historic sights, water recreation, and special German heritage events, including the popular New Braunfels Wurstfest. The county had 896 miles of public roads and 33,135 registered vehicles in 1982. In the same year, the county reported 1,131 traffic accidents and 16 fatalities. Because New Braunfels has grown from Comal into Guadalupe County, the local police must deal with officials of both counties in matters of law enforcement.

The county attorney's office reported 1,000 misdemeanor DWI cases filed in 1983; less than one-half the cases actually involved county residents. As for final disposition of misdemeanor DWI cases in 1983, 780 entered a guilty plea, 16 were found guilty by trial, and 142 were dismissed on deferred adjudication and pretrial diversions. One case received a fine only, 141 were sentenced to jail time, and 649 received a probated sentence. In the following year, the total number of misdemeanor DWI cases filed in the county dropped by one-half to 506, with 263 county residents and 243 nonresidents charged. As for final dispositions, 445 entered a guilty plea, 11 were found guilty, and 139 cases were dismissed due to pretrial diversions, a lack of available witnesses, or insufficient evidence. Disposition records indicate that 152 of these cases served jail time, while 319 received probation.

The county attorney attributes the drop in number of misdemeanor cases in 1984 to the changes contained in Senate Bill 1, pressure from the business community to decrease the number of tourist arrests, decreased tourist traffic due to the severe drought, and changes in local late-night closing laws. Aggressive prosecution and stiff, consistent punishment of DWI offenses also have helped to keep drunk drivers off the county's roads.

Focus of DWI Program Effort

Most agencies in Comal County give special priority to DWI. When asked, county officials most often point to law enforcement and adjudication as the most important program focus but state that public information and treatment programs are essential as well, in the effort to deter drunk driving. Working relationships among the county agencies and departments involved in the DWI process are extremely successful because county officials make a special effort to cooperate with one another. Occasionally, problems arise over a lack of communication with the sheriff's department or friction between the county and district attorneys' offices due to differing trial timetables or disagreements over specific upcoming cases. Overall, the agencies work to keep open the lines of communication in an effort to maintain the good reputation of the county's existing DWI program.

Special Programs

The county attorney and county court work closely with probation officials to utilize the offender's talents, help him make a constructive contribution to society, and learn from his mistakes. They recently initiated a program of pretrial diversion to replace the court's discretionary option of deferred adjudication, which was removed in Senate Bill 1. This process attempts to identify offenders who have a good driving record, have not endangered lives, and have a job problem (i.e., would lose their job if convicted). It allows the judge to assess punishment that would not mar their permanent record. The county actively supports a work release program, which allows the convicted offender to serve the sentence while continuing to earn a living, thereby maintaining his self-esteem. The court makes frequent use of the community service restitution program, which requires the offender to complete community projects that benefit the community and the offender more than a simple fine would.

The adult probation department provides an alcohol education program for all DWI offenders, as well as a follow-up program, "Discovery," run by people affiliated with Alcoholics Anonymous (AA). Probation officials provide an alcohol program in jail on a weekly basis. County officials emphasize the importance of treatment as an element of the punishment process.

During the annual Wurstfest celebration and the summer months, the Department of Public Safety (DPS) saturates the interstate highway with troopers specifically to look for DWI offenders. The DPS pulls six additional troopers from San Antonio, along with the eight Comal County officers, and supplements this with regular driver's license personnel to provide the extra necessary law enforcement. They feel these efforts have been extremely effective in the last few years.

Paul Harst, a member of the New Braunfels Police Department, initiated a successful public awareness program on his off-duty hours. The program consists of an anti-DWI film produced by the television program "60 Minutes" and a slide presentation of DWI accidents within the county. He now receives compensatory time and equipment from the police department to support the project due to the positive feedback from the community.

In an effort to inform visitors and remind residents of the county's commitment to DWI enforcement, the county attorney's office displays billboards with anti-DWI messages in prominent locations in New Braunfels. Other groups involved in the public awareness and education activities include the local Parent-Teachers Association (PTA), concerned parents' groups, and the local MADD chapter. The MADD chapter, incidentally, has kept a low profile in the past year in response to the county's successful and effective efforts to deter drunk driving.

Adult Probation Department

Adult probation services for Comal County cover the same territory as do the district judges: Comal, Caldwell, and Hays counties. Within the adult probation department, the supervisor and four probation officers deal with DWI for residents of Comal County, and one probation officer deals with DWI for residents of other counties. Agency officials estimate that 60 to 70 percent of the agency's caseload is related to DWI. The agency also recruits and maintains contract help for the required DWI and defensive driving programs.

A small amount of the agency's budget, about $10 thousand per year, is county tax money. The agency receives $15 per day funding from the state Adult Probation Commission for each probationer. Fifteen dollars per month is paid directly to the agency by each probationer.

DWI receives the most attention of all issues dealt with by the agency. In dealing with DWI, adult probation is in regular contact with the sheriff's department, local police, DPS officers, district court, district clerk's office, district attorney's office, county clerk's office, county court, and the county attorney, especially in regard to anyone who breaks probation. Such an occurrence is reported quickly by adult probation, and the court authorizes a warrant for arrest, which is served by the sheriff's department.

Senate Bill 1 affected adult probation in that the agency now is responsible for probationers for two years, rather than for one, as previously was the case. In addition, there are no longer early discharges from probation. Doing away with deferred adjudication did a great deal to impress an offender with the seriousness of a DWI offense. Senate Bill 1 also increased the paperwork requirements of the agency. It must now submit a report on completion of the DWI education program (Education Program for Driving While Intoxicated Form DL-17A) for each probationer. The form is mailed to the Driver Improvement and Control section of DPS.

While adult probation has lacked sufficient staff to mount a public awareness program on DWI, the agency has been instrumental in starting some Students Against Driving Drunk (SADD) chapters and in assisting with an Alcoholics Anonymous (AA) program in the county jail. The agency has funded an eight-week "Discovery" program for some years, which includes former AA people, as well as an offender's family members. The focus of the program is to encourage people to look at the problem of alcoholism and to participate in AA. A success rate of about 80 percent has been realized, although recidivism statistics have not been collected by the agency itself. Most statistics simply are reported to the state Adult Probation Commission. However, the agency has plans to begin to use a computer in the near future to maintain statistics on its clients.

The agency has been able to produce presentence reports for both the district court and the county court using DPS criminal history records. Driver's records also have been used for the past two years. One of adult probation's responsibilities is to review and to make recommendations to the county judge on requests for occupational driver's licenses for offenders whose licenses have been suspended. This responsibility was assigned to the agency by the legislature, which did not fund any additional staff to assist in carrying it out.

The average caseload per probation officer is about 149 active cases during any one month for clients who live in the county, plus about 15 clients who do not live or work in the county. During a recent month, one officer's clients included 98 misdemeanor and 58 felony cases, of which 90 to 100 were DWI cases.

A probation officer sees DWI clients once a week during the entire program. Probation officers have specialized training, particularly in administering the Mortimer-Filkins Test. All new staff are sent to be trained in Austin at the Council on Alcoholism program. Applicants for these positions must have a bachelor's degree in a social science and some minimal experience in a social service field. Some probation officers have a master's degree.

The agency maintains permanent records on DWI offenders who have been on probation. It recently has begun to enter some records into the county's computer in the auditor's office. When the information system is fully developed, maintaining and retrieving information on clients should be improved.

Record Keeping

In Comal County, the chief deputy county clerk and three other staff members monitor DWI reporting. DWI is the first priority of the county clerk's office, followed by other misdemeanor cases such as drugs and weapons cases.

Information on past DWI convictions is maintained on the county's computer, which is located in the county auditor's office. Information from Comal, Hays, and Lockhart counties is included. The computer is used by all county offices. Although the computer was installed about five years ago, the county clerk's office has used it for only about a year and still is working on refining the information system.

The county clerk's office reports final convictions and probations to DPS on a monthly basis. If there is a second offense, a Notice of Conviction Form (DL-17) is completed and mailed to the Driver Improvement and Control section of DPS for every case, except revocation of probation. DPS does not want revocation reports. The county clerk's office maintains a master list of DWI dispositions referred to DPS.

Although the sheriff's department reports arrests made by its officers, it is not very good at referring information to the county clerk. However, the adult probation department readily provides information for presentence investigations to the county judge when requested by him.

Disposition of DWI cases occurs very promptly, usually within three to four months from date of arrest. One problem noted is that attorneys may incur delays so they will appear to be earning their fees. Most time is lost from the date of arrest to filing, usually six to seven weeks. In some cases, an officer will not report a DWI promptly, particularly in the summer. When a case is filed, arraignment occurs within ten days. A defendant then has thirty days to enter a plea. There may be some continuances for other factors.

About 160 DWI cases are awaiting final disposition in the county at present, or about 80 percent of 200 outstanding warrants for arrest. This number is excessive primarily because the sheriff lacks personnel to serve the warrants. However, the sheriff recently has hired a new administrator who is improving the management of the office, and it is hoped that one result will be a reduction in the number of outstanding warrants.

In the district clerk's office, three clerks deal with DWI in addition to their other duties. Priorities in the office include felony cases: drugs, burglaries, murders, other felonies, and DWI as one of the last categories. Other local agencies are most cooperative in DWI matters, particularly the adult probation department.

The new reporting requirements of Senate Bill 1 would have been dealt with more efficiently if more information on implementing them had been made available. The record-keeping system sometimes fails to provide information about past convictions, and sometimes reports on judgments are delayed. The office is just beginning to use computers for record keeping. The district clerk reports final convictions and probations by completing and mailing a Notice of Conviction Form (DL-17) to DPS on a monthly basis. There are few felony DWI cases, only about three to six per month, but all cases are reported. A file of DWI dispositions is maintained. Information for presentence investigations is readily available from the adult probation department. Trials ordinarily are held promptly, unless a waiver is filed. Only eighteen felony DWI cases currently are awaiting final disposition in Comal County, not an excessive number compared to other types of cases.

Effectiveness of Senate Bill 1

Local officials overwhelmingly agree that the reforms contained in Senate Bill 1 establishing the per se level of intoxication at a blood alcohol concentration (BAC) of .10 percent and allowing the admission of a BAC test refusal in court have helped DWI enforcement and adjudication. They generally agree on the need to prohibit the practice of deferred adjudication in DWI cases due to the possibility of abuse, but the county attorney and judge would like to reinstitute a system of "limited" deferred adjudication in cases where the offender has a job problem, is extremely young, has a good past record, and/or no injury was involved with the offense. When used responsibly, deferred adjudication can be a very effective tool in the DWI process, as was the case in Comal County prior to Senate Bill 1. Prohibition of deferred adjudication raised the caseload for the already overcrowded court system. The county initiated the pretrial diversion program to replace the court's discretion previously allowed through deferred adjudication.

Officials responded that the provision in the law granting police officers authority to order blood tests could be effective, but has not been needed very often in the county. They pointed out that the law needs to further protect the officers and hospitals from liability in these cases. They like the new reporting procedures for convictions and probations but could see no impact on their agencies, since they already had been reporting in this manner.

County officials identified a tremendous drop in Intoxilyzer test refusals as a direct result of the Senate Bill 1 changes in implied consent license revocation procedures. However, they hold mixed opinions on the mandatory videotaping procedures. As a "double-edged sword," county officials noted that, in most instances, the videotape won cases or kept them from going to trial, but, at other times, it hurt the prosecution's case. The county attorney, however, shows the videotape one time uninterrupted. Then, if needed, the tape is replayed while an officer instructs the jury and points out more subtle signs of intoxication.

Stiffened penalties provided by Senate Bill 1 have not had a great effect on the county because the county court sentenced stiffly before the law took effect; however, the propaganda value of the reforms has been effective.

Recommendations for Making Senate Bill 1 More Effective

County officials identified several areas where the DWI law could be improved. Other than reinstating a form of limited deferred adjudication and protecting law enforcement officers and hospital staff from liability, they pointed out that the state should adopt and monitor uniform enforcement procedures among the Texas counties. In this manner, Texas residents could expect consistent enforcement as they travel from county to county.

The county attorney pointed out that expert Intoxilyzer witnesses are too busy with the increased workload to testify in court. The local expert currently serves eight counties in the area. He would like to see a provision in the law allowing the Intoxilyzer records to be admitted in trial along with the testimony of any expert witness, not just the one who originally completed the tests.

Probation officials would like to see changes in the notification procedures, such as the paperwork involved with the DL-17A, to signify when the probation program is complete. The adult probation department handles all the added paperwork required by Senate Bill 1, but it is given no additional funding for these responsibilities.

Conclusions

The DWI system in Comal County works reasonably well in all aspects of enforcement, adjudication, health and treatment, probation, administration, and public information. The roles of County Attorney Bill Reimer and County Court Judge Rolin Zipp seem pivotal in the success of the system and are recognized as such by all the concerned agencies. They provide consistency and fairness in the adjudication process and attempt to keep open the lines of communication among all participating agencies and departments. Their personalities play an important role in the public information aspects as well, as they work to maintain a credible reputation for the county's DWI program.

Although the local police do not yet feel comfortable with the videotaping equipment and dislike the lengthy processing time for weekend DWI arrests, when only one videotape unit is available, the videotapes have been quite effective for the Comal County program.

The few problems in the DWI system are dealt with as they occur. A problem mentioned by several individuals concerns the legislature and its propensity to enact laws without funding for their enforcement. Some agencies simply lack manpower to do the job with which they are charged. Other problems occur when Comal County needs DWI information from other counties. The sheer number of counties in Texas cause delays in providing information and in serving warrants.

The German heritage and culture of the area present a unique working environment for Comal County officials, one in which they have succeeded so far. They maintain a strict DWI program while trying to balance the interests of the business community, the local culture, and the lucrative tourist industry.

DALLAS COUNTY

Background Information

Dallas County covers 880 square miles and is located in north central Texas at the intersection of Interstate Highways 35-East, 30, and 45 in the Blackland Prairies region. The county seat of Dallas County is the city of Dallas, and other major cities with populations over 50,000 in the county include Garland, Irving, Mesquite, and Richardson. In 1982, the estimated population of the county was 1,641,400, with a continued strong growth rate indicated. During the same year, there were 1,475,542 registered vehicles and 45,528 reported traffic accidents including 298 fatalities.

In 1983, there were 16,486 misdemeanor and 1,676 felony DWI cases filed in Dallas County. Over the same span of time, 12,781 offenders entered a guilty plea, 237 were found guilty by trial, 5,731 cases were dismissed, and 2,572 cases involved deferred adjudication. In terms of punishment, 8,521 offenders were put on probation, 602 received a fine only, and 4,068 served time in jail.

In the following year, there were 15,527 misdemeanor and 723 felony DWI cases filed. Of the total 17,680 cases disposed, 12,677 offenders entered a guilty plea, 237 again were found guilty by trial, 3,992 cases were dismissed, and 774 cases involved deferred adjudication. As for punishment, 8,401 offenders were put on probation, 170 received a fine only, and 4,457 served time in jail.

Priority Given to DWI

Public awareness of both DWI and the problems involved with drunk driving has been increasing rapidly in the Dallas County area. As a result, many--if not all--agencies view combatting DWI as one of their top priorities. For example, in 1984, 48.25 percent of all cases tried by the district attorney's office were DWIs.

Focus of DWI Program Effort

The concentration of Dallas County's DWI program effort is on public information, law enforcement, probation, and to a lesser degree, health and treatment. Several programs run at various times during the year aim at increasing public awareness. Examples are the Holidays Ahead campaign, organized by the Dallas Police Department, private information campaigns run in conjunction with some area bars and restaurants, and a Safety Council of Greater Dallas program where people may dial a central number if they suspect a DWI (see below for further discussion of these programs). Efforts to apprehend DWI offenders have been stepped up throughout the county, and arrest rates have increased dramatically. Probation efforts and DWI education programs conducted by the Dallas Council on Alcoholism have been very effective.

Effectiveness of County Agency Relationships

Relationships among agencies throughout the county appear to be cohesive and effective. The agencies currently are working together on a DWI task force established by County Commissioner Chris Semos.

Special Programs

County Commissioner's Task Force

The task force originally was set up when County Commissioner Chris Semos realized that the message of Senate Bill 1 was not reaching the Hispanic community. The ten-member council later expanded its horizons and began looking at the problems on a community wide basis. The task force hopes to come up with recommendations for improving Dallas County's anti-DWI efforts and increasing public awareness.

Holidays Ahead Campaign

This program is sponsored by the Dallas Police Department. Its main focus is to remind drivers to be especially careful during the holiday season, and to avoid drinking and driving during the entire year. The program generally is thought to be very effective, especially with recent increased public concern over drinking and driving.

Suspect a DWI?

The Safety Council of Greater Dallas sponsors this program. They have distributed bumper stickers which state "Suspect a DWI? Dial this number ---." The program allows persons to anonymously report suspected DWIs or concerns.

Informal Programs

There are numerous informal programs within the Metroplex area sponsored by local restaurants and bars. Buttons, flyers, and table tents are distributed to remind the public to drink intelligently. Mothers Against Drunk Drivers (MADD) also runs many informational campaigns aimed at deterring drunk driving.

County Alcohol Council

The Dallas Council on Alcoholism employs eleven full-time staff members and twenty part-time instructors/consultants who teach DWI education classes. The agency's priorities are informational, educational, and referral programs.

The council currently is directing its efforts toward the Hispanic population. Criticism has been directed against the DWI system and Senate Bill 1 for not addressing the problems of the Hispanic community. To aid this group, the council is distributing pamphlets, which outline Senate Bill 1 in both Spanish and English. The council and the adult probation department work together in offering DWI education classes. These classes are required of every first-time offender. At these classes, specific categories are assigned to each person depending upon the severity of the alcohol problem. They range from the lowest level, social drinker; to medium level, problem drinker; and end with the chronic drinker, or abuser. Treatment and educational programs depend upon this categorization. The council would like to devise some sort of posttreatment effectiveness evaluation, but this is difficult, if not impossible, since the population which makes up Dallas County is highly mobile.

Adult Probation Department

The adult probation department is staffed by fourteen counselors. Only a portion of these counselors are certified alcohol counselors (three are currently trained, and two others are attending certification classes). The adult probation department handles a high number of cases; each counselor handles around three hundred cases at any one time. Several problems arise from this heavy caseload. First, the quality of care per case is lessened. Little time is available for the counselor to acquaint himself with every case, let alone understand the problem behind each drinker. Second, the department cannot afford to let its counselors take leave to receive the training they need to be more astute in their assessments. Essentially, the department needs greater funding to hire more staff and to offer more classes.

Record Keeping

As provided by Senate Bill 1, the county clerk's office coordinates the procedure of reporting convictions and probations to DPS. After a suspect has pled guilty, the county clerk's office makes a request to the sheriff's department for any information the agency may have on the individual. The sheriff's department runs a criminal history check and notifies the county clerk's office only if the suspect has a felony in his criminal record.

The county clerk makes a report for every case. Every seven to ten days, the types of DWI notices are categorized by the county clerk. They include the DL-17 series, which are the forms required by the Department of Public Safety (DPS). The notices that require a DL-17 form are separated, and copies of the following are made: judgment and sentence; complaint; information; waiver; and attorney of record.

The county clerk then compiles and requests information from the sheriff such as the defendant's signature, physical description, fingerprints, photograph, and driver's license number. A copy of this list, the clerk's copies, and the DL-17 form are held until the requested information is received from the sheriff. Notices are listed according to category, then alphabetized and listed by year. The notices are attached to the clerk's list and sent to the DPS with a certified return receipt requested. If the defendant received deferred adjudication, no reports on cases prior to 1984 are forwarded.

Copies of the county clerk's list sent to the DPS are kept on file. The clerk waits an average of two to three weeks for the sheriff to return the information to the court. Sometimes a reorder is necessary, if information has not been received or if information received on the defendant is incorrect.

The clerk's office currently has eighteen thousand pending misdemeanor cases on record. While this number is average for Dallas County, the county clerk's office, nevertheless, suffers from inadequate staff and an inadequate computer system.

The effectiveness of the district clerk's office is limited by administrative problems. The office has trouble retaining skilled staff. Pay generally is low and career mobility limited; therefore, competent staff have no incentive to stay. This problem is exacerbated by the limited ability of the clerk's office to replace vacant positions. Thus, the second problem is understaffing due to limited funding. Third, the information systems of the district clerk are inadequate; criminal cases are on a direct system while civil cases are on a batch system. This means that changes in a civil case cannot be readily organized, reducing the accuracy of the overall data collection. These combined problems limit the ability of the clerk's office to handle the county's growing number of DWI cases.

Problems with the DWI Process

Dallas County officials outlined a wide range of problems at all levels of the DWI process. The first problem concerns the court system. A general feeling exists among those interviewed that most judges need more education concerning the problem of drinking and driving. Specifically, judges need to be aware of all details of DWI laws to carry out the full degree of DWI legislation. This highlights another problem--that of consistency. Dallas County officials feel too much discretion exists among sentencing procedures by different judges throughout the state. To reduce the discretionary power, judges should adhere strictly to the DWI law. Officials feel that judges are too lenient in sentencing and are probating too many sentences. Also problematic is the excessive granting of occupational driver's licenses. Almost all county officials feel occupational licenses are being abused by those receiving them.

Another problem involves videotaping. The feeling is that videotaping is not working as intended. This is due, in part, to videotaping procedures and to the behavior of the experienced drinker. If a DWI case is presented before a jury, the jury tends to think of a drunk driver as exhibiting outrageous behavior. When the DWI offender is an experienced drinker, his videotape may not show the vile behavior expected by the jury. Juries tend to view this behavior as inconclusive and may base their decision on their judgment of the videotape rather than on the results of the breath or blood tests. This problem can be lessened if videotaping procedures are upgraded and standardized. An example of such upgraded procedures would include having the suspect walk into the room, move about the room, or exhibit any behavior showing reflex impairment. Better photographic skills also would aid videotaping procedures. Examples include a camera close to the suspect which is able to focus on the suspect's eyes, and a mobile camera which is able to detect any movement by the suspect. These changes would enhance the ability of videotaping to demonstrate physical as well as mental impairment.

Still another problem is the lack of focus in the DWI process on alcohol education and prevention. County officials feel that insufficient emphasis is placed on understanding the drunk driver. Related to this problem is the potential usefulness of alcohol problem assessment in the sentencing guidelines. The assessment is not being ordered by judges. If this process of orienting the court to the extent of the drinking problem would be used to its fullest extent, a better system of treatment could be designed for the offender.

Finally, county officials feel that too much paperwork is required within the DWI system. As a result of the paperwork, the length of time for case completion is growing. And as completion time grows, cases become lost or significantly delayed.

Effectiveness of Senate Bill 1

For the most part, Dallas officials feel the .10 percent BAC per se rule is very effective. The provision allowing admission of BAC test refusal at trial is given a rating of very to somewhat effective. The reason for this somewhat lower rating is that the justice of peace cannot probate suspension on refusal. The case then moves to the county court of appeals, producing a log jam in the system. Due to this problem, appeals have increased by 125 percent in Dallas County since the enactment of Senate Bill 1.

Prohibition of deferred adjudication in DWI cases is rated to be very effective, although Dallas County already followed this provision prior to the passage of Senate Bill 1.

In answering the next question, Dallas officials rated the authority for police officers to order blood tests as very effective. Several county officials feel that some law enforcement officers still are unaware of this aspect of the law. The lack of awareness prevents full use of this authority. To rectify this problem, the wording of Senate Bill 1 needs to be made clearer. It should outline in more detail who can order a blood test and under what circumstances.

The new procedure for reporting convictions or probations to the Department of Public Safety (DPS) is, for the most part, given a neutral rating. Several reasons are given for this rating. The staffing problems in the county and district clerk's offices prevent efficient routing of DWI records. Also, an inadequate computer system prevents accurate and speedy reporting to DPS. While the computer system currently is being upgraded, the limitations of the information system have nevertheless reduced the effectiveness of the new reporting procedures.

Reactions to the changes in implied consent license revocation procedures are mixed. Those rating the effect as no change outlined the general problem of appeals. Many judges in Dallas County are probating license revocation, thereby canceling this provision of Senate Bill 1. In addition, DPS is just now able to operate under the new procedures. DPS is unprepared both in manpower and data systems to handle the licensing revocation records. Consequently, although seventeen months have passed since the enactment of Senate Bill 1, DPS is just now suspending driver's licenses according to law.

The videotaping of all suspects proved to be somewhat controversial. Rated generally effective, Dallas officials outlined a variety of problems. First, if videotaping is to be performed effectively, it requires more funding than is often available. The time required for setting up a videotape system is the second problem. In Dallas County, the videotape system took six months to set up. Localities become frustrated with the time delays and set up their own systems, which does not allow for consistent videotaping. Finally, the problem of the experienced drunk is troublesome. Juries tend to favor acquittal in these cases. Enhanced videotaping procedures would help to lessen this problem.

In response to the final question, stiffened penalties were rated as somewhat effective. General problems with this provision include too much discretion left to judges in assigning jail sentences, fines not being sufficiently high to effectively deter drinking and driving, and judges still probating first offenders. Several respondents feel the law has not been in effect long enough to determine the extent of the effectiveness.

Recommendations for Making Senate Bill 1 More Effective

Dallas County generally is satisfied with its system of controlling drinking and driving. However, several changes are suggested for improving the DWI system. In general, Dallas County officials outlined two problem areas--administrative problems and specific changes in Senate Bill 1.

Administrative Problems

Updating DWI information systems is considered a must. Specifically, counties which currently have computerized data systems should be allowed to access DPS files and to update the information now being sent through the mail. This would reduce paperwork.

With regard to videotaping, a problem arises with the storage of videotapes. Some county officials voiced the need to set a time limit on the storage of videotapes. The space available for storage in most cases is limited. Once the case has been decided, videotapes should be erased after a certain amount of time has elapsed.

Specific Changes

Senate Bill 1 needs to be amended so that alcohol testing can be given at any public place such as shopping centers or parking lots, rather than only on roadways. Senate Bill 1 also should be amended to require that pictures be taken showing field tests--reciting the alphabet or testing coordination by walking lines. The authorization to administer blood tests needs to be expanded, allowing tests to be administered by paramedics and nurses as well as by doctors.

As for videotaping, the wording of Senate Bill 1 should be changed. Specifically, Senate Bill 1 should state that localities must use videotaping equipment and not just possess it.

The penalties for refusal of breath and blood tests need to be strengthened. The refusal to take a test should carry an immediate administrative revocation. At the point of trial, refusal should be a mandatory sentence of ninety days with no probation. To further strengthen this provision, Senate Bill 1 needs a codicil stating that the judge may not suspend or probate the ninety-day suspension.

The provisions concerning occupational driver's licenses also should be strengthened. On the first offense, the granting of a twenty-four-hour occupational license should not be allowed. On the second offense, no occupational license should be granted.

The use of alcohol evaluations should be enhanced. Alcohol evaluations need to be required on the first conviction even if the sentence is probated. Such an enhancement would allow a better understanding of the drinking problem of the DWI suspect.

Finally, a list of general changes were suggested. These changes include raising the drinking age, stiffer penalties for an open container found in motor vehicles, and strengthening the law enforcement power of the Alcohol Beverage Commission.

Conclusions

The DWI process in Dallas County seems to be running smoothly. Dallas County had been following many of the provisions of Senate Bill 1 before it became law; therefore, Senate Bill 1 did not significantly change the manner in which DWI is being handled. Officials participating in the DWI process agree, for the most part, with the existing DWI law but feel that much is left to be accomplished, including strengthening existing provisions of Senate Bill 1. To achieve that end, Dallas County has appointed a DWI task force to come up with a comprehensive list of proposed changes in existing DWI law to close perceived loopholes.

A strength of Dallas County is the cooperation exhibited by the major participants in the county DWI process. Typical of this cooperation is the aforementioned task force, which brought together the major participants. Another strength of Dallas County seems to be their courts. Despite criticism directed at sentencing procedures and the discretionary power of the judiciary, the great majority of the judges involved in misdemeanor and felony courts are concerned about and take an active role in the problem of DWI. One judge serves on the county task force.

Dallas County, not unlike the other counties in Texas, suffers from an inadequate record-keeping system. The problems include a wholly inadequate computer system for the type and number of cases to be processed. Problems of inadequate staff and funding for the record-keeping function also frustrate the DWI process.

EL PASO COUNTY

Background Information

Located in far west Texas and bordering the Mexican city of Juarez, El Paso County covers 1,014 square miles. The estimated 1982 population was 513,400. The county grew 34 percent between 1970 and 1980. The median age in the county is twenty-five, and over one-half the residents are of Hispanic descent. The major city in the county is the city of El Paso.

Located close to the Texas-Mexico border, El Paso is the site of a large military installation. The army's Fort Bliss employs nearly 25 thousand people and covers 118 thousand acres. Also located in El Paso are the U.S. Army Air Defense Command and school and special training facilities for the German Air Force and other NATO units.

In 1982, there were 315,763 registered vehicles and 1,958 miles of public roads in El Paso County. Traffic accidents totaled 13,055 with 103 fatalities. In 1983, there were 3,334 misdemeanor DWI cases and 1 felony DWI case filed in the county. Over the same span of time, 594 offenders entered a guilty plea, 11 were found guilty by trial, and 1,252 cases were dismissed. As for punishment, 213 offenders were put on probation, 65 received a fine only, and 327 served time in jail.

In the following year, there were 4,667 misdemeanor and 7 felony DWI cases filed. Final dispositions included 1,674 offenders entering a guilty plea, 18 found guilty by trial, and 1,989 cases dismissed. In terms of punishment, 1,131 offenders were put on probation, 8 received a fine only, and 553 served time in jail.

Priority Given to DWI

The priority given to DWI in El Paso County changed dramatically within the last two years. Due in part to the heightened awareness of DWI across the country, efforts in El Paso to reduce the problem of drunk driving can largely be considered as effective. The most forceful and visible change occurred in the county attorney's office. Luther Jones became El Paso County Attorney in March 1983 and made it clearly known to all that the DWI offender would not receive any sort of preferential treatment from the county attorney's office. Because of this commitment to strict prosecution of El Paso's DWI offenders, coupled with enhanced law enforcement and greater community awareness, El Paso's DWI process has begun to show marked improvement. However, it is not yet at a point where it could be considered ideal.

Focus of DWI Program Effort

The focus of El Paso's DWI program efforts lies largely in the area of prosecution. The county attorney's office has received high marks from nearly all parties involved with the DWI process in El Paso County. The county attorney's special task force (to be described later) seeks to combat drunk driving by encouraging a strongly perceived certainty of punishment. In addition, more DWI offenders are being apprehended as a result of increased enforcement by both the El Paso Police Department and the Department of Public Safety (DPS). El Paso police arrest an average of four hundred to five hundred DWI offenders per month, and the DPS--which patrols only Interstate 10 and the Transmountain Road--averages about one hundred DWI arrests per month. The lines of communication between these parties and the other actors in El Paso's DWI system appear to be open and functional.

Effectiveness of County Agency Relationships

The major actors in the El Paso DWI system are the El Paso Police Department, the Department of Public Safety, the county attorney's office, the county courts at law, the West Texas Adult Probation Department, the county clerk, and Mothers Against Drunk Drivers (MADD). All expressed relative satisfaction with the working relationships among the different offices. The El Paso police and the DPS conduct nearly all DWI enforcement in the county. It is only on rare occasions that the sheriff's department plays an active role in DWI enforcement.

Since most DWI offenders are charged with misdemeanors, the majority of DWI cases in El Paso are handled by the county attorney's office. When there are felony DWIs in El Paso, however, they need not be transferred to the district attorney's office. Rather, the county attorneys, who prosecute DWIs, also are certified as district attorneys, thereby obviating the need for any transfer of a case.

The county attorney's office works closely with the West Texas Adult Probation Department. In El Paso, a first-time DWI offender is eligible for a treatment program called "Pre-Trial Intervention" (PTI), if his or her record contains no evidence of prior alcohol abuse. If directed to PTI, the DWI offender undergoes six months of treatment and education, overseen by probation personnel. Pre-Trial Intervention is not considered to be a final conviction, whereas completion of probation, as ordered in sentencing, is considered a conviction. The intent of the PTI program is to reduce the burdens placed on the county court dockets, while offering an effective treatment option considered to be a deterrent. Although the record is not conclusive, there appear to be very few repeat offenders in El Paso County among those who successfully complete the PTI program.

The county clerk, as the official source of records for El Paso County, maintains the public information on DWIs in El Paso County. Access to the records is considered public, and the county clerk's office tries to accommodate those requesting information as quickly and thoroughly as possible.

Public information and education activities are conducted by many of the DWI-related agencies in El Paso. Efforts to publicize the dangers of drinking and driving appear to come from many corners. The police department alerts residents to increased law enforcement, and the courts' handling of DWI offenders receives coverage in the local papers. Mothers Against Drunk Drivers (MADD) is active in both public information and court monitoring. Also, the county attorney's office has one attorney focusing primarily on public education and awareness of the DWI problem.

Special Programs

County Attorney's Special DWI Task Force

As mentioned earlier, changes in the El Paso County Attorney's Office significantly altered the DWI process in El Paso. In March 1983, Luther Jones became the county attorney and took office with a commitment to improve prosecution of DWI offenders in El Paso County. Dismissal of DWI cases would no longer be readily considered by the county attorney's office. This commitment to enhanced prosecution was further strengthened through the formation of a special DWI unit within the county attorney's office.

There are three attorneys in this special task force. The funds to initially hire two of the attorneys--Frank Cram and Bob Abbot--came in September 1983 from the Criminal Justice Division of the Governor's Office. The third attorney, Laura Gordon, and the witness coordinator are funded by a grant from the Department of Public Safety. The efforts of these people are widely praised by all the participants in the DWI process in El Paso County. Attempts by the county commissioners to reduce funding to this unit failed, partly because of its overall acceptance in El Paso County.

The policy of the county attorney's DWI task force is to prosecute almost all DWI cases, unless an Intoxilyzer test is not administered and the suspect appears sober on videotape. The charge of driving while intoxicated is rarely reduced to careless driving or public intoxication. The unit works closely with the West Texas Adult Probation Department and the Pre-Trial Intervention program. Because the attorneys believe in the effectiveness of PTI as a deterrent, they often suggest PTI for DWI offenders. By doing so, they know that the DWI offender receives treatment conducted under appropriate guidelines.

In addition to prosecution of DWI cases, the special task force also promotes public information and education about DWI. One attorney, Laura Gordon, deals primarily with this function and works closely with various facets of the community to discourage drunk driving. In late February of this year, the Victims Panel Project was begun. The panel members were volunteers from MADD, and the audience was composed of first offenders enrolled in the PTI program. Apprehension and uncertainty were high prior to the first panel discussion, but afterward most were in agreement that it was a successful endeavor and should be continued. There was no real hostility between the panel and the audience, and both felt it provided valuable insight into "the other's perspective." Subsequent to the panel's first meeting, other victims in El Paso County, many not members of MADD, called expressing their desire to participate in the project.

At the time of the visit to El Paso, efforts also were underway to begin a "Project Graduation" at some of the local high schools. Originated in Maine, this event is designed to be "a chemical-free celebration of life" for graduating students and their friends. Two of these events were successfully carried out in Texas last year--one in Del Valle and the other in Lubbock. They involve close cooperation between the participating school and the local community. The students raise the necessary funds from local firms and businesses to conduct the many graduation activities. The emphasis is on having fun without consuming alcohol or drugs. Activities may range from picnics to camp-outs to swim parties and more. In the end, the success of these projects depends largely on the creativeness and enthusiasm of the high school students, coupled with the necessary financial backing and moral support of the community.

El Paso Police Department STEP Program

The El Paso Police Department has a Selective Traffic Enforcement Program (STEP) directed at DWI enforcement efforts. On Wednesday through Saturday nights and on all holidays, four police officers work overtime patrolling areas with a high incidence of alcohol-related injury accidents. These officers, who work from 10:00 p.m. to 2:00 a.m., receive extra in-house training for spotting and apprehending drunk drivers. Each officer is expected to make at least one DWI arrest per night.

The program began October 1, 1983, and since then DWI arrests have doubled. At the same time, the number of police department officers has not increased. One problem that has arisen is that drunk drivers are using alternate routes to avoid the patrol areas. However, this cat-and-mouse game has not discouraged the police department in its efforts to enforce stringently drinking and driving laws.

Adult Probation Department

The West Texas Regional Adult Probation Department considers itself a coordinator of anti-DWI efforts in El Paso County. The probation department has 42 probation officers, with each officer responsible for an average of 160 cases. Almost one-half of all cases are DWI offenders. All 42 officers have had alcohol training, and 30 officers soon will receive additional intensive training. Two of the probation officers work solely on Project Home (described below). Two other officers handle caseloads that are 80 percent DWI offenders, electing to keep the remaining 20 percent of their caseloads for other types of offenders for diversity.

In February 1985, 1,200 DWI offenders were participating in the PTI program, which is administered by the probation department. This is the only PTI program in the state that is in full operation and that is located within a probation department. The program appears to be very successful in El Paso County. Only a small number do not complete the program, and those who do not finish receive priority on the docket. The PTI program is three years old, and thus far probably less than twenty of those completing the program have had subsequent DWI arrests.

Without the PTI program as a diversion mechanism, the county attorney's office would be unable to handle all the DWI cases. By the time of the arraignment, it is already determined if the offender qualifies for the PTI program. This saves both time and paperwork. The prosecutor can meet and confer with the probation department if he disagrees with the recommended disposition.

The probation department also has developed a program called "Project Home." Participants in the program are confined to their home except during working hours. Two probation officers counsel the participants in their homes. "Project Home," with twenty-five participants in February 1985, has decreased the amount of required jail space.

Recently, the probation department and Fort Bliss finalized plans for the DWI Inpatient Evaluation and Education Program. Fort Bliss already had established a program whereby any military personnel picked up for DWI spent five days as a patient in the military hospital. During the five days, the offender underwent assessment and counseling, received alcohol education, and attended a panel discussion by El Paso County officials active in the anti-DWI effort. The expanded program includes the 5,800 civilian employees at Fort Bliss. Civilian employees of the military installation convicted of DWI now can be sentenced to the forty-hour program at the military hospital. They can obtain sick leave for the time of attendance. This program received the support of the commanding officer at Fort Bliss. Other military bases have expressed an interest in the five-day hospital stay concept for their personnel.

Record Keeping

The county clerk's office coordinates the procedure for reporting convictions and probations to DPS, as provided by Senate Bill 1. The process begins when an individual pleads guilty or is found guilty of DWI. The county clerk's office notifies the sheriff's department of a request for any information that they might have on the individual. The sheriff's department, which receives a request for information on everyone convicted or probated for DWI, runs a criminal history check to determine if the individual is guilty of a misdemeanor or a felony DWI. Criminal records are sent to the county clerk's office for only felony cases. The sheriff's department does not keep any type or record of the requests that it receives. It takes about three to four weeks for the county clerk's office to receive a response from the sheriff's department. Ninety percent of the requests for information are returned with "no record--police department arrest" noted on them. The county clerk's office makes copies of the judgment, the information from the sheriff, the sentence, and the complaint, and forwards this information to DPS, along with the driver's license if it was suspended.

For DWI offenders placed on probation, a separate copy of the probation report is sent to DPS. The DWI school that the offender attends also is given a copy which it returns to DPS when the individual completes the alcohol education program. If DPS does not receive the DWI school's copy within 181 days, meaning that the individual has not completed the program, DPS is obligated to suspend the individual's driver's license.

The county clerk's office makes a report of every case. It keeps a copy of the notice sent to the sheriff and a log, detailing by name and case number the date that the information was sent to DPS. Information for presentence investigations is filed in indexes, and the court cases are kept on microfiche.

At the end of 1984, 6,711 cases were pending on the docket. Officials did not consider this total to be excessive. The special DWI task force within the county attorney's office is helping to eliminate the backlog. Currently, the average length of time from arrest to disposition of a case in El Paso County is eight weeks.

Overall, record keeping in the county is not viewed as a problem area. Since Luther Jones became county attorney, record keeping has improved. Further improvements are expected as the county clerk's system is computerized and integrated with the sheriff's department, the police department, and the district attorney.

Problems with the DWI Process

One feature of the DWI system in El Paso County that has not changed, and that is cited as a problem, is the requirement that a justice of the peace (JP) be summoned to give the magistrate's warning after an arrest and before a BAC test can be given. If a justice of the peace is not available, a police officer may give the warning. Law enforcement officials are especially unhappy with this requirement because of the delay it causes in administering the test.

Other problems are difficult to ascertain at this time. Under the leadership of the new county attorney, many changes were implemented to deal with the problems in the DWI process in El Paso County. The results were immediate, as shown by the increase in DWI cases filed (the 1984 figure was 69 percent higher than in 1982). Also, Senate Bill 1 went into effect January 1, 1984, creating more changes. Due to the many recent changes and improvements in the DWI process, it is too early to tell if and where any problems remain.

Effectiveness of Senate Bill 1

Officials in El Paso County are pleased, for the most part, with Senate Bill 1. Establishing .10 percent BAC as a per se level of intoxication, allowing admission of a BAC test refusal as evidence, prohibiting deferred adjudication in DWI cases, and stiffening the penalties for DWI violations are viewed the most favorably. With a .10 percent BAC per se level of intoxication, more offenders will be forced to plead guilty. Admission of refusal to take a BAC test makes it seem as if the person had something to hide, inferring guilt. The prohibition of deferred adjudication in DWI cases should result in more offenders being given probation, which is a final conviction. The stiffened penalties also should help clarify probation as a final conviction and should help in handling repeat offenders.

Other changes created by Senate Bill 1 received mixed responses. The provision that allows police officers to order breath and blood tests gives officers more leverage, but it is too early to tell if it will be used. Officials felt it is a good idea in theory, but that it might be hard to find someone who will give a BAC test against the offender's will.

The new procedure for reporting convictions and probations to DPS has created much additional paperwork for the county clerk's office. If the arrest is made by the police department, the sheriff's department does not have the arrest information. The time spent contacting the sheriff's department is wasted. To obtain the information, the police department also would be required to conduct reporting. It is believed that the DPS is not acting on the information it receives from the counties because it is not suspending the licenses of offenders who fail to complete alcohol education programs. Centralization of the arrest and disposition information is necessary, but the process established by Senate Bill 1 has several weaknesses.

The changes in the implied consent license revocation procedures are viewed as good because the burden of requesting a hearing is shifted from the county attorney to the offender. However, offenders are not made aware of this until after they have been arrested. It would be a more effective deterrent if better publicized; justices of the peace are finding ways to evade this provision.

The videotaping of offenders is perceived as more negative than positive. It can work for the prosecution if the offender appears drunk, but it also can work against the prosecution, particularly for offenders with high alcohol tolerances. Because videotaping is not an accurate test of sobriety, its use should not be a requirement.

Recommendations for Making Senate Bill 1 More Effective

Since Senate Bill 1 only became effective in 1984, it is still too early to draw any conclusions concerning its effectiveness and where improvements are needed. One improvement recommended in the DWI process that would be in addition to Senate Bill 1 is sentencing guidelines. Within El Paso County, sentences for DWI offenders are very inconsistent. The county attorney's office and the West Texas Regional Adult Probation Department are collaborating to develop uniform sentencing recommendations for DWI offenders in the county. A review of the disparity among Texas counties in sentencing DWI offenders might encourage the development of uniform sentencing guidelines for the state.

Conclusions

In recent years, several factors have converged in El Paso County which have strengthened anti-DWI efforts. Luther Jones became county attorney and took a strong stand against DWI offenders. A special DWI task force was created within his office to increase DWI convictions. With the greater number of convictions, the adult probation department had to hire more probation officers. Police officers, realizing DWI offenders would be punished, increased the number of DWI arrests.

Additional factors have aided the county's efforts. National awareness of the DWI problem generated publicity and interest. A MADD chapter was formed in El Paso. Probation officers received better alcohol training and created a comprehensive treatment program for DWI offenders. The adult probation department and the West Texas Council on Alcoholism developed a closer working relationship. Fort Bliss and the probation department began cooperating in their anti-DWI efforts. The Texas state legislature passed Senate Bill 1.

Because of the many recent changes, the DWI system in El Paso County is in transition. The DWI system appears to be functioning effectively at this stage, however, and relationships among the participants in the system have improved. El Paso County provides an example of a county that is working to turn its program around and combat the problem of drunk driving.

GRAY COUNTY

Background Information

Gray County covers 921 square miles and is located in the Texas panhandle in the Rolling Plains region on Interstate 40. Pampa is the county seat and also is the major city in Gray County. In 1982, there were 1,120 miles of public roads and 31,695 registered vehicles in Gray County. Law enforcement agencies handled 934 traffic accidents including 21 fatalities. The county population has been on the decline since 1960; however, the rate of decline appears to have tapered off in the past few years. The estimated 1982 county population was 27,700.

In calendar year 1983, there were 272 new misdemeanor DWIs filed. There were 111 cases still pending from 1982, so the total on the docket added up to 383 misdemeanor DWI cases. Of those, 229 pled guilty, with all but 7 receiving probation and a fine. The remaining 7 served some jail time. In 1983, 45 cases were dismissed, leaving 109 misdemeanor cases still pending at the end of the year. Also in 1983, 13 new felony DWIs were filed, with 3 cases pending from the previous year. Nine entered a plea of guilty and 3 cases were dismissed, leaving 4 cases pending for 1984.

In fiscal year 1984, there were 230 new misdemeanor cases filed, with 130 pending from the previous year. Of the 195 cases convicted, 194 pled guilty and 1 was convicted who pled not guilty. A total of 60 cases were dismissed, leaving 105 cases pending from the previous year. Eleven of the felony cases pled guilty, 8 cases were dismissed, and two cases were left pending.

The numbers above give an estimate of the DWI situation in Gray County. They are not precise, however, because 1983 figures are for calendar year 1983, while the report for 1984 is for fiscal year 1984, covering September 1, 1983, through August 31, 1984. A hand count of the misdemeanor and felony DWIs filed in calendar year 1983 revealed that the figures available at the state level for Gray County are scrupulously accurate. The hand count uncovered 265 misdemeanors and 4 felonies in 1983, with virtually all receiving probation and a fine. The hand count came up with 7 fewer misdemeanors and 9 fewer felonies than the number shown at the state level. This indicates that reporting to the state is very thorough and that the discrepancies most likely are due to our error in the hand counting process.

No record is kept of the number of DWI offenders who are residents of Gray and those who are from other counties, but several people suggested that about 60 percent are probably residents, with the remaining 40 percent from the neighboring counties. The counties surrounding Gray are dry, whereas about one-fourth of Gray is a wet county. This fact contributes to the high DWI rate for nonresidents. Many people arrested for DWI in Gray County are just passing through on a one-time trip.

Priority Given to DWI

In 1983, a total of 400 misdemeanor cases were filed. Of these, 272 were misdemeanor DWI cases. This means that almost 75 percent of all misdemeanor cases in Gray County are DWIs. Therefore, due to its sheer volume, DWI is allotted a high priority. Enforcement of DWI is taken seriously, with frequent arrests. The number of DWI cases filed and the number of DWI arrests are not the same in Gray County, so the statistics may be misleading. In many counties, the flow of information is such that all DWI arrest reports are given to the county clerk to be filed in the county docket books. The clerk then forwards the reports to the county attorney, who decides whether or not the case is worth prosecuting. In Gray County, however, the DWI arrest report is forwarded directly to the county attorney's office. Only after the county attorney decides which cases he wishes to prosecute are the reports sent to the county clerk for filing. This prevents the misfiling of cases which will not be followed.

Although all county officials interviewed considered DWI to be a high priority, problems do exist. There is more concern for second offenders than for first offenders, but only 5 to 10 percent of all DWIs are second offenders in Gray County. There also is a concern for the overall effect the punishment will have on the community. In other words, too harsh a punishment for a first offense is seen by some in the county as hurting the offender's family through the loss of badly needed money or a job. Senate Bill 1 was not perceived as changing the priority placed on DWI. It is handled in much the same way it always has been handled.

Focus of DWI Program Effort

Gray County does not focus its efforts on any one program area such as law enforcement or prosecution. Instead, its efforts are evenly distributed among all elements of the DWI system. Each person interviewed feels that the effort in Gray County is diversified and no one has any problem with this approach. There is no treatment facility in the county, but offenders requiring treatment can be sent to nearby Amarillo or receive counseling through the local Mental Health and Mental Retardation (MHMR) counseling facilities. There also is no coordinated public information effort, but public awareness of the penalties for DWI appears to be high. Gray is a small, friendly county in which a word-of-mouth approach is adequate. The newspaper does publish a notice of those convicted of DWI, and ministers occasionally mention the problem in their sermons.

Effectiveness of County Agency Relationships

In general, agency relationships are close, with the offices of all but the Department of Public Safety (DPS) located in a one-block radius. Most of the offices are in the same building. This geographic proximity allows for the development of close working relationships and an understanding which would not be possible in a larger county.

However, there is a distinct difference in philosophy between the law enforcement and prosecution components, which leads to some frustration on the part of both. Law enforcement officers feel that they sometimes are wasting their time because many of their DWI arrests are not prosecuted. The county prosecuter, on the other hand, feels that the community is unlikely to convict the average DWI case, were it to go to trial. He looks, therefore, for mitigating circumstances or a BAC level a little higher than .10 percent before pressing charges, unless the offender pleads guilty. The prosecutor also feels that law enforcement officers issue DWI charges through "bar watching," that is, waiting for potential drunk drivers to come out of bars. He feels that the police officer is endangering the public by allowing a driver known to be impaired to get into the vehicle. The prosecutor feels that the offender should be given a public intoxication charge and stopped before he enters the car. Therefore, cases of this type are returned to the arresting officer, with the request that the charge be reduced to public intoxication.

Adult Probation Department

Gray County has two adult probation officers and a chief who also accepts cases. One of the officers takes intensive caseloads for felonies, but there is no probation officer specializing in DWI cases. There are a total of about 460 cases for the three officers. The adult probation department offers educational classes and counseling for DWI offenders, but it refers people to MHMR Family Services for treatment or to Amarillo, which is only sixty miles away, for serious cases.

Officers attend seminars offering specialized training in dealing with alcohol offenders when possible, but nothing is offered within the county. Records are kept on all offenders, but no particular data on recidivism rates are recorded. In spite of the apparently heavy caseload, the probation department seems satisfied with the current system.

Record Keeping

The county clerk submits a monthly report to DPS on all DWI cases filed in that month. Probations are reported in the same manner on a monthly basis. Offenses are kept in an index file according to name for easy cross-reference, with a notation on the disposition of the case. All those concerned with conducting presentence investigations feel comfortable about relying on state-provided data for all prior convictions. The county clerk is meticulously accurate and just assumes everyone else is as well, so that statewide data is seen as trustworthy. It also was mentioned that most people could be relied upon to tell the judge about any prior conviction when asked under oath.

The length of time which elapses from the arrest to the final disposition varies widely, depending largely on whether the offender hires a lawyer to contest the case. Cases may take anywhere from thirty days to two years to be resolved. There is not a significant backlog of cases in Gray County, with about 116 pending cases. In a typical nonholiday month, twenty-seven new cases are filed and forty are disposed of.

Problems with the DWI Process

No one in Gray County likes the changes provided by Senate Bill 1, but feel that they can live with them. They prefer the flexibility that was available before the changes. People surprisingly do not see any problem with information processing and record keeping, a problem which is a central concern in many counties. The residents of Gray County trust the accuracy of their clerks and, failing that, are likely to recognize a second offender's face anyway.

Effectiveness of Senate Bill 1

Senate Bill 1 has had no demonstrable effect in Gray County, except perhaps as an irritant. The passage of .10 percent BAC level as the definition of legal intoxication has had no effect in strengthening DWI convictions and may have hurt the local system. The county attorney looks for extenuating circumstances of a higher than .10 percent BAC level before pressing charges because juries in Gray County are unlikely to convict just because the driver registered a .10 percent BAC level on the Intoxilyzer test. Juries take into account the possibility of testing error and the fact that some people are impaired at less than a .10 percent BAC level, while others are not visibly impaired until registering a much higher rating. The .10 percent standard has discouraged the possibility of conviction at a lower than .10 percent rating regardless of the circumstances.

The provision in Senate Bill 1 which allows the admission of the refusal to take the breath test at the trial has had no effect in the county. The breath test virtually is never refused. On the few cases where it is refused, that fact would not be entered into evidence at the trial, even though allowed under Senate Bill 1, because it is seen as confusing to the jury. The jury is told that they cannot hold the refusal to take the test against the offender, so there is little use in presenting that evidence to them, according to the county attorney.

There is universal dislike of the removal of deferred adjudication. Deferred adjudication is seen as a useful tool which provided the court and the prosecuting attorney with needed flexibility in handling DWI offenders. It also is viewed as unfair that deferred adjudication still is permitted for more serious crimes. With the removal of deferred adjudication, the level of convictions looked remarkably high on a percentage basis because all that were not convicted were erased from the record.

The provision in Senate Bill 1 allowing police officers to order blood tests is seen as useless and unenforceable because there is no penalty for failure of hospital personnel to comply. It is not felt that blood tests aid in obtaining a conviction anyway, so they seldom are ordered. In general, hospitals in Gray County cooperate in the few cases where a blood test is requested, but this cooperation is not attributed to Senate Bill 1.

The new procedure for reporting convictions to the Department of Public Safety (DPS) is taken in stride, but not welcomed. The county clerk was relieved to know that someone at the state level uses the data and admitted that getting used to the new format took some time, but adjusting to changes is considered to be a normal part of the job. The new procedure is not seen as an improvement necessarily, but only as another change in reporting. There is a consensus that the forms change too often.

The changes in the law which allow for the administrative removal of licenses is not liked. It rarely has to be used because the offender rarely refuses the breath test. However, in a few cases where the breath test has been refused, it has been successfully challenged in court. The defense attorney has alleged that the arresting officer must be present at the administrative hearing to remove the license because he is the accuser. The lawyer will not permit a DPS hearing officer to perform the administrative function. There also is some sense that a poor offender would lose his job if his license were revoked, resulting in an entire family being forced to go on welfare. The option of obtaining an occupational driver's license is considered unrealistic, since it requires the hiring of a lawyer and several hundred dollars expense, which the average working-class person in the county cannot afford.

Gray County is not in compliance with the requirement to possess videotaping equipment. The county does not feel that videotaping is particularly useful and does not wish to expend precious resources for equipment which never would be used. There is a feeling that the state legislature sometimes ignores the financial situation of smaller counties. Gray County officials feel that cheap equipment, which is all the county can afford, would be worse than no equipment at all.

The changes in Senate Bill 1 which provide for stiffer penalties have resulted in slightly increased fines and longer probations. However, neither of these changes is viewed as an improvement. The average DWI offender in Gray County could not afford the old fines, so increasing the fines is an exercise in futility. Many of the stiffer penalties are directed at repeat offenders, and the county experiences very few of these cases.

Recommendations for Making Senate Bill 1 More Effective

County officials would like to see a return to the old law. Barring that, they at least would like the videotaping provision be made optional. A provision should be added mandating fines for noncompliance with the request for a blood test so that this part of the law is enforceable, if ever needed. The law should specify that a person may be prosecuted with a BAC level under .10 percent so that it would be clear that this is not a lower limit. Deferred adjudication should be restored, with a reporting mechanism attached, so that people are not lost in the system. Stiffer penalties are in order for second offenders, but increased fines or jail time is not the answer in Gray County. The average resident is too poor to afford the fines, and the jail is too full of other felons to permit any increased incarceration. With the new jail standards, Gray's jail capacity fell from twenty-six to fourteen persons, and it is virtually always full to capacity without any DWI offenders. An alternative to jail, which is suggested for investigation, is the impoundment of the offender's vehicle for felony DWI offenses. There is plenty of room for car storage in the county, so impoundment might prove to be a feasible option.

Conclusions

The interviewed officials often expressed a concern for the plight of the DWI offender. It is felt that the poor are overrepresented in the number of DWIs arrested and convicted. Fines and jail time are seen as having the effect of damaging the entire county by forcing families on welfare and seriously disrupting lives due to the poverty level of those usually found guilty. Some alternative form of punishment would be welcomed.

Public awareness of DWI as a problem and the severity of punishments, if convicted, are reported as high, in spite of a lack of any organized public information program. Due to the size of Gray County, word-of-mouth seems to suffice. Most offenders plead guilty, when caught, and acknowledge that they have committed a serious crime. Virtually all first offenders are given probation and a fine. There is some concern that there is no recourse when probation is violated, due to the crowded jail situation.

There were fourteen fatal accidents in Gray County two years ago, seven of which were DWI related. So far this year, there have been five fatal accidents, only one of which was DWI related. This indicates that in spite of some perceived setbacks, the county is making progress in solving its DWI problem.

HARRIS COUNTY

Background Information

Harris County covers 1,734 square miles and is located along the southeast portion of the Gulf Coast area on Interstate Highways 45 and 10 in the Coastal Prairie region. The county seat is Houston. The 1982 estimated population of 2,684,100 indicates a continuation of the very strong past growth. Forty percent of Harris County's population growth rate between 1970 and 1980 took place in urban areas where the county's population is concentrated. Persons of English descent make up 20 percent of the population, followed by 20 percent black, 15 percent Irish, and 15 percent German.

The county had 11,785 miles of public roads and 2,075,088 registered vehicles in 1982. In the same year, 100,464 traffic accidents including 683 fatalities were reported. In 1983, there were 26,011 misdemeanor and 1,873 felony DWI cases filed in Harris County. Over the same span of time, 18,588 offenders entered a guilty plea, 202 were found guilty by trial, and 4,026 cases were dismissed. As for punishment, 9,502 offenders were put on probation, 123 received a fine only, and 9,454 served time in jail.

In the following year, there were 22,270 misdemeanor and 598 felony DWI cases filed. Of the total 26,019 cases disposed, 20,744 offenders entered a guilty plea, 168 were found guilty by trial, and 5,107 cases were dismissed. Punishment involved 11,209 offenders put on probation, 9 receiving a fine only, and 10,364 serving time in jail.

Priority and Focus of Program Efforts

DWI is given a very high priority in Harris County by all agencies involved in the process. The focus of Harris County's efforts is on law enforcement and adjudication. Most agencies and departments recognize that enforcement and adjudication are imperative when addressing the drinking and driving problem. Attention also is given to other areas, namely probation and public information. Working relationships within the county are cohesive and effective. Knowledge of and respect for other agencies' activities are evident, although occasional problems do arise. The activities of the Houston Regional Council on Alcoholism, Inc., for example, are unfamiliar to most other actors involved with the county DWI system. Also, there are varying views on the efficacy of videotaping. Overall, there is mutual support of the county's objectives: to increase public awareness of the consequences of drinking and driving--both to the drinking driver and society--and to enforce the DWI laws aggressively.

Special Programs

In the area of law enforcement, Harris County has three special programs: a DWI task force, a Selective Traffic Enforcement Program (STEP), and a Houston Metro Area Safety Task Force. The first program is the Houston Police Department's DWI task force. Ten one-person units and two supervisors work five days a week--Tuesday through Saturday--from 9:00 p.m. to 5:00 a.m. to apprehend drunk drivers. Funded completely by the city of Houston, the ten hand-picked officers have been trained to spot intoxicated drivers; conduct field sobriety tests, including the Horizontal Gaze Nystigmus (HGN) eye test; perform traffic stops; and recognize other causes that may make one appear intoxicated, for example, insulin shock. In addition, the task force officers attend an eight-hour class every four months to review procedures, means of detection, and laws. Task force officers volunteer to assist regular officers, as the task force officers can process persons suspected of driving while intoxicated in much less time. Although the task force concept is new in law enforcement, it is working quite well in Houston.

STEP, the second special program, is similar to others conducted nationwide. STEP utilizes federal highway funds to hire off-duty police officers to patrol a designated area for intoxicated drivers.

The third special program is the Houston Metro Area Safety Task Force. This task force consists of representatives of the Houston Police Department, DPS, Harris County, and the city of Houston. Among other activities, this group sponsors four task force operations per year. DPS troopers, Houston police officers, and county police officers band together to patrol a publicized area for an evening. Friendly competition arises as the various law enforcement officers seek to exert that extra effort to see which department can arrest the most intoxicated drivers.

In addition to these special law enforcement programs, the Houston Regional Council on Alcoholism, Inc., sponsors a unique Advanced School for problem drinkers. The eighteen-hour program focuses on problem solving and family awareness of drinking and its effects. Although it is a relatively new program, the council sees the Advanced School as a promising way to reach problem drinkers.

County Alcohol Council and Adult Probation Department

Supplementing this special program, the alcohol council works closely with the adult probation department in evaluating and treating persons convicted of driving while intoxicated. The council serves mainly to counsel and refer social drinkers, potential problem drinkers, and problem drinkers. The council offers Alcoholism and Drug Awareness programs, administers evaluations, sponsors public information activities, and gives referrals. Representatives of the council expressed concern that only those convicted of DWI and given probation are evaluated for a drinking problem. In their view, all convicted DWI offenders should be evaluated. Moreover, council workers advise that treatment should be required by law whenever a person is identified as a problem drinker.

The alcohol council has an excellent rapport with the adult probation department. These two agencies collaborate frequently. The probation officers also administer evaluation tests and sponsor a DWI School. Fifty percent of the probation cases consist of persons convicted of DWI, with the average caseload of two hundred probationers per probation officer. The adult probation department does have specialized caseloads for DWI offenders who have been identified as problem drinkers. There is some effort to train all officers in dealing with alcohol offenders, and special caseload officers are certified in dealing with alcohol problems. Probation is seen as both a means of providing needed treatment and a deterrent to further drinking and driving. The terms of supervised probation generally are intrusive and inconvenient for the offender. Unsupervised probation, though, may be assessed; it involves no fee and no supervision by a probation officer. One judge in Houston regularly gives this punishment. Alcohol council representatives, as well as probation officers, find this practice bothersome and unacceptable. The probation department also conducts research and planning projects. One such effort culminated in "A Study of the Initial Effects of the New Texas DWI Law on Pretrial Sanctions and Probation Disposition in Harris County," published in December 1984.

Record Keeping

In Harris County, the district clerk's office is responsible for reporting felonies and misdemeanors to DPS. This is accomplished via a weekly report which documents all cases disposed of that week. This report is printed on paper and then copied onto microfiche. All cases with known disposition are reported. In March 1985, 10,908 misdemeanor cases and 293 felony cases awaited final disposition in Harris County. A seemingly large 40 percent of these cases still are awaiting disposition because they received deferred adjudication. This excessive number will be reduced as cases of deferred adjudication are disposed of. Thus, there is not an excessive backlog of current, active cases. The record-keeping system, according to the district clerk's office, is adequate and accurate.

Problems with the DWI Process

Several problems with the overall DWI process were identified. A major problem is the total number of people who need to be processed through the system. There were over twenty-two thousand arrests for DWI in Harris County during 1984. The problem is particularly evident on weekends, when there is an enormous increase in the number of arrests. The suspects quickly fill the outlying suburban and satellite jails. This necessitates the transportation of suspects to the larger county jail in downtown Houston for processing. This transportation reduces the time law enforcement officers have to patrol for additional offenders. The additional travel time can add upwards to an hour to the processing time. Additional delays result from the need for the arrest warrant to be in hand prior to transporting the prisoners from the substations to the main jail. The warrants are transmitted via a telecopier. This is a slow process, which adds to the bottleneck.

The videotaping of defendants also adds to processing time in two ways. All DWI arrests in Harris County are required to be videotaped. The backlog of those arrested can result in delays of two-and-one-half hours for taping. The videotaping also inhibits court scheduling and trials. Defense attorneys sometimes drag their feet in reviewing the tapes, thus extending the scheduling of trials. Although the average tape is approximately only fifteen minutes in length, the time needed for review during the trial can add to its length. The defense and prosecutor will refer to the tape periodically during the trial in their deliberations.

Record keeping and information processing are two other areas identified as being problematic. Law enforcement officers frequently are unable to determine the status of an individual's driving record quickly. Because of a large backlog in license suspensions, DPS has not confiscated all the licenses. Individuals do drive even though their license has been suspended. Additionally, officials believe the delay to be at the DPS facility in Austin, because information is not being entered onto the individual's driving record as rapidly as it should be. This creates problems in determining whether the individual has had previous DWI offenses.

Many of those convicted of DWI opt for jail time, rather than probation. Probation is viewed as a greater inconvenience because of the amount of time involved meeting the conditions; serving three days in the county jail often is viewed as more expeditious than making monthly contact with a probation officer. There also are additional costs associated with probation. The greatest displeasure with offenders choosing jail over probation is that it allows the offenders to skirt alcohol evaluation. Many individuals who should be receiving alcohol treatment are bypassed because they do not receive adequate screening. The problem is exacerbated by the fact that many of the individuals are in the repeat offender categories, indicating a problem drinker.

Tied closely to the frequent choice of jail time is a perceived failure to enforce the minimum jail standards. Because the sheriff provides credit for time already served, those scheduled for jail time do not serve the entire sentence. Some of the time accrues during processing for arrests, making jail confinement only a minor inconvenience.

Even with the apparent effect of Senate Bill 1, officials emphasize that DWI is not considered a major problem by the public. Some judges are hesitant to convict individuals of DWI even after a review of the available evidence. Some officials expressed the need for developing a better community understanding. It is believed that people need to be educated as to the health implications, as well as to the legal aspects, to expect adequate local support and compliance.

Effectiveness of Senate Bill 1

County officials expressed overall support for Senate Bill 1. There is general agreement that the .10 percent BAC as the per se level of intoxication is very effective. However, because all DWI offenders are videotaped, there is concern that the effectiveness of the .10 percent BAC level is not as great as it could be. The videotaping of suspects is perceived as hindering prosecution in many cases. Even though many defendants register a .10 percent or higher level, if they perform well during the videotaping they are usually found not guilty. However, situations were cited that indicated that the videotaping has enhanced the state's case by resulting in many cases being resolved through plea bargaining.

The admission of the BAC test refusal is deemed to be effective. Some agencies cited it as the best point of the new legislation. Mandatory blood testing also is adjudged to be effective. However, this provision is issued only in cases of severe injury and/or death. Several agencies noted hospital personnel not wanting to conduct the test as another problem.

County officials stated that the prohibition of deferred adjudication is effective. It is believed that anything that would be accomplished by deferred adjudication could be covered under a probated sentence.

The initiation of stiffer penalties is not deemed to be an effective measure of the bill. Some agencies expressed the opinion that the penalties are really not stiff and that as an inhibitor to DWI, they are much less effective. Others indicated that the penalties are not being enforced.

The reporting of convictions and probations is not deemed effective. Problems and concerns were voiced regarding whether the information is being reported in a timely manner, if at all, since it requires more time of the district clerk to process the necessary information. Some agencies would like to see a more centralized reporting system to facilitate the retrieval of enforcement and judicial information.

There is mixed opinion regarding the effectiveness of the implied consent license revocation procedures. Most agencies feel that the concept is good, but that there exists too much discretion in its use. It also is believed to exert a disproportionately unfair impact on the poor and less-educated residents of the county.

Recommendations for Making Senate Bill 1 More Effective

Most of the suggested improvements to Senate Bill 1 address those areas overlooked during the drafting of the initial legislation. County officials believe that these minor but important changes would resolve some difficulties currently being encountered in applying Senate Bill 1.

Licensed morticians should be covered under the same immunity afforded physicians. Morticians have been reluctant to draw blood specimens without the protection of immunity. The implied consent sections should be expanded to include all areas, such as shopping malls and apartment complexes. No area should be exempt from the law. All DWI offenders should be required to undergo alcohol evaluation. The evaluation would be an incentive for choosing probation, which includes a treatment regime. Additionally, funding grants should be provided for those individuals who are not able to afford the cost of treatment. Funding also should be provided for research into the effectiveness of the programs already in place. DWI educational programs should be included as part of the driver's license renewal procedure.

Officials expressed a desire for a modification of the videotaping procedure. Some believed that the videotaping should not be used at all. Action should be taken regarding the ability to charge a defendant with aggravated bodily injury. The need for flexibility in filing the most appropriate charge is deemed to be very important.

Finally, opinions were offered regarding occupational driver's license requests. Requests should be heard by the convicting judge. Far too often, those convicted of DWI apply to judges who are unfamiliar with the case. Additionally, a provision should be made to revoke the license plates from the vehicle used in a felony DWI.

Two additional laws were cited by many county officials as being necessary to complement the existing provisions of Senate Bill 1. The drinking age should be raised to twenty-one years. Officials also favor the banning of open alcoholic containers within the passenger section of a motor vehicle.

Conclusions

DWI is given a very high priority in Harris County by all agencies involved in the process. The major focus is on the law enforcement and adjudication components of the system. Special programs primarily are found in the enforcement component. Problems within the system can be traced to the sheer number of cases needing to be processed through each system component. Bottlenecks occur, particularly during high arrest periods. Videotaping also is identified as an area where officials acknowledge that problems exist. Slow and inadequate information processing and access exacerbate the ability to properly charge individuals. While the system has been successful in Harris County, there is a need to integrate the treatment and probation components more effectively. By providing a mechanism to evaluate all DWI offenders, those individuals suffering from the underlying disease of alcoholism can be identified and provided the opportunity to obtain treatment.

HARRISON COUNTY

Background Information

Harrison County covers 908 square miles and is located in the East Texas Timberland region on Interstate Highway 20. The county seat is Marshall. The 1982 estimated population was fifty-five thousand; between 1970 and 1980, population increased 16 percent. This relatively low-income agricultural county has a population mix of approximately 32 percent black, 22 percent of English decent, and 17 percent of Irish decent. Harrison County had 1,457 miles of public roads and 42,228 registered vehicles in 1982. In that same year, the county reported 1,504 traffic accidents with 22 fatalities.

The district attorney's office reported 571 misdemeanor DWI cases filed in 1983, with more than three-fourths of these cases involving county residents. Over the same span of time, 483 entered a guilty plea, 2 were found guilty by trial, and 79 were dismissed for various reasons. Only 31 of these final dispositions received jail time. A total of 146 received only a fine, and 306 received probation. In the following year, 1984, the total number of misdemeanor cases dropped almost 40 percent from 571 to 368, with the overwhelming majority attributed to county residents. As for final dispositions, 310 entered a guilty plea, 3 were found guilty by trial, and 67 were dismissed. Punishments consisted of 216 receiving probation, 48 receiving fines only, and 35 receiving jail sentences.

In 1983, there were 25 felony DWIs filed. A plea of guilty was entered 21 times, and 6 cases were dismissed for various reasons. Punishments consisted of 12 probations and 9 jail sentences. In 1984, only 10 felony DWIs were filed. Twelve felony cases entered a guilty plea and 7 were dismissed for various reasons. Nine cases received probation and 3 received jail sentences. There has not been a felony trial for DWI in Harrison County during the past two years.

In Harrison County, the typical punishment for a misdemeanor DWI is a $400-$600 fine and two years probation. This usually is reduced to a $300-$400 fine and thirty-sixty days probation. A DWI felon usually receives five years probation and, increasingly, a jail sentence.

Priority Given to DWI

Most Harrison County officials believe that DWI has received a high priority since the passage of Senate Bill 1. This general belief, however, sometimes is contradicted by responses to perceived problems with the DWI process, recommendations for improvement, and differing views regarding the degree of public concern about DWI. And despite apparent strong and cohesive interagency relationships within the county, the actions of some public officials do not represent behavior which reflects a high priority. The demographics of the county also have played an important role in fashioning the current DWI system.

Focus of DWI Program Efforts

The focus of the Harrison County efforts is on probation. The overwhelming majority of offenders enter a guilty plea and receive probation as the sole punishment. A secondary emphasis is on treatment and rehabilitation. All persons convicted of DWI offenses are sent to the Sabine Valley Regional Mental Health and Mental Retardation Center (MHMR) for a Mortimer-Filkins Test evaluation, as well as to DWI school to be educated about the hazards of drinking and driving. Both of these activities appear to be the foundation of the county DWI efforts, although no clear focus is apparent in many of the agencies.

This apparent lack of focus probably is the result of two factors. First, most agencies simply perform the routine tasks that are required by Senate Bill 1. Second, though most of the agencies feel that there exists a deep citizen concern, there is no regular expression of this concern; the citizens appear content with the prevailing activities and practices in the county. This attitude is exemplified by the dissolution of the MADD chapter, which officials attribute both to a lack of interest and to the fact that MADD members found few grievances about abuses in the criminal justice system.

Effectiveness of County Agency Relationships

In general, the interagency relationships within Harrison County are cohesive and strong. Many officials stated that within the county, the relationships could not be better. This probably results from the small size of the county and the proximity of the agencies, as well as their general accessibility. Furthermore, the county's small size facilitates friendships among officials, thereby easing communication.

One potential problem exists in the relationship between the Department of Public Safety (DPS) and the district attorney. Since DPS feels that the district attorney's office is not prosecuting borderline cases where videotapes exhibit only a few signs of inebriation, a resentment might develop. This, in turn, might result in strained communication between the two agencies, although it does not appear to have happened yet.

Special Programs

Several special programs for dealing with DWI offenders are in effect in Harrison County. The county court at law makes frequent use of the county work release program so that the offender can serve jail time and continue to work and support the family. All people found guilty of DWI in the county must attend a DWI school or education program, coordinated by the Sabine Valley Regional Mental Health and Mental Retardation Center (MHMR). Two instructors are under contract to handle this program.

Harrison County also has two alcohol treatment facilities, the outpatient program at MHMR and the inpatient program at the Oak Haven Recovery Center, which also is financed by MHMR. Oak Haven serves a six-county area in East Texas and is located five miles northwest of Marshall, Texas. Referrals from the courts are based on the alcohol assessment performed for the courts by MHMR. MHMR also established a program that offered to drive people home who had too much to drink, during the 1984 Christmas and New Year holidays. Officials credit this program with making the community more aware of the problem through the publicity it received. However, actual response to the service was extremely light.

A unique relationship exists in Harrison County between the county court at law, which hears misdemeanor cases, and Alcoholics Anonymous (AA). AA normally takes only voluntary participants, but in Harrison County they accept referrals from the court. This avenue frequently is used in the county as a required part of probation in cases where this type of program is needed.

Finally, the Department of Public Safety in the county participates in Selective Traffic Enforcement Program (STEP) in conjunction with the neighboring counties along Interstate 20. The program has been successful, netting an estimated one hundred additional DWI arrests than normal over a four-month period.

County Alcohol Council

The Harrison County Council on Alcoholism is not a leading actor in the county DWI system. With an annual budget of $500, their activities are severely limited. Therefore, the rehabilitation function within the county is handled by MHMR. MHMR is the referral agency for all Mortimer-Filkins testing, as well as for general presentence investigation interviews. Data are recorded on all people treated, although follow-up data are missing due to the lack of funds. This lack of funds also appears to be the reason behind the lack of increased program efforts in the rehabilitation and treatment areas. MHMR has one staff person and one secretary dedicated solely to DWI, indicating a low priority for DWI in the agency. Approximately $42 thousand is budgeted to DWI, which helps pay the instructors for the DWI school that MHMR operates in a three-county area. All instructors employed by these facilities have special training in Mortimer-Filkins testing as well as National Council Against Alcoholism seminars.

Adult Probation Department

Because most persons accused of DWI plead guilty, probation is the most common punishment. One adult probation officer has a specialized caseload of DWI offenders and handles approximately 95 percent of all DWI cases. The rest of the probation officers assist with the DWI caseload whenever possible. Average caseloads for the probation officer normally exceed two hundred cases, although the number may vary. All probation officers undergo twenty hours of training per year, much of it geared toward alcohol treatment.

As might be expected, the most pressing need for probation is manpower. With Senate Bill 1 in effect, the adult probation department is receiving more cases than can be adequately supervised. Records are kept for every case, and data are kept on the recidivism rate of DWI offenders. No problem is perceived on the part of the adult probation department with the records kept in the county; many of those convicted of DWI in the county are local residents, and county records apparently are complete.

Record Keeping

In Harrison County, the district and county clerks appear to maintain accurate records of the cases handled by their courts. Within the county clerk's office, there is a time lag in reporting to DPS. Because he does not have the felony conviction information necessary to complete the forms, the county clerk feels it inappropriate to send in the form to DPS. The procedure is that DPS comes to the office approximately three times per year to follow up on the cases. The basic attitude within the county clerk's office is that the clerk follows standard filing procedures and anyone can get the information that is needed.

There is a disparity, however, in the record keeping for felony DWI offenders. The district clerk's office claims it files all cases with DPS on the appropriate forms, although no log or record of this exists. A duplicate copy of the form apparently is filed in the office, but the number of duplicates was less than the number of felony dispositions. Therefore, either the clerk does not report all cases to DPS or there is a problem in the filing system of the receipts of dispositions sent to DPS. The district clerk's office currently is undergoing an automation of the docket.

The irregularities in record keeping have not proved to be a major liability thus far. Neither the district clerk nor the county clerk had trouble obtaining the necessary information; moreover, no agency within the county complained about a lack of information or the efficiency of the clerks.

Problems with the DWI Process

Harrison County officials cited various problems within the DWI process. One basic complaint is that public awareness concerning the seriousness of the DWI offense needs to be heightened. They believe that most people feel a DWI conviction is merely an inconvenience, thereby ignoring the potential hazards involved in drunk driving. Reasons cited for this perceived ambivalence is that disposition is slow and people can simply enter a guilty plea and undergo probation. Another common problem is insufficient manpower and money, especially in the areas of probation, treatment, and rehabilitation. In these areas, caseloads are heavy, and officials expressed the desire to spend more time with each offender.

A final problem noted is that the overall conviction rate would be higher if police officers were trained better in the use of videotaping equipment. This view is related to another complaint that prosecution is not always equitable in borderline cases and in DWI cases involving prominent citizens.

Effectiveness of Senate Bill 1

All parties interviewed agreed that the provisions included in Senate Bill 1 generally have been effective with certain exceptions. The provisions requiring new reporting procedures have no effect in Harrison County because the county clerk's office does not fill out the forms. Instead, DPS officers follow up on the arrests themselves. Videotaping of all DWI suspects received a mixed reaction. Some officials were strong advocates of the procedure because it enhances the prosecution's case; others were strongly opposed because an alcoholic may not appear drunk on the videotape. The reduction in cases prosecuted in the county partly is attributed to a reluctance to pursue these questionable cases.

Due to the low per capita income of the county, the effectiveness of implied consent license revocation procedures also is questioned. Many people who drive in the county cannot afford driver's licenses in the first place; thus, a revocation will not deter their driving. Finally, the stiffening of penalties under Senate Bill 1 is perceived as having a negligible effect on the penalties given in the county. Increased public pressure--though somewhat sporadic--generally is credited with the stiffer penalties that are now given in Harrison County, rather than specific provisions included in Senate Bill 1.

Recommendations for Making Senate Bill 1 More Effective

One recommendation for making Senate Bill 1 more effective is an automatic, or stronger, suspension of licenses even with probation. This would make punishment more severe and perhaps would lead to a change in public attitudes. This also would concur with a district attorney's recommendation for mandatory penalties for felony offenders.

Another recommendation from treatment officials is a provision requiring more money to be spent on treatment within the county. This would allow for a more efficient method of assessing and aiding DWI offenders with serious drinking problems.

Throughout the county, officials generally were pleased with Senate Bill 1, and could think of few recommendations for change. One judge said that the bill gave the county all the tools necessary to establish an effective program to confront the drinking driver problem.

Conclusions

Being a relatively small county, Harrison operates under several difficulties that small counties often encounter. The people in the county are in daily contact with each other, making it awkward to accuse acquaintances of neglecting duties, not to mention prosecuting and sentencing them for a crime. Elected officials appear particularly susceptible to the "good-old-boy" network (depending on who knows whom or a person's standing in the community); within this system, equal and just administration of penalties may or may not occur. Furthermore, for many elected officials, each vote is believed crucial due to the small size of the county. There is therefore a tendency to gloss over potential problem areas, asserting that all is working properly in the county. One does not want to be labeled a troublemaker in a small county. Given this working environment, Harrison County does a respectable job of assuring that convicted DWI offenders receive some form of penalty.

However, the county does have problems that warrant attention. The county clerk's office, while maintaining accurate county records, apparently does not, or is not able to, report DWI convictions to DPS, meaning that most convictions never appear on state records. Public information on DWI still is minimal in the county, despite the large strides that have been made nationally in the past several years. The district attorney exercises a great deal of discretion in prosecuting borderline cases, even with the .10 percent per se BAC level for defining legal intoxication.

Finally, although probation definitely is a viable sentencing alternative, it seems to be an overworked option in Harrison County for the support systems that are in place. Probation is the most common punishment for a DWI conviction in Harrison County, yet the funding for health and treatment has not increased accordingly. Harrison County should either diversify its punishment modes or find alternative funding sources for the probation/treatment system components. Existing problems must be addressed before a strengthening of the program can begin. Once this occurs, a program suited to the demographics of the county could have a substantial impact on curbing the problems of DWI in Harrison County.

WEBB COUNTY

Background Information

Webb County borders Mexico on the south and is west of Corpus Christi. The county covers 3,363 square miles, and had an estimated population in 1982 of 109,900. Between 1970 and 1980, the population increased by 33 percent. Almost 96 percent of the inhabitants live in urban areas, with approximately 100,000 living in Laredo, the county seat. Ninety-two percent of those residing in Webb County are of Hispanic ancestry. The county has a total of 999 miles of public roads. In 1982, there were 61,622 registered vehicles and 2,739 reported traffic accidents, including 11 fatalities.

In 1983, prosecutors filed 809 DWI misdemeanor cases and 9 felony cases. Over this period, the courts convicted 441 persons and dismissed 194 persons. In 1984, there was a significant decrease in DWI arrests. County officials attribute the decrease to citizen concerns over stiffer penalties for DWI convictions and a strong awareness campaign concerning the new law. During 1984, prosecutors filed 406 misdemeanor DWI cases and no felony cases. There were 283 convictions and 146 dismissals during 1984. County officials claim that the lack of felonies is due to both the extra caution exercised by those previously convicted and the difficulties in verifying previous DWI convictions. Many individuals in Webb County have the same name, and indictments filed before 1984 often had no date of birth or residence listed. Without additional documentation, it is impossible to tell whether the individual currently being charged also was the person convicted earlier. Some cases filed as misdemeanors should be filed as felonies; however, by the time prosecutors have verified the previous convictions, it is too late to change the charges. While such charges could be refiled, it is a complicated procedure for the already overworked district attorney's office.

The latter part of 1984 and early 1985 showed an upswing in DWI arrests. County officials believe that concern over the new law has subsided and people are being less conscientious. Moreover, public information campaigns are not as frequent, which probably results in a drop in public awareness.

Priority Given to DWI

The number of DWI arrests are of concern in Webb County. Most of the DWI arrests take place within or near the city of Laredo because the rest of the county is sparsely populated. Webb County officials who have duties involving DWI generally agree that it is high on their list of priorities and that DWI-related matters take up a significant amount--often over 50 percent--of their job time.

Focus of DWI Program Efforts

Law enforcement and adjudication are the focal points of the DWI system in Webb County. A large number of people are arrested for the DWI offense. Prosecutors charged over 800 people in 1983, and more than 400 in 1984. All misdemeanor DWI cases are handled by the county court at law judge. The current judge has a reputation of being strict with drunk drivers, especially where the DWI offense resulted in an accident. If restitution has not been made prior to the accused's hearing, the judge is likely to place the defendant in jail in addition to ordering restitution.

The Webb County district attorney's office, which prosecutes all misdemeanor DWI cases, has a policy of no plea bargaining on misdemeanor DWI cases. Currently, there are two assistant district attorneys working on the cases. Most individuals charged with DWI in Webb County plead guilty, so there are few jury trials. The average sentence for a first-time DWI offender in Webb County is a $300-to-$500 fine, two years probation, and any costs relating to the probation, such as the DWI school.

The adult probation department is becoming more concerned with DWI problems. Beginning in 1985, the Webb County probation staff is administering the Mortimer-Filkins Test to all those placed on probation for DWI. This evaluation is to determine whether these individuals have a drinking problem. The testing is being done as the result of a Texas Adult Probation Commission recommendation for all county adult probation departments. All Webb County probation officers who work with DWI offenders have learned to administer the test.

Effectiveness of County Agency Relationships

The county agencies appear to have congenial and cooperative relationships. The principal problem among the agencies appears to be the frequently stalled flow of information. All county officials expressed the desire for computerized record keeping; the efficiency and effectiveness of the county clerk's office could be greatly improved. The clerk feels that he needs additional staff and space to perform his tasks more effectively. However, some county officials seem to feel the current staff in the clerk's office could be operating more efficiently. Information flow among the district attorney's office, the county clerk, and the sheriff needs to be improved as well. Often, the district attorney will dismiss a case without immediately telling the county clerk. The clerk will issue an arrest warrant, which the sheriff serves, only to find out the district attorney had previously dismissed the case. This practice wastes time and creates tension among the three offices.

Special Programs

There are no special Webb County programs dealing specifically with DWI. However, the area does have programs concerned with drug and alcohol abuse. The district attorney's office sponsors a program which works with the Parent-Teachers Association (PTA) and the Governor's War on Drugs to bring drug and alcohol information into the schools. The SMILE program, a student alcohol awareness group, is active at the United High School. The BASTA program (Barrios Alerta Siempre Toman Accion) is a branch of Mental Health and Mental Retardation (MHMR) in the area which primarily deals with drug abusers. In addition, local television and radio stations air some public service announcements concerning drinking and driving. There are two private treatment centers in Webb County: the Laredo Alcoholism Treatment Center and Charter Rio Grande. These two programs cost more money than the other county programs, which are supported by state and local funds. The higher cost means that many problem drinkers arrested for DWI are unable to take advantage of the intensive alcohol treatment offered by such private facilities.

Adult Probation Department

Webb County has three probation officers who deal with misdemeanor offenders. Current caseloads average one hundred probationers per officer. Webb County does not use specialized caseloads, but about 60 percent of the misdemeanor caseloads are DWI offenders.

In 1983, the office had 420 clients who had been charged with driving while intoxicated. In 1984, this number dropped to 220. The Webb County Adult Probation Department is funded, in part, through the collection of probation fees and court fines, and the reduction in the number of those convicted of DWI and placed on probation has meant a significant loss of funds. This financial problem has been exacerbated by high unemployment in the area, meaning that many of those who are convicted of misdemeanor crimes, including DWI, cannot afford to pay their probation fees and court fines. Recent estimates are that fine and fee collections are averaging 35 percent of the total owed. In order to assist their clients financially, the adult probation department recently asked the agency which runs the required DWI school to reduce its fees from $50 to $30.

Record Keeping

The Webb County clerk's office has two assistant county clerks and a number of support staff. Although Laredo and Webb County as a whole have grown in recent years, the clerk's staff has not expanded enough to adequately deal with the increased paperwork. Inadequate personnel and space have resulted in delayed information flow. The provision in the recent DWI law which prohibits deferred adjudication helped the clerk's office somewhat. However, according to the county clerk, the increases in the volume of misdemeanor cases also has resulted in a certain number of cases being lost among all the paperwork. Recently, a task force of representatives from different county offices has been formed to improve information flow to and from all offices working with DWI cases.

Another problem with increased paperwork occurs when Mexican nationals are arrested for various misdemeanor crimes, including DWI. Such arrests require extra paperwork to be processed, and such individuals usually cannot be held accountable for their crimes because they post bond and leave the country. The county cannot afford to detain the individuals because the county jail is constantly full. Webb County is under a court injunction to limit the number of persons in the existing jail.

Still another concern the clerk's office must deal with is distinguishing county residents who have been charged with a crime, but have the same last and first name as other county residents. Addresses may be used to help identify an individual, but many people relocate, so that this is an inadequate form of identification. Social security numbers are not always helpful in the identification process because many residents of Webb County do not have social security numbers. Birth dates seem to be the most effective aid, and the district courts have just begun to note date of birth on indictment papers.

Although each county must report all DWI convictions to the Department of Public Safety (DPS), Webb County is only forwarding information on those individuals who are placed on probation and complete DWI school. The county clerk's office receives a form which verifies that an individual placed on probation has completed the DWI class; the form then is certified and forwarded to DPS in Austin. There is no notification regarding individuals who receive jail terms, are fined, or who have been sentenced to probation but have not attended or completed the DWI class. However, with the new requirement making the DWI class a required condition of probation, this data problem may be alleviated.

The district clerk's office and the district judges only deal with DWI felonies. In 1984, there were no felony cases filed in Webb County. In 1983, there were nine cases of DWI on the district docket. The district clerk's office soon will be automated, so when felony cases are presented to the district courts, the district clerk's office should be able to deal with such cases efficiently.

Problems with the DWI Process

The principal problem in Webb County concerning misdemeanor DWIs, as well as other misdemeanors, is the slow flow of information. These data flow problems could result in cases being filed as misdemeanors when, in fact, they should be filed as felonies. The difficulties in preparing a presentence investigation without adequate data may mean prosecutors will be reluctant to expend the effort on each DWI case. Data flow problems also result in cases being served by the sheriff's office after they have been dismissed by the district attorney or in court, which creates additional complications in fine and fee collection procedures. Other problems include the lack of conviction data forwarded to DPS on individuals not attending the DWI school.

Another problem in the local system is that only seven police officers are qualified to administer breath tests. Without a BAC level to present at the trial, some officers feel the chances of conviction are slim and the prosecution of the suspect is unlikely. The Laredo Police Department currently is training additional personnel to run the Intoxilyzer. In addition to the low number of qualified Intoxilyzer personnel, the police station is not centrally located. This means it takes a great deal of time to process most DWI suspects. Some county officials think officers are less likely to arrest people who are not flagrantly violating traffic laws because of the DWI processing requirements.

Some Webb County officials feel the biggest problem in streamlining the DWI process is the lack of commitment by the county commissioner's court. They claim the commissioners have not allocated enough funding to the county clerk's office or the county court at law to enable the offices to maximize job performance. Moreover, the commissioners have not made a push to computerize county records.

Effectiveness of Senate Bill 1

Most county officials feel the provisions of Senate Bill 1 are effective. Some note that the videotaping of suspects can be both a help and a hindrance, depending on the accused's performance during the taping. Others feel the fines and other penalties are too stiff. Some officials think that although the law has improved, people are looking for loopholes in the legislation. Law enforcement officials agree that the .10 percent BAC level as the definition of legal intoxication has led to an increase in the number of people being arrested for DWI. They claim officers are more confident of a conviction of a suspect when the Intoxilyzer test showed a .10 percent BAC or higher level. The provision allowing Intoxilyzer test refusal as evidence has had very little effect in Webb County, since there are very few DWI trials.

Recommendations for Making Senate Bill 1 More Effective

Possible improvements to the law noted by county officials include mandatory jail sentences for all those convicted, increased funding to automate the records on previous convictions, stiffened penalties for refusing to take the Intoxilyzer test, stricter requirements for occupational driver's licenses, and stiffer penalties for second offenses.

Conclusions

Because of Webb County's proximity to the Mexican border, it has some distinct problems and concerns involving DWI. DWI offenses by Mexican nationals require extra paperwork, and the offenders usually do not return to face prosecution. Also, many individuals in the county have the same name, which makes identification a complicated process. County officials pointed out that the Hispanic culture affects DWI problems because drinking plays a significant role in their frequent celebrations. Also, county officials claim the average Mexican-American wife is submissive and is unlikely to complain when her husband drinks and drives.

Webb County also has experienced severe economic problems. The county's primary industry is tourism and trading with Mexico, and the recent devaluation of the peso severely affected the area. Unemployment is around 15 percent, which is much higher than that of most Texas counties. This unemployment has two consequences relating to DWI. First, those who are arrested for DWI may be unemployed or underemployed, and may be unable to pay the fines and fees. Also, employed individuals who are sentenced to jail are likely to lose their jobs. Often these individuals have families to support, and judges are reluctant to levy prison sentences. License suspensions also cause problems. Laredo does not have a good mass transit system, and an individual whose license has been suspended will have a hard time getting to work. Again, this may cause family hardship.

Most Webb County officials realize that drinking and driving is a problem. They have a commitment to improving the situation in their area, and Senate Bill 1, in general, has aided them in reducing the number of drunk drivers on the county's roads. However, without better information flow, Webb County will continue to have difficulties adjudicating its DWI cases efficiently and effectively.

WILLIAMSON COUNTY

Background

Williamson County covers 1,137 square miles and is located north of Austin on Interstate 35 in the Blackland Prairies region. It ranked thirty-fourth among the nation's counties in highest population growth rate between 1970 and 1980. The 1982 estimated population of 85,700 indicates continued growth. The county has 1,805 miles of public roads. The county seat is Georgetown. In 1982, there were 69,571 registered vehicles and 1,813 reported traffic accidents, including 19 fatalities. In 1983, there were 868 misdemeanor DWI cases filed and 64 felony DWI cases filed. The final disposition of almost 90 percent of misdemeanor cases and 93 percent of felony cases was a guilty plea. About one-half of the felony cases were given probation, and half served time in jail. About 75 percent of the misdemeanor cases were given probation, about 20 percent were assessed a fine, and about 6 percent were given jail terms.

Priority Given to DWI

DWI is given high priority in Williamson County by all agencies and officials involved in the system. The exception seems to be the local police department, which has a divergent policy for dealing with some DWI cases. As reported in the Williamson County Sun, October 31, 1984, it is the policy of Georgetown local police to issue charges of drunk driving only if an accident is involved, a Breathilyzer test is requested, a police pursuit takes place, extremely reckless driving is involved, or the driver previously has been charged with DWI.

Focus of DWI Program Efforts

The DWI program does not focus on any particular area to the exclusion of others, yet officials take pride in the areas of treatment and adjudication. Within adjudication, the example of plea bargaining is an important focus. Plea bargaining is used extensively in Williamson County, but without its traditional negative connotations. Judges and adult probation officers in Williamson County have a great deal of confidence in the prosecutors and in their ability to use plea bargaining in the manner in which it is intended.

Effectiveness of County Agency Relationships

County agency relationships seem to be very effective and cohesive. No interviewed officials reported any specific problems in communicating with other agencies in the system. Little mention was made of the divergent DWI policies of Georgetown local police and county officials.

The county has a large Alcoholics Anonymous (AA) organization, participates in the Dial-a-Ride program during the holiday season, and treats DWI offenders in a program developed by the county alcohol council. This program, the Advanced Alcohol Education Program, is the cornerstone of treatment for DWI. It involves an eight-week, sixteen-hour curriculum at a cost of eighty dollars per person. A large portion of the class enrollment is by order of the court as a condition of probation, but the course is open to the public. Public information programs are conducted by the alcohol council on the subject of alcoholism and its prevention, but these programs are not devoted specifically to DWI.

Plea bargaining is used so extensively that it is considered a major component of the Williamson County DWI program. Officials feel that plea bargaining is an effective tool if it is used as intended. In this county, plea bargaining is used in a strictly controlled manner in the discussion of punishment. Its effectiveness is seen as a major asset in the Williamson County system.

County Alcohol Council

The Williamson County Alcohol Council plays an important part in the county's DWI treatment efforts. The council includes four professionals, two of whom are directly involved in the DWI system. About one-third of the council's budget goes toward DWI-related programs. These funds come from Williamson County, United Way of Round Rock, Georgetown and Taylor, and the Texas Commission on Alcoholism. The county contracts with the alcohol council to conduct alcohol evaluations and assessments. In its evaluations, the council uses the Mortimer-Filkins Test as well as other measures. It prescribes different treatments for social drinkers, who comprise about 41 percent of convicted offenders; presumptive problem drinkers, who comprise about 18 percent; and problem drinkers, who make up about 41 percent. The council makes no recommendation for social drinkers, and recommends from two to ten AA meetings for presumptive problem drinkers. For problem drinkers, they recommend at the very least membership in AA and, for most cases, the council's Advanced Alcohol Education Program.

Adult Probation Department

DWI-related offenses comprise the majority of the Williamson County Adult Probation Department's caseload. The department makes a substantial number of referrals for treatment, many of those to the county alcohol council. Its working relationships with the alcohol council, the district and county attorneys' offices, and the district and county courts is strong and has proven beneficial to all. They consider their probation program to be effective because its stringent guidelines for probationers have caused those defendants--given the choice--to opt for a short jail term rather than probation.

All probation officers are trained in alcohol abuse, and each averages forty hours of training each year by attending various continuing education programs throughout the state.

Record Keeping

The county clerk reports final convictions to DPS using a standard form (known as the D-17) provided by the U.S. Department of Justice. The county clerk's office does not report felony convictions or deferred probation. The automated system records all DWI dispositions referred to DPS. Responses from the sheriff's department to requests for criminal record information are immediate. The average time from the date of arrest to docket call is about two weeks.

Records as of December 31, 1984, show 275 cases awaiting disposition. According to the clerk's office, this number is about average. They expect a backlog to develop soon due to the unprecedented growth in Williamson County. The increase in population will result in an increased workload, which existing staff will not be able to handle efficiently.

Problems with the DWI Process

The problems pinpointed by those involved in the county DWI system are general in nature:

-- a lack of personnel at all levels, making it
   difficult to comply with speedy trial requirements
   and to keep up with the increased numbers
   of cases;

-- a lack of personnel and resources to deal with
   treatment; and

-- a lack of personnel certified to administer
   Breathilyzer tests, causing a slowdown in
   processing time for DWI arrests.

Effectiveness of Senate Bill 1

Certain provisions of Senate Bill 1 were rated as ineffective or less effective by county officials. The prohibition of deferred adjudication in DWI cases has had little effect on the system because deferred adjudication was used only in limited cases. New procedures for reporting convictions or probations to DPS also has had relatively little effect because the county already was in compliance with existing procedures. Finally, the reform giving police officers the authority to order blood tests is considered to have little effect because this sort of situation rarely occurs in Williamson County.

Videotaping is considered by some officials to be an effective reform, but several others termed it a "double-edged sword." The problem lies with people performing extremely well on videotape even though their BAC level is in excess of .10 percent. This has proved to be a particular problem in jury trials, where jurors give more credence to a defendant's "normal" performance than to his blood or breath test results. An additional problem is the lack of personnel familiar with the video equipment and knowledgeable in its use.

Most officials feel the stiffer penalties are useful, but are having little effect in Williamson County due to the previously existing policy of levying stiff penalties.

Recommendations for Making Senate Bill 1 More Effective

County officials expressed a belief that reforms making law enforcement more effective should have been accompanied with greater levels of funding. This would enable more Intoxilyzer testing and more extensive training and certification for officers to administer the alcohol tests. In general, a substantial increase in funding should have accompanied the reforms to ensure proper compliance with the new law. Another recommendation focused on what county officials view as problems in the status of defendants given probation. They recommend that probations be classified as convictions in order to gain a future felony conviction for repeat offenders.

Conclusions

Williamson County is an example of effective coordination and enforcement in the DWI process. The county's strength lies in its past history of strong DWI enforcement. This strength appears to continue in the face of tremendous population growth, with no corresponding increases in staff and budget. Thus, its strength also has the potential of becoming its "Achilles' heel" in its inability to meet the challenges of a changing county.

INTERVIEWS

COMAL COUNTY (New Braunfels)

Martin Allen Court Administrator, District Court for Comal, Hays, and Caldwell Counties, March 19, 1985.

Sheriff Walter Fellers, Sheriff of Comal County, March 19, 1985.

Diana Guerrero, Chief Deputy County Clerk, Comal County, March 19, 1985.

Sargeant J.R. Holder, Highway Patrol Supervisor for Comal/Northern Bexar, Texas Department of Public Safety, March 19, 1985.

Hazel Kuhn, District Clerk for Comal and Caldwell Counties, Telephone Interview, March 12, 1985.

William Reimer, County Attorney, Comal County, March 19, 1985.

William Schroeder, District Attorney for Comal, Hays, and Caldwell Counties, March 19, 1985.

Jack Williamson, Supervisor, Adult Probation Services for Comal, Hays, and Caldwell Counties, March 19, 1985.

Lieutenant John Wommack, Patrol Lieutenant, New Braunfels Police Department, March 19, 1985.

DALLAS COUNTY (Dallas)

Cami Alexander, Administrative Assistant to Chris V. Semos, Dallas County commissioner, District 4, March 1, 1985.

Earl Bullock, County Clerk, Dallas County, February 28, 1985.

Kay Chandler, Director of Special Services, Adult Probation Department, Dallas County, mail reply, March 15, 1985.

Judge Harold Entz, Criminal Court No. 4, Dallas County, February 28, 1985.

Mike Gillette, Assistant District Attorney, Dallas County, February 28, 1985.

Milo Kirk, President, Dallas Area Chapter, Mothers Against Drunk Drivers, February 27, 1985.

Judge Pat McDowell, Criminal District Court No. 5, Dallas County, Dallas, March 1, 1985.

Captain Leo Savell, Traffic Division, Dallas Police Department, February 27, 1985.

EL PASO COUNTY (El Paso)

Waldo Alarcorn, Supervisor, County Clerk's Office, El Paso County, February 28, 1985.

Ben Castro, Court Administrator, El Paso County Court, February 28, 1985.

Sargeant Robert F. Collins, Texas Department of Public Safety, El Paso County, February 28, 1985.

Frank Cram, Assistant County Attorney, El Paso county, February 28, 1985.

Laura Gordon, Assistant County Attorney, El Paso county, February 28, 1985.

Gloria Gravalos, Court Administrator, District Court, El Paso County, March 1, 1985.

Tomma Harris, Office Manager, el Paso County Chapter, Mothers Against Drunk Drivers, February 27, 1985.

Officer Harry Kirk, El Paso Police Department, Telephone Interview, March 5, 1985.

Richard Lasater, West Texas REgional Adult Probation Department, March 1, 1985.

Dr. Frank Lozito, Director, West TExas Regional Adult Probation Department, March 1, 1985.

Lieutenant Jack Marshall, Patrol Division, Sheriff's Department, El Paso County, March 4, 1985.

Edie Rubalcaba, District Clerk, Thirty-Fourth Judicial District, El Paso County, March 1, 1985.

Officer Larry Tipton, Traffic Division, El Paso Police Department, February 28, 1985.

GRAY COUNTY (Pampa)

Lucille Brown, Chief Deputy District Clerk, 31st and 223d Judicial Districts, March 21, 1985.

Wanda Carter, County Clerk, Gray County, March 22, 1985.

Ken Keith, Chief Deputy Sheriff, Sheriff's Department, Gray County, March 22, 1985.

Judge Carl Kennedy, County Court, Gray County, March 22, 1985.

Robert McPherson, County Attorney, Gray County, March 21, 1985.

Dovye Massie, Chief Adult Probation Officer, Adult Probation Department, Gray County, March 22, 1985.

Chief J. J. Ryzman, Chief of Police, Pampa Police Department, March 21, 1985.

HARRIS COUNTY (Houston)

Marlene Durst, Counselor, Alcohol Safety Training, Houston Regional Council on Alcoholism, Inc., March 21, 1985.

Judge Shelly P. Hancock, Criminal Court at Law No. 7, Harris County, March 21, 1985.

John P. Holmes, Jr., District Attorney, Harris County, March 22, 1985.

Travis Jackson, Director, Alcohol Safety Education and Training, Houston Regional Council on Alcoholism, Inc., March 21, 1985.

Judge Ted Poe, 228th District Court, Harris County, March 21, 1985.

Lieutenant Ricky D. Smith, Texas Department of Public Safety, Harris County, March 21, 1985.

Andy Tobias, Assistant District Attorney, Harris County, March 22, 1985.

Sargeant R.C. Watson, Supervisor, DWI Task Force, Houston Police Department, March 21, 1985.

Gerald Wheeler, Director of Planning Community Resources, Adult Probation Department, Harris County, March 21, 1985.

Charles Workman, Systems Analyst, District Clerk's Office, Criminal Division, Harris County, March 21, 1985.

HARRISON COUNTY (Marshall)

Betty Cawood, District Clerk, Seventy-first Judicial District, February 28, 1985.

Judge Ben Z. Grand, District Court, Seventy-first Judicial District, February 29, 1985.

Nancy Howell, Director, Substance Abuse, Education, and Program Development, Sabine Valley Regional Mental Health and Mental Retardation Center, February 29, 1985.

Judge J. Ray Kirkpatrick, County Court at Law, Harrison County, February 28, 1985.

Bonnie Leggat, Assistant District Attorney, Harrison County, February 28, 1985.

Glen Link, county Clerk, Harrison County, February 25, 1985.

Joe Moore, Director, Adult Probation Department, Harrison County, February

28, 1985.

Sargeant Michael Payne, Texas Department of Public Safety, Harrison County, February 28, 1985.

WEBB COUNTY (Laredo)

Carlos Barrero, Assistant District Attorney, Forty-ninth Judicial District, March 14, 1985.

Ana Cavazos, Assistant District Attorney, Forty-ninth Judicial District, March 14, 1985.

Henry Flores, County Clerk, Webb County, March 14, 1985.

Judge Manuel Flores, County Clerk, Webb County, March 14, 1985.

Isidro Garcia, Chief Adult Probation Officer, Adult Probation Department, Forty-ninth Judicial District, March 14, 1985.

Judge R. Garcia, District Court, Forty-ninth Judicial District, March 14, 1985.

Chief Eliodoro Grandados, Assistant Chief of Police, Laredo Police Department, March 14, 1985.

Manuel Guitierrez, District Clerk, Forty-ninth Judicial District, March 15, 1985.

O.J. Hale, Assistant District Attorney, Forty-ninth Judicial District, March 14, 1985.

Roberto A. Magnon, Deputy County Clerk, County Court at Law Division, Webb County, March 15, 1985.

Cresencio Pena, Adult Probation Officer, Adult Probation Department, Webb County, March 14, 1985.

Sheriff Marion Snatos, Sheriff of Webb County, March 15, 1985.

Sargeant Dioncio Valdez, Texas Department of Public Safety, Webb County, March 14, 1985.

WILLIAMSON COUNTY (Georgetown)

James Boydston, County Clerk, Williamson County, February 20, 1985.

Betsy Burba, Counsel for, Georgetown Council on Alcoholism, February 20, 1985.

Judge John Carter, District Court, 277th Judicial District, February 19, 1985.

Judge Timothy Maresh, County Court, Williamson County, February 19, 1985.

William Stubblefield, County Attorney, Williamson County, February 19, 1985.

Chief Travis Thomas, Chief of Police, Georgetown Police Department, February 20, 1985.

Edward Walsh, District Attorney, Williamson County, February 19, 1985.

Richard Zinsmeyer, Chief Adult Probation Officer, Adult Probation Department, Williamson County, February 20, 1985.

APPENDIX 2

QUESTIONNAIRE FOR VISITED TEXAS COUNTIES

COUNTY NAME:

General Questions (for all agencies to answer)

1. Office Name and Address:

2. Respondent's Name, Title, and Phone Number:

3. How many people within your office deal specifically with DWI? (Please attach an organization chart.)

4. How much of your budget is dedicated to DWI? (In dollars and percentage.)

5. Do you receive any special or grant funding for DWI work?

6. Prioritize your agency's functions. Where does DWI fall?

7. With which of the following agencies are you in regular contact on DWI cases?

	Yes	No
Deptartment of Probation	_____	_____
Sheriff	_____	_____
Local Police	_____	_____
DPS	_____	_____
District Court	_____	_____
MADD	_____	_____
District Attorney	_____	_____
Alcohol Council	_____	_____
County Clerk	_____	_____
Other	_____	_____

8. Senate Bill 1 (S.B. 1) made several changes in the DWI law which are considered major reforms. Have these changes made the process of dealing with DWI offenders more or less effective in your county?

	Very effective	Somewhat effective	No change	Less effective	Much Less effective
.10 BAC per se drunk					
Provision allowing admission of BAC test refusal at trial					
Prohibition of deferred adjudication in DWI cases					
Authority for police officers to order blood tests					
New procedure for reporting convictions or probations to DPS (i.e., the county clerk)					
Changes in implied consent license revocation procedures (administrative)					
Videotaping of all suspects					
Stiffened penalties					

9. Are there any improvements that could be made in the

existing law?

10a. Would your efforts be more effective if statewide records of DWI arrests and convictions were available to you?

Yes _____   No _____

10b. Would you like a statute to provide this?

Yes _____   No _____

11a. Are you satisfied that the required reporting of DWI convictions/dispositions to DPS from your county is carried out in a timely and objective manner?

Yes _____   No _____

11b. If not, what changes could be made at the state level to improve it?

12. Would the establishment of standard state-approved procedures for videotaping DWI suspects improve the usefulness of such evidence in prosecution?

Yes _____   No _____

Comment:

Questions for the County Alcohol Council
(In addition to the general questions.)

1. How many and what kinds of alcohol treatment facilities do you have in the county?

2. Does your agency have any unique or special programs

for DWI offenders?

3. Do you have special staff training programs for handling DWI offenders?

4. Do you conduct public information programs on drinking and driving for groups or clubs in the community? Please describe.

5. Do you have countywide guidelines for assessment and treatment programs?

6a. Describe the assessment process.

6b. What kinds of "drinker categories" do you use?

7. Do you have a different treatment process for each set of drinker category?

8. Do you have data concerning numbers treated, recidivism, and types of persons treated (social drinker, problem drinker, etc.)?

9a. Do you have any type of posttreatment effectiveness evaluation? (System for following up on patients?)

9b. Why or why not?

Questions for Probation Officers
(In addition to the general questions.)

1. What is the average caseload per probation officer?

2a. Do you have specialized caseloads for DWI offenders

2b. If not, where does treatment of DWI offenders usually fall within your probation program?

3. Do any of your probation officers have specialized training to deal with alcohol offenders? If yes, please describe.

4. Can you think of ways to improve the probation process as it applies to DWI offenders?

5a. Do you keep permanent records on persons who have been on probation?

5b. Do you have data on recidivism for DWI offenders (follow-up records)?

Questions for Probation Officers
(In addition to the general questions.)

1. What is the average caseload per probation officer?

2a. Do you have specialized caseloads for DWI offenders?

2b. If not, where does treatment of DWI offenders usually fall within your probation program?

3. Do any of your probation officers have specialized training to deal with alcohol offenders? If yes, please describe.

4. Can you think of ways to improve the probation process as it applies to DWI offenders?

5a. Do you keep permanent records on persons who have been on probation?

5b. Do you have data on recidivism for DWI offenders (follow-up records)?

Questions for County Clerks
(In addition to the general questions.)

1. Please describe your procedure for reporting final convictions in DWI cases to the DPS.

2. Are probations reported to the DPS in the same manner?

3. Is a report made in every case? If not, why (or what are the exceptions)?

4. Do you keep a log, record, or file of DWI dispositions referred to DPS?

5. On the average, how long does it take for the sheriff to respond to your requests for criminal record information?

6. Is information for presentence investigations readily available? If not, how could the process or information be improved?

7. What is the average number of days from the date of arrest to final disposition of DWI cases in your jurisdiction?

8a. How many DWI cases are currently awaiting final disposition in your county?

8b. Do you feel this number is excessive?

8c. If so, what is causing this backlog?

8d. What is being done to eliminate the backlog?

Questions for Sheriffs
(In addition to the general questions.)

1. How often do you receive requests for criminal record information on persons convicted or probated for DWI?

2. Do you keep a log, record, or file on such requests?

APPENDIX 3

MAIL-OUT QUESTIONNAIRE FOR TEXAS COUNTY AND DISTRICT ATTORNEYS

1. Office Name and Address:

2. Respondent's Name, Title, and Phone Number:

3. How many people within your office deal specifically with DWI?

4. How much of your budget is dedicated to DWI? (In dollars and percentage.)

5. Do you receive any special or grant funding for DWI work?

6. Prioritize your agency's functions. Where does DWI fall?

7. With which of the following agencies are you in regular contact on DWI cases?

	Yes	No
Deptartment of Probation		
Sheriff		
Local Police		
DPS		
District Court		
MADD		
District Attorney		
Alcohol Council		
County Clerk		
Other (Specify)		

8. Senate Bill 1 (S.B. 1) made several changes in the DWI Law which are considered major reforms. Have these changes made the process of dealing with DWI offenders

more or less effective in your county?

	Very effective	Somewhat effective	No change	Less effective	Much Less effective
.10 BAC per se drunk	_____	_____	_____	_____	_____
Provision allowing admission of BAC test refusal at trial	_____	_____	_____	_____	_____
Prohibition of deferred adjudication in DWI cases	_____	_____	_____	_____	_____
Authority for police officers to order blood tests	_____	_____	_____	_____	_____
New procedure for reporting convictions or probations to DPS (i.e., the county clerk)	_____	_____	_____	_____	_____
Changes in implied consent license revocation procedures (administrative)	_____	_____	_____	_____	_____
Videotaping of all suspects	_____	_____	_____	_____	_____
Stiffened penalties	_____	_____	_____	_____	_____

9. Are there any improvements that could be made in the existing law?

10a. Would your efforts be more effective if statewide records of DWI arrests and convictions were available to you?

   Yes _____   No _____

10b. Would you like a statute to provide this?

   Yes _____   No _____

11a. Are you satisfied that the required reporting of DWI convictions/dispositions to DPS from your county is carried out in a timely and objective manner?

   Yes _____   No _____

11b. If not, what changes could be made at the state level to improve it?

12. Would the establishment of standard state-approved procedures for videotaping DWI suspects improve the usefulness of such evidence in prosecution?

   Yes _____   No _____

   Comment:

APPENDIX 4

QUESTIONNAIRE FOR FLORIDA

ORANGE COUNTRY

Organization/Agency:

Interviewee:

Interviewers:

Date:

Place:

Time:

GENERAL QUESTIONS

1. What are the functions/purposes of your agency? What role does it play in the DUI processing system?

   Organizational structure (diagram, etc.)

   Training

   Workload

   Staffing

   Job responsibility

   Special programs

2. What jurisdiction does your agency have within the DUI system?

3. In terms of processing DUI cases, with whom does your agency interact?

DATA

1. What is your agency's capacity to collect and analyze data concerning DUI?

2. Who receives the final data and how is it used?

3. Are there any deficiencies in the data itself, or in the process of collecting and compiling it?

EFFECTIVENESS OF 1982 LEGISLATION

1. How effective is the practice of refusing to grant operational licenses to repeat offenders? What was the practice before 1982? Any attempt to evaluate this in numbers?

2. How effective is the mandatory license suspension after conviction? What was the practice before 1982? Evaluation attempts?

3. How have the restrictions against plea bargaining affected the conviction rate? Overload on the court system? Was plea bargaining allowed prior to the 1982 legislation? What caused the change?

EFFECTIVENESS OF SPECIFIC PROGRAMS

1. What prompted the Department to initiate the DUI program? Did the 1982 legislation or public opinion provide the incentive?

2. Will the grant that supports the DUI project for three years be continued? If not, where will the funding come from? Are any evaluations done by those that provide this grant?

Videotaping

1. What is your procedure for videotaping? Is it always used or just for those who refuse the breath and/or blood tests?

2. Is mandatory videotaping necessary or is the voluntary system adequate?

3. Because videotaping is not mandated by legislation, what do you think accounts for its widespread use? Its success?

Batmobiles

1. What are the advantages/disadvantages of Batmobiles as opposed to fixed testing centers such as those used in Clearwater?

2. What role do Batmobiles play in the DUI system (public information, increased mobility, greater accuracy in police reports, increased chance of prosecution, etc.)?

3. What costs are involved in operating Batmobiles (man-hours, purchasing cost, equipment maintenance, training, etc.)? Cost-effective?

Public Education and Information

1. How are DUI presentations arranged? Who generally makes the initial contact--the schools and organizations, or the law enforcement staff?

2. Should DUI training for law enforcement officials be legislated? Need more or less? Advantages? Evaluation techniques?

RECOMMENDATIONS

1. Give your opinion of the successes in the DUI programs and/or legislation. Areas for improvement?

2. Any ideas, suggestions for change within the DUI system?

PINELLAS COUNTY

1. How many officers do you have who work with DUI enforcement?

2. What is the jurisdiction of your agency?

3. In terms of DUI work, with whom does your agency interact? Describe these interactions. If possible, include an organizational chart.

4. In terms of the "Arrest Drunk Driving" program, whom do you work with most closely?

5. How significant is videotaping in getting convictions? Statistics kept on before-and-after figures for videotaping convictions?

6. Have your funding grants been renewed (in reference to articles and descriptions in packet)?

7. What is the most common punishment for a first-time DUI conviction in your jurisdiction? What have been the judges' reactions to your DUI programs?

8. How common is the granting of occupational licenses? How do you feel about occupational licensing?

9. What kinds of treatment and rehabilitation facilities are available to DUI offenders, besides the required basic course?

10. With the streamlining process, how long does it take to complete an arrest?

11. What is the current status of the roadblock constitutionality issue?

12. What has been the overall reaction of citizens to the program?

13. How is your reporting system organized with respect to DUI? Are any statistical analyses done with your data?

14. How effective is the statewide reporting system?

15. What recognition have you received from the National Highway Traffic Safety Administration (NHTSA) for being a model

program?

16. How often do you set up roadblocks?

17. What training do officers receive concerning DUI detection?

18. Who formed the advisory board on special programs?

19. What is MADD's (and SADD's) role in the DUI system? Are there other similar groups in the area?

20. Could you provide information about the Task Force and when it meets?

21. How often are PSAs given?

MADD INTERVIEW

1. How many members are there locally in your MADD chapter?

2. How does MADD interact with the different law enforcement agencies? What is the level of cooperation?

3. Is MADD involved in the "Arrest Drunk Driving" program. What is its role?

4. What is your perception of your local MADD's role in the DUI system?

5. What activities are done locally by MADD?

6. How effective are the current Florida laws in dealing with those arrested for DUI?

7. How have local judges reacted to the "Arrest Drunk Driving" program? More strict? Cooperative?

8. What is citizen opinion of the roadblocks?

9. What are current flaws in local procedures concerning DUI/state laws?

10. What are the chances in Florida of raising the drinking age?

BACCHUS INTERVIEW

1. What are BACCHUS' sources of funding?

2. What services and programs do you provide?

3. What are the organization's objectives?

4. How many chapters are there nationwide?

INTERVIEW WITH BACCHUS SECONDARY PREVENTION EFFORTS STAFF

1. With whom does BACCHUS interact on DUI matters?

2. What are your program objectives and functions? Where does your funding come from?

3. What programs do you have concerning DUI? Public information?

APPENDIX 5

QUESTIONNAIRE FOR MINNESOTA

<u>Interview with Jim Abercrombie, Cofounder of MADD in Minnesota</u>

1. What are the strongest features of Minnesota's DWI legislation?

2. In what ways has the administrative per se law improved the effort to deter drunk driving?

3. What are the weak points in Minnesota's DWI laws?

4. Could you suggest any recommendations for improvements?

5. Do you feel plea bargaining is a problem in Minnesota? How so?

6a. What types of citizen groups are there in the state active in the anti-DWI campaign (MADD, RID, SADD, etc.) and numbers of participants?

6b. Which is the strongest of these groups?

7. Are citizen groups effective in furthering Minnesota's anti-DWI efforts?

8. What or who are the driving forces for improving DWI laws in Minnesota?

Interview with Major Glen Gramse, Minnesota State Patrol

1. What is the average DWI arrest processing time (statewide)?

2a. What training do officers receive for DWI enforcement?

2b. Who provides the training?

3. Officers in Minnesota are allowed to stop drivers for "reason to believe" instead of "probable cause" that the driver is intoxicated, and they also decide which type of test to give the driver. What, if any, impact have these policies had on enforcement?

4. In 1978, officers were allowed to act for the Commissioner of Public Safety in revoking the license of the driver at the time of test refusal or for a test result at or above .10. What impact did this have on enforcement?

5. What are your feelings regarding the use of videotapes in DWI trials?

6. Do you feel that plea bargaining in DWI cases is a problem in Minnesota?

7. Minnesota is known for its two-track system for handling DWI offenders--the automatic license suspension for refusal to take the test or for receiving a result at or above .10 percent, and the separate criminal charges against those believed to have been driving while intoxicated. Do you feel that this two-track system is the most effective means of dealing with the problem of drinking and driving?

8. What are the strongest features of Minnesota's drunk driving legislation?

9. What are areas needing improvement?

10. Does your department have any special programs for handling drunk drivers?

Interview with Judge Debra Hedlund, Hennepin County Municipal Court

1. What type of training do judges receive regarding DWI laws and cases?

2. What is the average time from arrest to disposition for DWI criminal charges?

3. What punishment is normally imposed for a first-time DWI offender? A second conviction?

4. Do you feel that sentencing for DWI offenders should be standardized?

5. What are the factors used in determining whether to refer an offender to treatment and/or probation?

6a. Are you satisfied with the alcohol assessments reported to you?

6b. How much emphasis do you place on the assessment when determining punishment?

7. Do you feel that plea bargaining undermines the DWI laws in Minnesota?

8a. What are your feelings about the use of videotapes in the hearing?

8b. Are your feelings the same as the majority of the judges?

9. What is the average time from the filing date to disposition on an appeal for a judicial hearing for a license revocation? Are revocations often reversed in the hearing?

10. Minnesota is known for its two-track system for handling DWI offenders--the automatic license suspension for refusal to take the test or for receiving a result at or above .10 percent, and the separate criminal charges against those believed to have been driving while intoxicated. Do you feel that this two-track system is the most effective means of dealing with the problem of drinking and driving?

11. In what ways could DWI laws or the DWI process be improved in Minnesota?

Interview with Forst Lowery, Safety Program Coordinator, Minnesota Department of Public Safety

1. Could you briefly describe Minnesota's administrative per se law, highlighting the most important points leading to its effectiveness?

2. Could you describe the impact of the administrative per se law on the DWI control system areas of:

   enforcement:

   prosecution:

   adjudication:

probation:

treatment:

driver licensing:

3. Can you think of any recommendations for a state contemplating an administrative per se law that would make the implementation process a smooth one?

4. Some of the recommendations made by the Presidential Commission on Drunk Driving have not been adopted in Minnesota. For example, establishing twenty-one as the legal drinking age; providing for a self-financing system through the use of offenders' fines and fees; a .08 percent presumptive level of intoxication; a task force to increase public awareness of anti-DWI activities; elimination of plea bargaining; and setting state standards for alcohol education, treatment, and rehabilitation services. Are such changes being considered or are there specific reasons for their exclusion?

5. Are any other changes being considered?

6. How is the system for handling drunk drivers currently financed?

7. In Minnesota, officers are allowed to stop drivers for "reason to believe" that they are under the influence rather than for "probable cause," and the officer has the choice as to which type of test should be administered. What effect has this had on the enforcement effort in Minnesota?

8. What is the statewide average DWI processing time?

9. What training do officers receive for DWI enforcement? Who provides the training?

10. What training, if any, do judges receive for handling DWI cases and hearings for license revocations?

11. How difficult is it to obtain an occupational license?

12a. What percentage of drivers request an administrative hearing when their license is revoked?

12b. What percentage request a judicial hearing?

13. Do administrative or judicial hearings often reverse the revocation?

14. If a driver is tested and found to have an alcohol concentration of .07 or more for the second or more times within two years, the Commissioner of Public Safety can require an alcohol assessment of the driver.

   a. How often is an assessment required?

   b. What is included in an alcohol assessment?

   c. Who performs the assessment?

15a. For a DWI conviction, who determines whether an alcohol assessment is performed?

15b. What happens in counties with populations under ten thousand?

16a. What punishment is normally imposed for a first-time DWI conviction?

16b. A second conviction?

17. Are these standardized?

18. What punishment is normally imposed for driving while one's license is revoked?

19. Is plea bargaining considered a problem?

20. What is the conviction rate based on the original charge?

21. What are the requirements for referring an offender to probation and/or treatment?

22. What percentage of those convicted are placed on probation?

23a. How effective is treatment?

23b. What is the recidivism rate for those referred to treatment?

23c. Would licensing treatment facilities lower the recidivism rate?

24. What is the percentage of licensed drivers arrested for DWI each year?

25. What is the average alcohol concentration per DWI conviction?

26. What is the average time from arrest to disposition for DWI criminal charges?

27. What are your feelings regarding the use of videotapes in DWI hearings?

28. Regarding publicity for anti-DWI activities:

    a. Is there anyone in charge or any coordination?

    b. What types of activities are present in Minnesota?

    c. Type of media involved?

    d. What group is most active in publicity efforts?

29. What types of citizen groups are there in the state active in the anti-DWI campaign (e.g., MADD, RID, SADD, etc.) and numbers of participants?

Interview with Richard Neuner, Executive Director, The Minnesota Institute

1. Is enough emphasis placed on treatment in Minnesota?

2. What screening or referral system is used for determining type of treatment?

3. How effective is treatment? What is the recidivism rate for those receiving treatment?

4. At present, how are alcohol education, treatment, and rehabilitation programs regulated in Minnesota?

5. Would providing state standards for alcohol education, treatment, and rehabilitation improve the effectiveness of these programs?

6. Are judges consistent in their recommendations for education and/or treatment or does it vary greatly by each judge?

7. Would uniform sentencing requirements be an improvement or does flexibility outweigh the benefits of uniform sentencing guidelines?

8. Minnesota is known for its two-track system for handling DWI offenders--the automatic license suspension for refusal to take the test or for receiving .10 percent or above on the BAC test, and the separate criminal charges against those believed to have been driving while intoxicated. Do you feel that this two-track system is the most effective means of dealing with the problem of drinking and driving?

9. Is license revocation a good deterrent to drinking and driving?

10. What are the strongest features of Minnesota's drunk driving legislation?

11. What are the areas for improvement?

Interview with Harold Peterson, Assistant Director, Drivers License Division, Minnesota Department of Public Safety

1. Describe the process for a license revocation for both refusal to take the alcohol concentration test or for receiving a BAC test result at or above .10 percent.

(Does the process differ?)

2. How soon after the officer revokes the license does it appear on the driver's record?

3. What percentage of administrative or judicial hearings reverse the revocation?

4. What training do the administrative hearing officers receive?

5a. How are Minnesota's driver's records used for the alcohol assessment?

5b. Are the records complete?

6. Many other states have adopted laws similar to Minnesota's administrative per se law. What are the strengths of Minnesota's law?

7. Are there any improvements that should be made in the law?

Interview with Steve Simon, Clinical Attorney, Criminal Justice DWI Task Force

1. Why is Minnesota's administrative per se law stronger than similar laws in other states?

2. Do you feel that there are any bottlenecks in the current DWI system?

3. Are any improvements being considered?

4. Could you describe the impact of the administrative per se law on the DWI control system areas of:

   enforcement:

   prosecution:

   adjudication:

   probation:

   treatment:

   driver licensing:

5. Some of the recommendations made by the Presidential Commission on Drunk Driving have not been adopted in Minnesota. For example, establishing twenty-one as the legal drinking age; providing for a self-financing system through the use of offenders' fines and fees; a .08 percent presumptive level of intoxication; a task force to increase public awareness of anti-DWI activities; elimination of plea bargaining; and setting state standards for alcohol education, treatment, and rehabilitation services. Are such changes being considered or are there specific reasons for their exclusion?

6. Has a self-financing DWI system been considered? If yes, why hasn't it been enacted?

7. Do you feel plea bargaining is a problem in Minnesota? Why or why not?

8. In Minnesota, officers are allowed to stop drivers for "reason to believe" that they are under the influence rather than for "probable cause," and the officer has

the choice as to which type of test should be administered. What effect has this had on the enforcement effort?

9. What or who do you feel are the driving forces for improving DWI laws in Minnesota?

10. What would you describe as the "ideal" piece of DWI legislation?

Questions Regarding the Alcohol Problem Assessments

1. What is included in the alcohol assessment?

2. Are recommendations made in the assessments?

3. Who performs the assessments? What type of training do they have?

4. Who determines whether to conduct an alcohol assessment?

5. Are judges well trained for handling DWI cases?

6. How are the assessments financed?

7. Do counties with populations under ten thousand have alcohol assessments?

8. Do the assessments play a large role in sentencing?

Interview with Tim Turnbull, Fridley Police Department

1. What is the average DWI arrest processing time?

2. Is this similar to other police departments?

3a. What training do officers receive for DWI enforcement?

3b. Who provides the training?

4. Officers in Minnesota are allowed to stop drivers for "reason to believe" instead of "probable cause" that the driver is intoxicated, and they also decide which type of test is to be given to the driver. What, if any, impact have these policies had on enforcement?

5. In 1978, officers were allowed to act for the Commissioner of Public Safety in revoking the license for BAC test refusal or a BAC test result at or above .10 percent. What impact did this have on enforcement?

6a. Do you use videotaping for evidence at trials?

6b. What are your feelings regarding the use of videotaping?

7. Do you feel that plea bargaining in DWI cases is a problem in Minnesota? If so, why?

8. Minnesota is known for its two-track system for handling DWI offenders--the automatic license suspension for refusal to take the BAC test or for receiving a result at or above .10 percent, and the separate criminal charges against those believed to have been driving while intoxicated. Do you feel that this two-track system is

the most effective means of dealing with the problem of drinking and driving?

9. What are the strongest features of Minnesota's drunk driving legislation?

10. What are areas needing improvement?

11. Do you have any special programs in your police department regarding DWI?

Interview with Rep. Kathleen Vellenga, Minnesota House of Representative

1. Why is Minnesota's administrative per se law better than similar laws in other states?

2. Are there any improvements that you feel should be made?

3. Have any changes in the DWI laws been proposed for this legislative session? If so, please describe.

4. Some of the recommendations made by the Presidential Commission on Drunk Driving have not been adopted in Minnesota. For example, establishing twenty-one as the legal drinking age; providing for a self-financing system through the use of offenders' fines and fees; a .08 percent presumptive level of intoxication; a task force to increase public awareness of anti-DWI activities; elimination of plea bargaining; and setting state standards for alcohol education, treatment, and rehabilitation services. Are such changes being considered or are there specific reasons for their exclusion?

5a. Are DWI laws an important concern to constituents?

5b. What recommendations have constituents conveyed to you?

6. What or who do you feel are the driving forces for improving DWI laws in Minnesota?

7. What lobbying groups are particularly strong?

Interview with Ed Vennewitz, Division Director, Municipal Probation Division, Hennepin County Municipal Court

1. What percentage of those convicted of DWI are placed on probation? (Is this figure for Hennepin County or statewide?)

2a. Is probation used in conjunction with alcohol education, treatment, and/or public service?

2b. What kind of emphasis is placed on treatment?

3a. What is the average caseload of probation officers handling DWI offenders?

3b. Are there different levels of probation?

3c. Are they reflected in the caseload assignments of different officers?

4. Do the probation officers have specialized caseloads or receive any special alcohol education training?

5a. What factors are used by judges in determining whether to place a DWI offender on probation?

5b. Is this standardized or does it depend on the judge?

6. Would standardized decisions for placing a DWI offender on probation be beneficial or is flexibility more valuable?

7. Could you describe alcohol problem assessments and when they are performed?

8. Are you satisfied with the process and result of these assessments?

9. Minnesota is known for its two-track system for handling DWI offenders--the automatic license suspension for refusal to take the BAC test or for receiving a result at or above .10 percent, and the separate criminal charges against those believed to have been driving while intoxicated. Do you feel that this two-track system is the most effective means of dealing with the problem of drinking and driving?

10. What are the strongest features of Minnesota's drunk driving legislation?

11. What are areas needing improvement?

APPENDIX 6

QUESTIONNAIRE FOR NEW YORK

State Officials

Date:

Name:

Title:

Affiliation:

1. What was the original intent of STOP-DWI legislation?

2. What is the role of the state in this program? What are the program requirements?

3. Is this the proper role? Too much? Too little?

4. What is the county's role?

5. Do they bear too much or too little of the burden in confronting the drunk driving problem?

6. How autonomous are the counties? State requirements for county STOP-DWI program?

7. Is there a need for more coordination among the counties, such as a coordinating association?

8. What is the communication between state and counties like? Too much? Too little?

9. Do you think fine monies are wisely spent?

10. If not, is this the fault of the STOP-DWI Programs or county and desires?

11. In regard to your agency, how effective is the STOP-DWI Program?

12. What improvements do you feel are necessary to correct any problems in this program?

13. What is the largest benefit of the STOP-DWI Program?

14. What is the biggest disadvantage of this program? How could you improve these disadvantages?

15. Has the program fulfilled its original design?

16. If yes, what is its future? Any changes?

17. If not, why? Any changes?

State Coordinators

Date:

Name:

Title:

Affiliation:

1. What is the state's role in STOP-DWI Programs?

2. Are the counties autonomous enough?

3. How stringent is the state in its requirements for adequate programs and spending?

4. What change is needed in the state's role?

5. Should there be more contact among various counties?

6. Is there the need for a prototype program which each county can adapt to its needs?

7. As coordinator, what is your role?

8. What type of data do you collect? Is there any difficulty in collecting data?

9. What is the purpose and function of the coordinating association?

10. Do you see the need for changes in the association? If so, what are they?

11. What is the communication between state and counties like? Is the communication regular?

12. Is the communication too much, too little, enough?

13. What are some disadvantages of the STOP-DWI Program? How could you improve this program?

14. What was the original intent of the program?

15. Has it fulfilled its role?

16. What programs, research, and activities does your office sponsor?

17. How is your county's DWI program evaluated?

18. What is the average budget for each county STOP-DWI Program?

APPENDIX 7

QUESTIONNAIRE FOR PENNSYLVANIA

1. Date:

2. Name:

3. Title:

4. Affiliation:

5. Address:

6. Phone Number:

7. What kinds of things does your agency do which relate to the problem of drinking drivers?

8. How many people in your agency administer these programs?

9. How does your agency's work with computers fit in with Pennsylvania's dealings with the drinking driver?

10. Is there a legal requirement for an assessment of a person (charged with DUI or being treated)?

11. If your agency does an assessment, what is the average time needed to collect the data?

12. Do the persons administering the assessment have to be trained and/or certified? What kinds of training? Is this standardized over the state?

13. Is there someone in your agency responsible for overseeing the assessment process?

14. Do you have a standardized form for the assessment? How was this form developed (in-house, consultant, etc.)?

15. What types of reports do you compile from the data you gather (types and frequency)?

16. Who are the major actors in your agency's part of the computerized tracing system? What are their rules and responsibilities?

17. How does your agency interact with other actors in the DUI process? Is there any kind of formal coordination between the agencies and actors? Informal agreements?

18. How do you collect the information you need for the tracking system?

19. Do convicted offenders have to pay a fee or fine? If so, is any of this money used to support your program?

20. What are the funding sources for your program?

21. What percentage of DUI offenders are referred for alcohol treatment?

22. What is the average amount of time between arrest and treatment? Conviction and treatment?

23. What percentage of persons arrested for DUI/clients admitted for treatment are considered to be social drinkers? midrange drinkers? problem drinkers?

24. What kinds of evaluation processes do you do in regard to your agency's functions?

TREATMENT/UNIFORM DATA COLLECTION SYSTEM

1. When you admit someone for treatment, are they categorized by drinker types or groups? If so, are these related to the Court Reporting Network (CRN) system categories?

2. What is the authority for the alcohol treatment program (legislation, etc.)?

3. Do you designate persons as DUI offenders in the Uniform Data Collection System (UDCS)? Do you have plans to do so? (Please elaborate.)

3. If someone needed to find out the status of a person convicted of DUI and sentenced to treatment through the Department of Health, how would they go about doing so?

4. After a person finishes treatment, do you have any sort of follow-up system?

5. Do you have a posttreatment evaluation regarding changes in attitudes toward drinking? Do you have any other type of posttreatment evaluation?

6. Do you keep records on recidivism rates in your program? If so, what are your percentages for 1983 and estimates for 1984?

7. Do you have different types of referral and/or treatment options for persons convicted of DUI (or just persons in your program in general)? If so, please describe the objectives and length of each option.

8. What are the dropout rates for your treatment programs?

9. What provision do you have for ensuring that DUI offenders complete their court-ordered treatment (any sort of legal mechanism)?

10. Do you have any sort of special programs for DUI offenders? If not, do you have plans for any?

11. What kind of plans does your agency have for expanding its role in Pennsylvania's DUI process?

COURT REPORTING NETWORK

1. How does the CRN evaluation fit in with the DUI system?

2. What is the conviction rate for persons charged with DUI (based on the original charge)?

3. Do you think the conviction rates have been affected by the use of the CRN? How?

4. What percentage of DUI cases involve jury trials? Are the CRN results given to the jury? If so, do you think the outcome of jury trials is affected by the CRN results?

5. Are there special DUI courts and prosecutors?

6. What is the average time from arrest to disposition? Has this been affected by the use of the CRN?

7. Does the court provide a record of all convictions/dispositions to the CRN? If so, is this information entered into the person's record?

8. What are your laws regarding license suspensions? Is there any provision for "hardship cases?"

9. What is your agency's role in the Accelerated Rehabilitative Disposition (ARD) process?

10. What kinds of plans does your agency have for expanding and/or improving your functions relating to Pennsylvania's DUI program?

APPENDIX 8
PENNSYLVANIA COURT REPORTING NETWORK — CLIENT INTAKE FORM

1 ____

SOURCE:

1. Referral source (Place letter in space at left)

   A. ARD (Pre-trial Diversion)
   B. Post Adjudication (District Justice)
   C. Post Adjudication (Court of Common Pleas)
   D. (If other, specify) _____
   (Non-DUI offense, referral from another source, etc.)

CRN Evaluation Instruments

2 ____

2. CIF could not be completed because: (Place letter in space at left)
   Leave blank if CIF can be completed; Submission of CIF optional if not completed beyond this question.

   A. Client appears to be under the influence of drugs or alcohol
   B. Language problem
   C. Client was too ill
   D. Client's lack of cooperation or failure to appear for interview

HEALTH:

3 ____

3. How is your general health? (Place letter in space at left)

   A. Better than average or very good, excellent
   B. Average or good
   C. Less than average, fair, poor, bad

4. Do you experience any of the following?
   (Place Yes 'Y' or No 'N' in space below)

   ____ 4A. Being tired or fatigued   ____ 4E. Inability to concentrate
   ____ 4B. General weakness   ____ 4F. Difficulty sleeping
   ____ 4C. Just feeling bad all over   ____ 4G. Increased irritability
   ____ 4D. Weight loss or inability to eat   ____ 4H. Difficulty doing your job or taking care of your home

5 ____

5. Do you have a chronic disease or illness?
   (Place Yes 'Y' or No 'N' in space at left)

6. Have you had any of the following?
   (Place Yes 'Y' or No 'N' in space below)

   ____ 6A. Fatty liver   ____ 6F. Diabetes
   ____ 6B. Cirrhosis   ____ 6G. Ulcers or stomach problems
   ____ 6C. Pain and/or weakness of legs   ____ 6H. Mental or emotional illness
   ____ 6D. Anemia   ____ 6I. Any severe bleeding problems
   ____ 6E. Convulsions or epilepsy   ____ 6J. Pancreatitis

   Other mentioned _____

7. Are you disabled or do you have any physical defects?
   (Yes 'Y' or No 'N')   ____ 7.
   (If yes): What? _____

8.
   A. Have you had a serious injury or illness in the past?
      (Yes 'Y' or No 'N')   ____ 8A.
      (If yes): What was its nature? _____

   B. Are you completely well from this? (these)?
      (Yes 'Y' or No 'N')   ____ 8B.

MARITAL STATUS:

9 ____

9. What is your marital status? (Place letter in space at left)

   A. Married   B. Single/never married   C. Widowed   D. Separated   E. Divorced

10. If married

    A. How long have you been married? (Years)   ____ 10A.
    B. Have you ever been married before? (Yes 'Y' or No 'N')   ____ 10B.
    C. (If yes): How many times?   ____ 10C.

10D ____

    D. Do you and your (present) wife/husband get along pretty well?
       (Place Yes 'Y' or No 'N' in space at left)

    E. Do you have any children at home? (Yes 'Y' or No 'N')   ____ 10E.
    F. (If Yes): Do you have any serious problems with them?   ____ 10F.
       (Yes 'Y' or No 'N')

10G ____

    G. Are there any (other) family problems?
       (Place Yes 'Y' or No 'N' in space at left)

       (If Yes): What? _____

10H ____

    H. Do you ever have arguments about drinking?
       (Place Yes 'Y' or No 'N' in space at left)

APPENDIX 8 (cont.)
PENNSYLVANIA COURT REPORTING NETWORK — CLIENT INTAKE FORM

2

11. If single
    A. Do you find that you drink more than your friends? (Yes 'Y' or No 'N') _____ 11 A
    B. Has drinking interfered with any marriage plans? (Yes 'Y' or No 'N') _____ 11 B
    C. Are there any children at home? (Yes 'Y' or No 'N') _____ 11 C
    D. Do you live alone? (Yes 'Y' or No 'N') _____ 11 D

12. If widowed
    A. How long have you been widowed? (Years) _____ 12 A
    B. Have you been married more than once? (Yes 'Y' or No 'N') _____ 12 B
    C. (If Yes): How many times? _____ 12 C
    D. Are there any children at home? (Yes 'Y' or No 'N') _____ 12 D
    E. (If Yes): Do you have any serious problems with them? (Yes 'Y' or No 'N') _____ 12 E
    F. Has your drinking increased since you lost your wife/husband? (Yes 'Y' or No 'N') _____ 12 F
    G. Are you alone most of the time? (Yes 'Y' or No 'N') _____ 12 G

13. If separated or divorced
    A. How many times were you married? _____ 13 A
    B. Were there any children? (Yes 'Y' or No 'N') _____ 13 B
    C. (If Yes): Do you have any serious problems with them? (Yes 'Y' or No 'N') _____ 13 C
    D. Did you have family arguments over drinking? (Yes 'Y' or No 'N') _____ 13 D
    E. Has your drinking increased since the separation or divorce? (Yes 'Y' or No 'N') _____ 13 E
    F. Are you alone most of the time? (Yes 'Y' or No 'N') _____ 13 F

INCOME and EMPLOYMENT STATUS:

14. _____ How many days of work did you miss due to drinking during the month prior to your arrest? (Place letter in space at left) **EVALUATOR NOTE:** Include days when sick or vacation days were taken on short notice because of effects of drinking.

    A. None   B. 1 - 2   C. 3 - 5   D. 6 or more

15. _____ Have you ever been fired? (Place Yes 'Y' or No 'N' in space at left)

    (If Yes): Why? _____

16. _____ Are you presently employed? (Place Yes 'Y' or No 'N' in space at left)

17. _____ What was the highest grade you completed in school? (Place letter in space at left)

    A. Received graduate degree
    B. Received undergraduate degree
    C. Partial college training (1 - 3 years)
    D. High school graduate
    E. Partial high school (10th - 11th grade)
    F. Junior high school (7th - 9th grade)
    G. Less than 7 years of school

18. _____ What is your current or most recent occupation? See list of occupations at Appendix A of CRN Manual and insert proper number in space at left.

    Describe occupation briefly. If client is a housewife or student, so state and indicate the occupation of the primary supporter. If unemployed for less than two years, state last job held; if more than two years rate as permanently unemployed. _____

19. _____ What is your main source of support? (Place letter in space at left)

    A. None
    B. Salary/wages
    C. Income other than salary
    D. Family/friend
    E. Savings, pension
    F. Disability benefits, social security
    G. Unemployment insurance
    H. Public assistance
    I. Other _____

20. _____ What is your yearly income to the closest thousand? (Place amount in space at left)

    EVALUATOR NOTE: Please be reluctant to accept a refusal to provide this information. Enter 9999 if unwilling to state or does not know.

21. How many full time jobs have you had during the past three years? (Place number in space at right) _____ 21.

22. If unemployed
    A. How long have you been unemployed? _____ 22 A
    B. Reason for unemployment: _____ 22 B
       A. Laid off previous job   B. Fired   C. Strike   D. Illness
       E. Other _____
    C. Did drinking contribute to your job loss? (Yes 'Y' or No 'N') _____ 22 C

APPENDIX 8 (cont.)
PENNSYLVANIA COURT REPORTING NETWORK — CLIENT INTAKE FORM

3

23. A. Have you had any problems with your job(s) in the last 3 years? _____ 23 A
(Yes 'Y' or No 'N')

What kinds of problems are (were) they? (Place Yes 'Y' or No 'N' below)

_____ 23 B Occasional friction with fellow workers or boss

_____ 23 C Frequent friction with fellow workers or boss

_____ 23 D Occasional trouble with work

_____ 23 E Serious difficulty doing work, or accidents

_____ 23 F Occasional absence

_____ 23 G Frequent absences

_____ 23 H Difficulty finding employment

_____ 23 I Other_____

DRIVING and ARREST HISTORY:

24. What was the reason the policeman initially approached you? (Place letter at left)

A. Vehicle violation (e.g., no headlights, etc.)
B. Weaving (reckless driving)
C. Moving violation (e.g., speeding, etc.)
D. Accident
E. Other_____

25. A. At the time of your arrest were you or the vehicle you were driving insured? (Place Yes 'Y' or No 'N' in space at left)
B. Was there any property damage? (Yes 'Y' or No 'N') _____ 25 B.
C. Was there any personal injury (Yes 'Y' or No 'N') _____ 25 C.

EVALUATOR NOTE: *Questions 26 through 29 should include arrests in any state.*

26. Other than this arrest, how many times have you been arrested for driving under the influence of alcohol or for impaired driving? (Place number at left)

27. A. Have you ever been arrested for being drunk and disorderly or for public intoxication? (Place Yes 'Y' or No 'N' in space at left)
B. (If Yes): How many times? (Place number in space at right) _____ 27 B.
C. Was driving related to any of these? (Yes 'Y' or No 'N') _____ 27 C.
D. (If Yes): How many times? (Place number in space at right) _____ 27 D.

28. A. Have you ever been cited for reckless driving? (Place Yes 'Y' or No 'N' in space at left)
B. (If Yes): How many times? (Place number in space at right) _____ 28 B.

29. A. Have you ever been arrested before? (Any type of arrest not including this DUI) (Place Yes 'Y' or No 'N' in space at left)
B. **Evaluator:** Establish prior arrest record to include any type of arrest except the DUI. (Place letter in space at left)

A. No prior arrest record B. Prior arrest record alcohol related
C. Prior arrest record non-alcohol related

ARREST DATA

Questions refer to the entire episode surrounding the arrest.

30. What was your blood alcohol level at the time of arrest - The breath test results? *Not available = 99; Refused = 98* (Place number in space at left)

31. What was the time lapse, in minutes, between your arrest and breath test? *Not available = 000* (Place number in space at left)

32. The day of your arrest, what did you have to drink? (Fill in the number of drinks for each category)

12 oz. beer *Make necessary adjustment if fortified beer e.g., malt liquor, Colt 45, etc. (12 oz. malt liquor ≅ 24 oz. regular beer)* _____

oz. wine *Make necessary adjustment if fortified wine, e.g., sherry, muscatel, port, etc. (5 oz. sherry ≅ 10 oz. wine)* _____

oz. hard liquor *(80 proof or above)* _____

33. Over how many hours were you drinking from start to finish prior to your arrest? _____ 33.

34. How many hours had it been since you ate a meal prior to the beginning of drinking the day of your arrest? *(Anything more than and including a sandwich)* _____ 34.

35. During the time you were drinking the day of your arrest, how would you describe your eating pattern? (Place letter in space at right) _____ 35.

A. Ate nothing
B. Ate snacks *(e.g., pretzels, peanuts, crackers & cheese, etc.)*
C. Ate a light meal *(e.g., hamburger, club sandwich, hoagie, etc.)*
D. Ate a full meal *(e.g., steak platter, chicken & potatoes, spaghetti dinner, etc.)*

36. Client's weight? _____ 36.

LICENSE STATUS:

37. While driving have you ever been stopped by police, but not ticketed, when you knew you had been drinking too much? (Place Yes 'Y' or No 'N' in space at left)

APPENDIX 8 (cont.)
PENNSYLVANIA COURT REPORTING NETWORK — CLIENT INTAKE FORM

4

38A. _____

38. A. Has your driver's license ever been suspended or revoked?
(Place Yes 'Y' or No 'N' in space at left)

B. (If Yes): How many times? (Place number in space at right) 38 B. _____

38C. _____

C. (If Yes to A): Was drinking related to the suspension(s) or revocation(s)?
(Place Yes 'Y' or No 'N' in space at left)

39. _____

39. Did you have a valid license at the time of your arrest? (Place Yes 'Y' or No 'N' at left)

CLIENT'S PERCEPTION:

40. _____

40. Do you feel that drinking is causing any problems in the following areas of your life? (Place Yes 'Y' or No 'N' in spaces below). **NOTE:** If all answers are No, place 'N' in 40 at left. If one or more answers are Yes, place 'Y' in 40 at left.

A. Marriage   40. A _____   C. Health   40. C _____
B. Job or employment   40. B _____   D. Court or other legal difficulties   40. D _____

41A. _____

41. A. Do you feel that you always drink like a social drinker? (Place Yes 'Y' or No 'N' at left)

B. (If no): How do you differ from the social drinker? (Show frequency and amount below)
41. B _____

42. _____

42. Do you ever find that you drink more than you had intended to drink?
(Place Yes 'Y' or No 'N' in space at left)

43. _____

43. Have you gone on a drinking spree or binge in the last five years?
(Place Yes 'Y' or No 'N' in space at left)

44. _____

44. Do you ever get the feeling that you "need" or "really want" a drink when (you feel):
(Place Yes 'Y' or No 'N' in spaces below). NOTE: If all answers are No, place 'N' in 44 at left.
If one or more answers are Yes, place 'Y' in 44 at left.

_____ A. Angry?   _____ F. With friends?
_____ B. Depressed?   _____ G. Things go wrong?
_____ C. Lonely?   _____ H. At parties?
_____ D. Happy?   _____ I. At certain times of day?
_____ E. Tense or nervous?   _____ J. Other (List) _____

Questions 45-65 (Place Yes 'Y' or No 'N' at left)

45. _____ 45. Have you ever hidden a bottle of liquor?
46. _____ 46. Do you drink to feel less self-conscious and more at ease around people?
47. _____ 47. Do you ever feel that it is easier to start something after you have had a drink?
48. _____ 48. Does drinking sometimes give you courage or self confidence?
49. _____ 49. Do you feel more quarrelsome or angry after you have had several drinks?
50. _____ 50. Have you been told that you become rowdy or noisy when drinking too much?
51. _____ 51. Have you ever destroyed property or gotten into physical fight(s) when you were drinking?
52. _____ 52. Have you ever thought about cutting down on drinking?
53. _____ 53. Have you ever felt bad or guilty about drinking?

THE PERCEPTION OF OTHERS:

54. _____ 54. Have any of your friends or members of your family suggested that you watch or cut down on your drinking?
55. _____ 55. Have you ever been treated for drinking? (If yes): When? _____

PHYSICAL SYMPTOMS:

56. _____ 56. Have you ever taken medicine or pills other than aspirin to help sober up?
57. _____ 57. Have you ever found that you can't remember or wonder what you did the night before when you were drinking?
58. _____ 58. Did you ever fall or seriously injure yourself when you were drinking?
59. _____ 59. After drinking the night before, have you ever decided not to go to work the next morning? (If Yes): How many times a year does this happen? _____
60. _____ 60. Have you ever found that your hands shake and tremble in the morning?
61. _____ 61. Have you ever vomited or been very sick to your stomach, not while drinking, but the morning after drinking?
62. _____ 62. Do you ever drink in the morning before breakfast or before going to work?
63. _____ 63. Do you feel that your health would be better if you decreased or stopped drinking?
64. _____ 64. Do you ever take tranquilizers, anti-depressants or pep pills?
65. _____ 65. Have you ever been told that your drinking was injuring your liver?

66. A. Have you ever had bad stomach or abdominal pain?
(Place Yes 'Y' or No 'N' in space at right)   66 A. _____

B. (If Yes): Did this occur after drinking?
(Place Yes 'Y' or No 'N' in space at right)   66 B. _____

APPENDIX 8 (cont.)
PENNSYLVANIA COURT REPORTING NETWORK — CLIENT INTAKE FORM

5   PSYCHOLOGICAL SYMPTOMS: *(Place a Yes 'Y' or No 'N' in spaces at left)*

67. _____ 67. Would you describe yourself as being lonely a good deal of the time?

68. _____ 68. Do you feel that your life is difficult to manage and you are not sure how to straighten it out?

69. _____ 69. Do you feel that you are a problem drinker?

BEHAVIORAL ASPECTS of DRINKING: *The following questions (70 through 83) pertain to the client's drinking pattern for the month prior to arrest - up to and including the day of arrest. Questions 70, 71, 73 thru 81, and 83, place letter in space at left.*

70. _____ 70. How many times did you get high (drunk) in that month? *Use quantity sufficient for client to reach .10% BAC as definition of "high".* ***Does not*** *include present DUI*
     A. None   B. 1 – 2   C. 3 – 4   D. 5 – 10   E. 11 or more

71. _____ 71. Generally, where were you when you got high? Leave blank if answer to Question 70 is A.
     A. Home   C. Party or social gathering, riding/driving in an automobile
     B. Friend's or relative's house   D. Bar or restaurant   E. Other _____

72. How did you get home? *(Place letter in space at right)*   72. _____
     A. Did not go home   D. Public transportation   G. Other _____
     B. Drive   E. Someone else drove (Police, friend)
     C. Walk   F. At home

73. _____ 73. What was the longest period that you went between drinks in the month prior to your arrest?
     A. 12 hours or more   B. Less than 12 hours

74. _____ 74. What was your longest period of continual drinking in the month prior to your arrest?
     A. Less than 6 hours   B. 6 – 12 hours   C. More than 12 hours

75. _____ 75. What was the number of days you had a drink before or with breakfast in the month prior to your arrest?   A. None   B. 1 – 4   C. 5 – 10   D. 11 or more

76. _____ 76. How many meals did you miss due to drinking in the month prior to your arrest?
     A. None   B. 1 – 4   C. 5 – 10   D. 11 or more

77. _____ 77. What percent of the time did you drink alone in the month prior to your arrest?
     A. 0 – 9%   B. 10 – 25%   C. 26 – 50%   D. 51% or more

78. _____ 78. How often did you have memory lapses or "blackouts" in the month prior to your arrest? (Could not remember events during drinking episodes)
     A. None   B. 1 – 2   C. 3 – 5   D. 6 or more

79. _____ 79. How often did you experience nausea or trembling (must be alcohol related like "shakes" or "hangover") in the month prior to your arrest?
     A. None   B. 1 – 2   C. 3 – 5   D. 6 or more

80. _____ 80. How many times did you have difficulty sleeping in the month prior to your arrest?
     A. None   B. 1 – 2   C. 3 – 5   D. 6 or more

81. _____ 81. How many times did you quarrel with others when you drank in the month prior to your arrest? (Heated argument, not discussion of different views)
     A. None   B. 1 – 2   C. 3 – 5   D. 6 or more

82. _____ 82. Did you drink while on the job (including lunch-time) or during daily activities in that month? (e.g., while painting the house on Saturday) (Place Yes 'Y' or No 'N' at left)

83. _____ 83. How many days of work did you miss or were you inactive for a day due to drinking in that month? (Does not include the day after arrest)
     A. None   B. 1 – 2   C. 3 – 5   D. 6 or more

MEDICATION USAGE DATA *(For medical use only)* 84. For the three months prior to your arrest did you use any of the following medications, with or without a prescription? ***EVALUATOR NOTE:*** *Read the following list of medications to client. Additional Controlled Substance information contained in Appendix B of the CRN MANUAL. (Place Yes 'Y' or No 'N' at left)*

84A. _____ A. Amphetamines (Diet tablets, "speed", refer to local jargon)

84B. _____ B. Antabuse

84C. _____ C. Antidepressants (Elavil, Tofravil, etc.)

84D. _____ D. Barbiturates (Sleeping pills, Quaalude, etc.)

84E. _____ E. Cocaine

84F. _____ F. Marijuana or hashish

84G. _____ G. Opiates (e.g. Heroin) or Methadone

84H. _____ H. Tranquilizers (e.g. 'Valium', 'Librium', etc.)

84I. _____ I. Other (Specify) _____

QUANTITY/FREQUENCY SCALE: ***EVALUATOR NOTE*** *the following questions pertain to the client's drinking pattern for the month prior to arrest — up to and including the day of arrest.*
     Drinking Quantity and Frequency – Beer

85. _____ 85. About how often did you drink any beer during the month prior to your arrest?
     (Place letter in space at left)
     A. Never   E. 3 – 4 days a week
     B. Less often than weekly   F. Nearly every day
     C. Weekends only (Fri. after work; all day Sat. & Sun.)   G. Every day
     D. 1 – 2 days a week   H. Constantly

APPENDIX 8 (cont.)
PENNSYLVANIA COURT REPORTING NETWORK — CLIENT INTAKE FORM

6

QUESTIONS 86 thru 90 and 95 thru 97 - Place letter at left.

86. _____ 86. About how much did you drink in a typical day? **EVALUATOR NOTE:** 1 Quart — three 12 oz. bottles (cans) or four 8 oz. glasses

    A. None   C. 1 – 2 quarts   E. 4 quarts   G. 6 quarts or more
    B. 1 – 3 glasses D. 3 quarts   F. 5 quarts

Drinking Quantity and Frequency – Wine

87. _____ 87. About how often did you drink any wine in that month?

    A. Never   C. Weekends only   E. 3 – 4 days a week   G. Every day
    B. Less than weekly (Fri. after work - all   F. Nearly every day   H. Constantly
                         day Sat. & Sun.)
                      D. 1 – 2 days a week

88. _____ 88. About how much did you drink in a typical day? **EVALUATOR NOTE:** 1 fifth is a standard size bottle and is equal to about three 8 oz. or six 4 oz. wine glasses. There are five fifths to a gallon or 2½ fifths to a half gallon.

    A. None   E. 2 fifths
    B. 1 water glass or 1 to 3 wine glasses   F. 3 – 4 fifths
    C. 2 or 3 water glasses or 4 – 6 wine glasses (Pint) G. 5 fifths or more
    D. 1 fifth (Quart)

Drinking Quantity and Frequency – Liquor

89. _____ 89. About how often did you drink any hard liquor in the month prior to your arrest?

    A. Never   C. Weekends only   E. 3 – 4 days a week   G. Every day
    B. Less than weekly (Fri. after work - all   F. Nearly every day   H. Constantly
                         day Sat. & Sun.)
                      D. 1 – 2 days a week

90. _____ 90. About how much did you drink in a typical day? **EVALUATOR NOTE:** 1 pint = 16 oz. or sixteen 1 oz. shots. There are a little over 1½ pints in a fifth

    A. None   D. 7 – 10 shots   G. 2 pints
    B. 1 – 3 shots E. 11 – 14 shots H. 3 pints
    C. 4 – 6 shots F. 1 pint   I. 4 pints or more

INTERVIEWER'S INITIAL EVALUATION
(This section can be filled in after the interview is over)

Drinking Pattern:

91. _____ 91. How experienced is this person at drinking? (Select a value from 1, very inexperienced, to 5, very experienced, and place number in space at left.)

Interviewer's Conclusion:

92. A. Do you feel that this drinking situation was unique and unlikely to happen again? (Place Yes 'Y' or No 'N' at right.) 92 A. _____

    B. Did the client give you evidence of a past behavior pattern of heavy drinking? (Place Yes 'Y' or No 'N' at right.) 92 B. _____

    C. Do you feel that without any therapeutic intervention he/she is likely to repeat this drinking behavior within the next 5 years? (Yes 'Y' or No 'N') 92 C. _____

93. Problem evaluation: (Place letter in space at right) 93. _____

    A. Person has no problems related to drinking
    B. Person has a temporary drinking problem
    C. Person has a long standing drinking problem

94. Interviewer's physical observation of client (Place Yes 'Y' or No 'N' in appropriate spaces.)

94A. _____ A. Looks older than stated age   F. Has language difficulty   94 F. _____
94B. _____ B. Looks ill   G. Appears to be markedly
94C. _____ C. Has a hand tremor   below average in intelligence 94 G. _____
94D. _____ D. Has bloodshot or glassy eyes   H. Nicotine stains
94E. _____ E. Has a flushed face   or blisters on fingers.   94 H. _____

95. _____ 95. Objective evaluation of reliability of client's responses to this interview:
    A. Excellent B. Good C. Fair D. Poor

    Explain: _____
    _____
    _____

96. _____ 96. Client's sobriety at time of interview:
    A. Appears sober   D. Admits to being intoxicated
    B. Appears mildly under the influence of alcohol. E. Appears to have had a drink
    C. Appears to be intoxicated   F. Admits to having had a drink

97. _____ 97. Race (By observation)
    A. Black
    B. Hispanic
    C. White
    D. Other (Specify) _____

APPENDIX 8 (cont.)
PENNSYLVANIA COURT REPORTING NETWORK — CLIENT INTAKE FORM

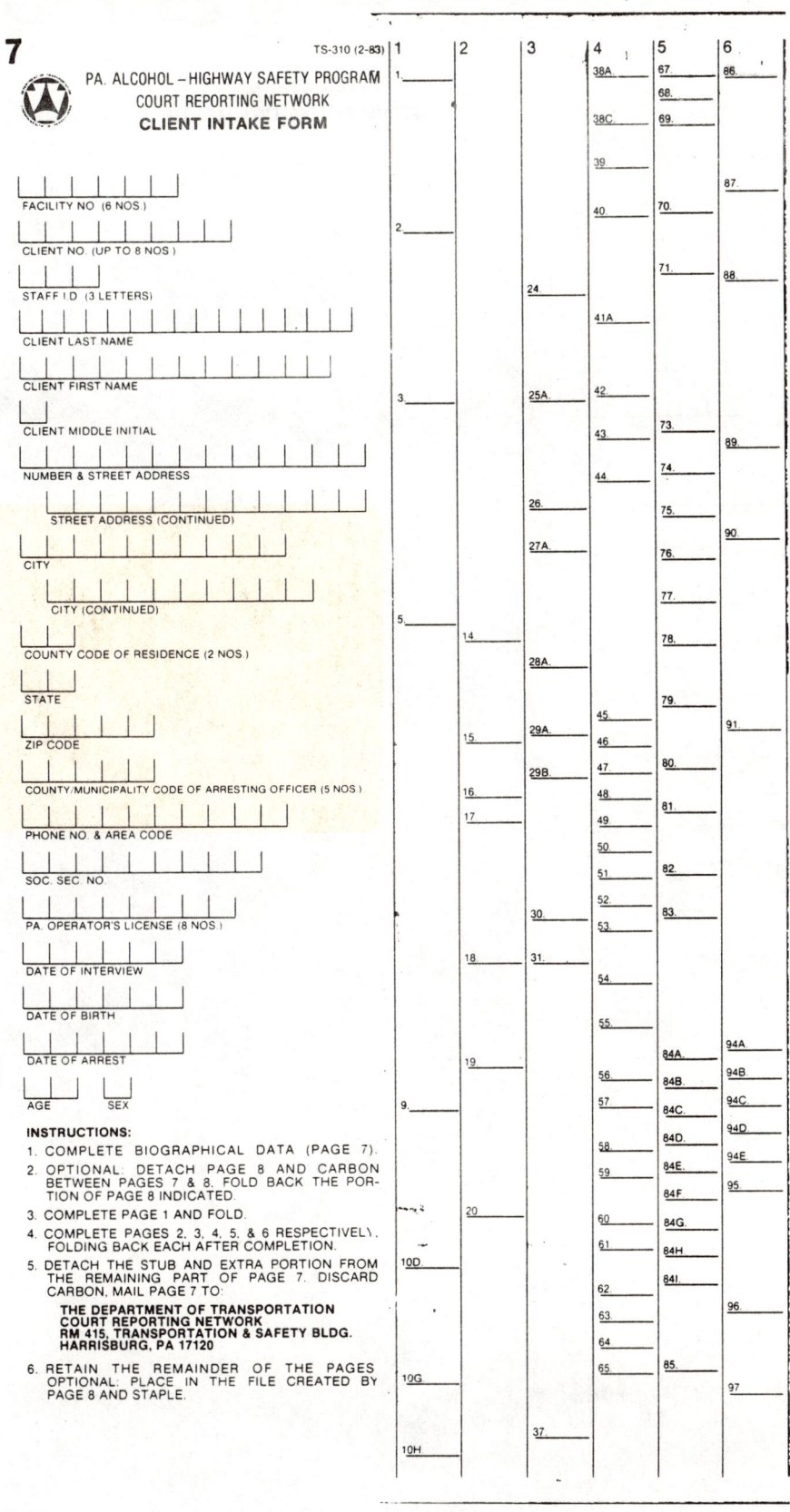

APPENDIX 8 (cont.)
PENNSYLVANIA COURT REPORTING NETWORK — CLIENT INTAKE FORM

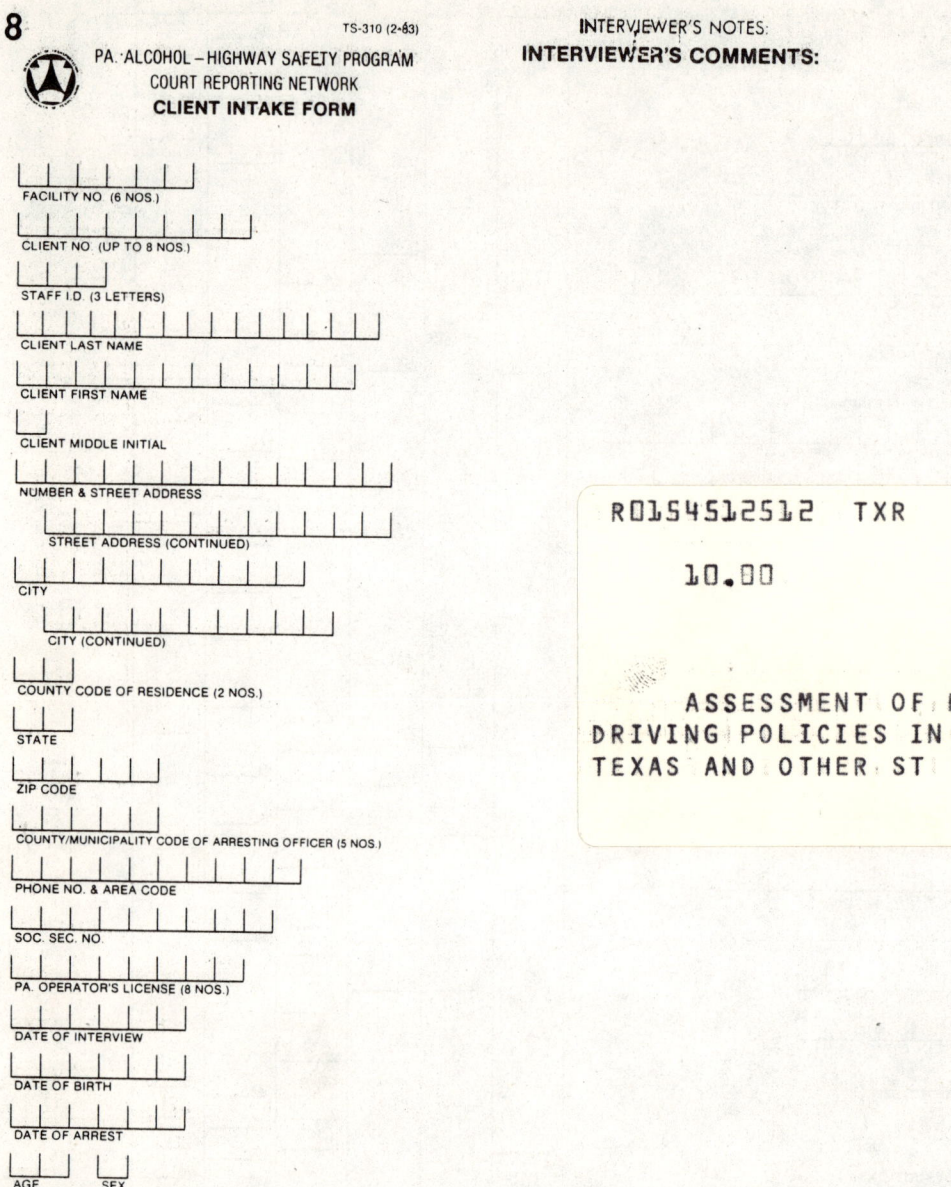